Business
Continuity
FOR
DUMMIES®

Business Continuity
FOR
DUMMIES®

by Stuart Sterling, Brian Duddridge,
Andrew Elliott, Michael Conway and Anna Payne

A John Wiley and Sons, Ltd, Publication

Business Continuity For Dummies®

Published by:
John Wiley & Sons, Ltd
The Atrium
Southern Gate
Chichester
West Sussex
PO19 8SQ
www.wiley.com

This edition first published 2012

© 2012 John Wiley & Sons, Ltd, Chichester, West Sussex.

Registered office

John Wiley & Sons Ltd, The Atrium, Southern Gate, Chichester, West Sussex, PO19 8SQ, United Kingdom

For details of our global editorial offices, for customer services and for information about how to apply for permission to reuse the copyright material in this book please see our website at www.wiley.com.

Wiley publishes in a variety of print and electronic formats and by print-on-demand. Some material included with standard print versions of this book may not be included in e-books or in print-on-demand. If this book refers to media such as a CD or DVD that is not included in the version you purchased, you may download this material at http://booksupport.wiley.com. For more information about Wiley products, visit www.wiley.com.

Designations used by companies to distinguish their products are often claimed as trademarks. All brand names and product names used in this book are trade names, service marks, trademarks or registered trademarks of their respective owners. The publisher is not associated with any product or vendor mentioned in this book.

For general information on our other products and services, please contact our Customer Care Department within the U.S. at 877-762-2974, outside the U.S. at (001) 317-572-3993, or fax 317-572-4002. For technical support, please visit www.wiley.com/techsupport.

A catalogue record for this book is available from the British Library.

ISBN 978-1-118-32683-1 (pbk), ISBN 978-1-118-48203-2 (custom pbk)

ISBN 978-1-118-32680-0 (ebk), ISBN 978-1-118-32681-7 (ebk), ISBN 978-1-118-32682-4 (ebk)

10 9 8 7 6 5 4 3 2 1

WILEY

Contents at a Glance

Table of Co[ntents]

CHAPTERS TO READ:
1 ☒ - THU
6 ☒ - FRI
7 ☐ - SAT
8 ☐ - SUN
10 ☐ - MON
12 ☐ | X-tra:
18 ☐
19 ☐

Part II: Starting Out on Your Business Continuity Journey 51

Part IV: Examining Business Continuity in Specific Contexts 193

Chapter 12: Calling in the Experts 195

Chapter 13: Viewing Business Continuity from a Manufacturing Perspective 207

Chapter 14: Developing a Retail Business Continuity Programme 217

Introduction

*B*usiness continuity (BC) involves building resilience in your business: identifying its key products and services and the critical activities that underpin them, and devising strategies so that you can trade through a disruption and recover afterwards. We see BC as being a bit like New Year resolutions: go on a diet, do more exercise, eat more fruit – you know the drill. People promise themselves they're going to do these things because they know that they *should* be doing them and can't deny that they won't benefit from making the effort. But in the end – normally, by 2 or 3 January – they just don't do them. 'It's too hard', 'I can't be bothered', 'I don't have enough time' . . . people use any number of excuses that don't really stack up.

Similarly, businesses know that they should be doing BC, and yes, believe it or not, would rather like to have it in their business. The problem is that people see BC as being too expensive and time-consuming, and the guidance available isn't aimed at smaller businesses.

But no longer. Although any size of business can use this book, we aim it specifically at small- and medium-sized enterprises (or SMEs). As the Prime Minister reminded people at the 2011 World Economic Forum, SMEs are the 'engines of job creation', and this has been the case for a long time. Their resilience and continuity is important for all sorts of different reasons, but most prominently to:

- ✔ Provide a source of jobs.
- ✔ Provide a market for goods and services.
- ✔ Strengthen local communities.
- ✔ Provide necessary economic flexibility through outsourcing.
- ✔ Create and spread innovation.
- ✔ Assist in re-invigorating the economy.

About This Book

We produced this guide to help SMEs introduce vital business continuity into their firms. We write especially with the small business in mind and keep coming back to the core principles: does this make sense for a small business; can a small business easily achieve this; can a business do this within a reasonable amount of time; and is it affordable for a small business?

In essence, we continually ensure that what we're telling you is:

- ✔ Accessible
- ✔ Affordable
- ✔ Achievable

Yet we haven't produced something completely new that doesn't recognise previous developments in the area of BC; on the contrary! This work is sponsored by the Business Continuity Institute (BCI), the Emergency Planning Society (EPS) and the Cabinet Office, and supported by the British Standards Institution (BSI). Each of these organisations has made great steps forward in promoting the adoption and use of BC.

In recognition of this, we draw inspiration and thoughts from the following:

- ✔ BCI's Good Practice Guidelines
- ✔ British Standard for Business Continuity BS25999:2006, Parts 1 and 2
- ✔ Cabinet Office's National Risk Register
- ✔ Crisis Management – Guidance and Good Practice PAS 200:2011

The content of this book was originally produced by the Emergency Planning Society's Business Continuity Professional Working Group and co-opted subject matter experts.

What You're Not to Read

The great thing about this guide is that, like all *For Dummies* books, you can choose exactly how you want to approach it. We've written and designed the content so that each chapter is self-contained. Therefore, you can read the book page by page and in the order that we present it, or you can dip in and out as you want.

Each chapter makes sense when read on its own, and so if you want to know about protecting your IT, flip straight to Chapter 17; or if you're interested in advice for forming a Business Impact Analysis (BIA), head to Chapter 4. Don't think that you have to study this book from cover to cover if you don't want to – as with anything to do with BC, focus on what's most important for you and your business.

Conventions Used in This Book

We use *italics* to indicate a defined term or a point of emphasis. And we put not so crucial, but none-the-less useful, information in grey-tinted sidebars. You can gloss over these if you're in a hurry, or save them to re-read at a later date when you want more detail on a topic.

When referring to a website, we use the official-looking `monofont`. If you're reading this as an ebook, the website is hyperlinked. When a web address breaks across two lines of text, just type exactly what you see (we don't put in any extra characters to indicate the break).

We use the terms *business*, *organisation* and *firm* interchangeably throughout this guide. Usually, economists refer to businesses as firms, academics refer to them as organisations and businesses refer to them (unsurprisingly) as businesses. In any case, it's all the same to us. Firms are firms; or rather firms are organisations, which are, of course, businesses – if you see what we mean!

Foolish Assumptions

We aim this book at the small to medium-sized business owner. In doing so, we assume that you're aware that BC is something that you should, but don't yet, have. Perhaps you didn't want to spend valuable money, resources and time on instilling something expensive and complicated. No doubt you're rushed off your feet already with the day-to-day running of your business and have a relatively small workforce who work hard enough as it is: they certainly don't want to take on a vast extra workload in order to embed BC into the business.

For this reason, we make BC simple and accessible, breaking it down into easy stages with tips to help you make your business more resilient from the outset.

How This Book Is Organised

We divide this book into five parts, which we outline in the following sections. If read in order, the first three parts take you through setting up and instilling BC into your business, Part IV gives some specific and practical guidance and Part V comprises some top tips for at-a-glance advice. Alternatively, dip in and out of chapters as you see fit, focusing on the ones most appropriate to your business.

Part 1: Discovering Business Continuity

The three chapters in this part lay the foundations. We explain in simple terms what BC is and why it's important to your business, and offer some simple but effective ways to get you started on the path to becoming more resilient. Chapter 1 provides an overview of the subject, introduces some key terms and gives a flavour of what the book provides for you. Chapter 2 explains why BC is important to your business and the benefits that it offers. In Chapter 3, we go full-steam ahead to get you moving, providing a few ideas on quick wins and ways to make your business more resilient right from the start.

Part 11: Starting Out on Your Business Continuity Journey

This part puts the world of BC at your fingertips. Chapter 4 helps you to identify the important areas of your business and what you need to focus on as you build your BC system. Chapter 5 discusses risks and looks at ways to identify the ones that your business faces. In Chapter 6 we show you how to build resilience in your supply chain and protect the elements that you can't afford to let fail. Chapter 7 helps you establish your BC framework, by planning out the strategies that are going to form part of your BC plan, and Chapter 8 walks you through developing the plan, which may prove crucial to the survival of your business in the future. We discuss ways to simplify the process and make sure that what you develop is going to be effective in the unfortunate event of your business suffering a serious disruption.

Part 111: Embedding Business Continuity into Your Company

This part is about making your BC system part of the everyday activities of your business. Chapter 9 explains how to build your BC team. You already have the staff; this chapter shows you how to ensure that they have a good awareness of BC, know what to do if the time comes and can champion BC across your business. Chapter 10 on managing a crisis is one that many of you may want to turn to first, but in any case make sure that you don't turn to it when it's too late. Crises require different ways of thinking and present new and unexpected challenges, and this chapter explains the considerations and the actions that your business can take when the worst happens. Chapter 11 is about testing and exercising your plans, an important aspect of BC, because unless you practise your plans you're taking a gamble on them working when you really need them to.

Part IV: Examining Business Continuity in Specific Contexts

In this part we help you put BC theory into practice. We take a practical look in Chapter 12 at areas where you may want to seek external help and assistance. You need to make sure that you take good advice about aspects of your business that are unusual or vulnerable, but the most important principle is that if you need expert help and advice, go get it! Chapter 13 looks at BC from a manufacturer's point of view and shows you how you can adapt BC to suit your business needs. In Chapter 14 we cover the main issues and dilemmas that retailers face when developing a BC programme, and how they can interpret and implement BC, and Chapter 15 examines adapting BC to the professional services arena. Chapter 16 gives you practical advice for wading through the somewhat murky waters of insurance, telling you exactly what you do and don't need as a small or medium-sized business.

Part V: The Part of Tens

The three chapters in this part provide reminders or inspiration for protecting your business. We look at top tips for protecting your IT system (in Chapter 17), and the importance of ensuring effective internal and external communication when the worst happens (in Chapters 18 and 19, respectively).

Icons Used in This Book

To ensure that your BC journey is an easy ride, we use the following icons to highlight certain points.

Here you can find handy tips and expert advice to speed up your progress and make life that bit easier.

Certain paragraphs of text are particularly worth remembering, and so we indicate these for you.

Think of this icon as a danger sign, because we use it to highlight common (and even some unusual) errors that you want to avoid.

The text beside this icon is really worth reading, because it's one of our special pieces of advice that give you a competitive edge or help you keep a step or two ahead of trouble.

Where to Go from Here

If you're completely new to business continuity and the whole subject seems a bit daunting, we suggest that you start with Part I, which takes you through understanding your business from a BC perspective. You're then ready to read Part II, which guides you through forming your BC programme.

If you're already clued up on this sort of thing, however, by all means dive in wherever you please. If you're, say, a retailer looking for specific advice, head directly to Chapter 14. If your need is immediate and you want to know what to do in a crisis, turn straight to Chapter 10, and look at it in conjunction with Chapters 18 and 19, which have great tips on internal and external communication during an incident.

Wherever you choose to start and whatever path you take through the book, we hope you enjoy reading *Business Continuity For Dummies* and find the content useful, practical and reassuring. Good business!

Part I
Discovering
Business Continuity

The 5th Wave · By Rich Tennant

SWIM WITH THE GIANT SQUID

SWIM WITH THE MORAY EELS

SWIM WITH THE JELLYFISH

SWIM WITH OCTOPI

"Since we lost the dolphins, business hasn't been quite the same."

In this part . . .

We lay the business continuity foundations, discussing the subject simply and showing why it's vitally important for your business. We define the key terms and offer up suggestions for quick wins so that you can start making your business more resilient straight away.

Chapter 1

Introducing Business Continuity

*I*f you think that business continuity (BC) is only for big businesses and companies, get ready to have that myth well and truly busted, because that's far from the case. BC is simply taking responsibility for your business and giving it every chance of staying on course when harsh winds come a-blowing. BC can help give you a good idea of the risks you face, as well as providing plans and strategies to assist you if any of these events materialise. You don't need to hire specialist consultants, create a project team, have a full-time BC manager, spend big bucks or stop doing anything that you usually do.

The fact is that firms practising BC can more confidently embark on new ventures and projects or launch new lines because they have a better understanding of their business and the risks it faces. After all, it's your business and your responsibility to strengthen the firm's resilience. The decisions and actions that you take are what differentiates you from your competitors and determines whether your business is successful or not.

In this chapter, we introduce you to business continuity, including its main concepts and an overview of how it works. We also define a few key terms that you encounter throughout this book, which help you to get the most out BC.

Introducing the Idea of Business Continuity

We're going to keep things simple, as we try to do throughout this book; in fact doing so is pretty easy because BC is in the main pretty straightforward. *Business continuity* is understanding your business, devising strategies based on this knowledge and recording these strategies into plans to enable you to trade through a disruption and recover afterwards.

Whatever the size of your business, the key principles of BC and the steps to follow remain the same:

1. **Business Impact Analysis (BIA):** Understanding your business so that you're able to work out what's really important to it and the activities that produce these aspects or make them happen. In this part you identify:

   • Your key products and services

   • The critical activities on which they depend

   Flip to the next section, 'Revealing the Key Terms and Concepts', where we define these terms for you. Also, Chapter 4 has loads more on BIA.

2. **Maximum tolerable period of disruption, recovery time objective and then recovery point objective:** The next part of your BIA is working out these three items, which are when you need to resume your critical activities, your objective time for resuming them and the level or point to which you need to resume them.

3. **Risk assessment:** Looking at the risks to the critical activities of your key products and services. Assess Chapter 5 for more about risk.

4. **Supply chain:** Understanding what influence you can have on those that supply to you and looking at what you can do to make your key products and services more resilient when others fail. (The later section in this chapter 'Considering your supply chain' and Chapter 6 have more information.)

5. **Building resilience:** Creating strategies to ensure the continuity and recovery of your critical activities.

6. **Business continuity plans:** Pulling everything together. You need to record all the above elements into plans, so that everyone knows what to do when disaster strikes. Flip straight to Chapter 8 for how to put together your plans.

Revealing the Key Terms and Concepts

Just like anything else – well, anything of use! – BC involves the use of some specific and helpful terms. However, one of the many good things about BC is that you need to get to grips with only a few terms, and when you know and understand them, the whole concept becomes much clearer.

We touch upon most of these terms in the preceding section, but now we take a closer look at the terms that you encounter in the world of BC, and so get you ahead of the game. All the terms and concepts that we discuss in this section have one thing in common: they're about understanding your business.

As we take you through BC's key terms and concepts, keep in mind that these apply only to the most important aspects of your business: your key products and services, as we discuss in the next section.

Protecting your key products and services

Business continuity is about stopping problems occurring, keeping things going when they do arise and recovering afterwards. Although the idea sounds quite simple when expressed like that, you soon realise that to do this for your entire business and everything in it would be unwieldy, complicated and near-impossible to achieve without something going wrong.

To avoid this situation happening, in BC you need to focus only on your *key products and services*: the important things that your business produces or delivers. We're talking about your flagship products or the services that draw customers to you; in a lot of cases, these are the aspects that make the most money or upon which your good reputation relies. We focus our attention on key products and services in this book for the simple reason that they're the most important things for your business's survival.

By looking at your business from the point of view of your key products and services, you discover what's most important and therefore what you need to keep running during a disruption.

Covering your critical activities

Your business's key products and services rely upon activities to make them happen: these *critical activities* are what your products and services really need and rely upon. When operating together, they deliver your products and services to avoid the process failing.

Critical activities are time-critical; if a critical activity stops, before long a key product or service is also going to stop.

You identify your critical activities (and indeed your key products and services) by carrying out a *Business Impact Analysis*. In this analysis, you collect information from different areas in your business, the combination of which allows you to work out the activities that are really important to keep running during a disruption and the timeframes for recovering these before their failure causes irreparable damage.

Examining your critical activities allows you to identify the activities that must carry on to ensure that your key products and services continue.

Never exceeding your maximum tolerable period of disruption

After you identify your key products and services, and the critical activities that you need to carry out to make them happen (check out the preceding two sections), you can calculate their *maximum tolerable period of disruption*.

Your maximum tolerable period of disruption tells you how long you have to get activities up and running before they become irrecoverable.

If you think that this all sounds rather drastic, you've put your finger on exactly why you identify this maximum period: to make sure that you never get to the end of it!

Calculating your recovery time objective

To help ensure that you never reach a point from which your business can't recover (see the preceding section), you define a *recovery time objective.*

Your recovery time objective is the time by which you aim to have your critical activities up and running; it's usually far enough away from your maximum tolerable period to avoid ever getting too close to that sinking feeling. The recovery time is simply when you want to resume your critical activities by, looking at things ideally but realistically. The recovery time objective is always a shorter time than the maximum tolerable period of disruption.

Handwritten margin note (right side): Risk - 'IERR-ing' on the side of caution.

Process:
Identifying
Evaluating
Recording
Responding

Doing what's necessary: Your recovery point objective

To help you with systems such as information technology (IT), you need to find a balance between complete recovery and restoring them to a 'that'll do for now' point. This latter point mainly concerns your data, with the most obvious question being: will yesterday's backup data suffice?

This stage is your *recovery point objective* and needs to be sufficient to keep you going so that you can focus on recovering other areas.

By creating a recovery point objective, you know to what level or point you need to recover these systems.

Assessing the risks to your critical activities

You have to decide what specific risks you need to watch out for and protect your business against. You experience *risk* in the BC context when you face an uncertain outcome or the chance of something happening that may be good but inevitably is bad.

Here are the steps to take in assessing this area of your business, concentrating as always on the risks to your organisation's critical activities:

1. **Risk assessment:** Although this step sounds daunting, we break it down into the simple mnemonic 'IERR-ing' on the side of caution, which leads you through the process of **I**dentifying, **E**valuating, **R**ecording and **R**esponding to risks.

2. **Risk management:** In this step you regularly update and review your risks: the process and procedures for keeping your business covered against new and fluctuating risks by ensuring that your plans stay relevant to the current dangers.

3. **Risk appetite:** When identifying your risks in Step 1, you no doubt come across some risks that you have to accept because they're too expensive to mitigate or their likelihood is so low, or a combination of both. The level that you accept depends on your *risk appetite,* which is the level of risk that your business is willing to accept, when you're aware of the likely consequences of certain events occurring. Risk appetite (like that for lunch!) varies from organisation to organisation and with the nature of your business and who runs it.

Turn to Chapter 5 to find out all about risk.

Discovering How Business Continuity Works

When you have a handle on the aspects that we describe in the earlier section 'Revealing the Key Terms and Concepts', your BC journey is well underway. You can now go ahead and start identifying your crucial areas and appraising your risks – Chapters 4 and 5 show you how.

You also have the information to start thinking about practical aspects such as the resilience of your supply chain, creating your plans and testing them, and getting in people to help out.

Considering your supply chain

Looking into how the various elements of your supply chain can affect your identified critical activities is a vital part of the BC process.

Your supply chain is indeed a chain of supply, usually beginning with the acquisition of raw materials or components and extending through to the delivery of products or services to the customer. This chain can include suppliers, manufacturing plants, logistics providers, distributors, wholesalers and many others.

Within your supply chain are a number of processes and focusing closely on them allows you to identify any *single points of failure* that exist. As the name indicates, these points are those in your processes that if lost or disrupted lead to the failure of the activity.

When you're aware of your single points of potential failure, you can do something about them. We break down this process by using the key aspects to building resilience in your supply chain: CHAIN for **C**ontracts and Relationships, **H**ierarchies, **A**ssurance, **I**nitiative and **N**eeds.

Chapters 3 and 6 contain more on BC as it connects with your supply chain.

Selecting continuity strategies and building business continuity plans

Of course, doing all the initial preparation and thinking about BC (as we discuss in the earlier section 'Revealing the Key Terms and Concepts') is pointless if you don't then put everything to good use. The real value here is in the planning and identifying of the strategies that you're going to adopt, but your plans are what enable you to pull it all together in a coherent way. You're going to need to use the information that you gather, along with your identified potential supply chain weaknesses, to devise your BC strategies and build your BC plans, as follows:

1. **Continuity strategies:** In these strategies you decide what action to take to ensure that your critical activities continue in a crisis. You aren't devising a detailed, step-by-step guide for dealing with trouble at this stage, but instead working out the best, broader strategy for ensuring that your critical activities continue. In Chapter 7, we discuss options to use two different suppliers (known as *dual sourcing*), having a backup location, being able to access the servers remotely, having contingency stock and your staff being able to cover the key processes needed to deliver your critical activities.

2. **Business continuity plans:** When you've thought about the sort of things that you can do to ensure the continuity of these activities, draw them together into a coherent set of BC plans that you can press into action when disruption strikes (see Chapter 8).

   BC plans are usually referred to as a singular plan, which gives the impression that it's a single document covering everything. This is not the case, and the sensible approach is to break them down. Your own approach depends, of course, on the nature of your business, but in this book we break plans down into the following:

   - **Emergency response and incident management:** What your immediate actions are going to be in an emergency, such as an evacuation. In effect, this is the management of the response to the incident and is likely to include things such as a communications plan.

   - **Continuity:** Covers what you need to do to ensure that you can continue to deliver your critical activities and in turn deliver your key products and services during a disruption.

   - **Recovery and resumption:** The plan to recover activities to a sustainable level, leading to resumption of operations to what your business describes as normal.

COMPONENTS OF A BC PLANS

After you devise continuity strategies and pull them together into a plan or set of plans, you can start to look at ways of *embedding BC into your business*. The core of this activity is, of course, your staff.

If staff members understand what BC is and why it's important, they're more likely to take it seriously and ensure that it happens.

In Chapter 9, we cover the sorts of roles useful for your business to have in this area, while recognising that these aren't going to be full-time posts. We look at ways to use your staff in the best way through building your plan with a flexibility that gets around having a small workforce.

Exercising and testing

Carefully thinking through strategies and plans is all very well, but you need to test them to make sure that they work. The middle of a disruption isn't the time to find out that your backup supplier can't actually supply you!

The best and most cost-effective way to validate your plans is to test them out. The key concept is to stretch your arrangements with a scenario and look for things that don't go according to plan. An *exercise* – a simulation of an event to test staff and the capability of your business to deal with a situation – rehearses a situation to discover whether a plan is fit for purpose. An exercise may affirm a good job done and boost confidence just as much as identify vulnerabilities.

Several different levels of testing exist, right up to a full-blown live exercise. Here are the four levels that we cover in this book:

PRACTICE!

- **Walkthrough:** Key staff get together and discuss whether, based on their combined knowledge of the business, a BC plan has everything it needs.

- **Desktop scenario:** Key staff members meet again to discuss a plan, but this time they take a deeper look at it under specific circumstances.

- **Time-pressured desktop scenario:** Here you progress to tackle some real business over a period of, say, two hours or so. This level involves feeding in fresh pieces of information to a scenario at certain points.

- **Active test in real time:** Also known as live play and what is, in effect, an exercise. All involved concentrate on a time-pressured scenario with fresh information, tackled in real time with normal operations suspended. The aim is to test staff and see whether people can do what you expect of them.

Chapter 11 has a whole lot more on testing and running exercises.

Consulting experts and insurers

When you have your critical activities, dangers, weaknesses and plans clear, you may find that getting in an expert is easier than tackling some areas yourself (and certainly better than ignoring the problem entirely). For tricky areas such as IT, health and safety, fire safety, testing and trading standards, getting it right is essential, so unless you're certain, consulting those in the know is important (check out Chapter 12).

↳ Bringing in EM Consultants.

Ask your local authority whether it provides free BC guidance to businesses within its area and whether anyone can help your business by pointing you in the direction of local trade associations.

Generally, in this book the advice we provide is relevant to all businesses, no matter what sector or type. We do, however, give some more specific advice for manufacturing, retailers and professional services. Not to say that you should ignore this advice if you aren't a manufacturer, retailer or in a business providing professional services. On the contrary, Chapters 13, 14 and 15 contain a great deal of useful points for your business and are valuable if you come into contact with businesses in these sectors.

All businesses need to have insurance, but getting it right can be difficult with so many different policies available and so many different levels of cover and options. We give you some straightforward, common-sense advice in Chapters 2 and 12 on how to make sure that your insurance works for you. We also sift through the terminology to make it a subject that you no longer dread approaching.

It'll never happen to me . . .

If you aren't sure whether BC is an essential initiative for your business, here's a plea for you to reconsider.

When most people think of disruptions they normally consider the big, newsworthy events that always shock but never seem quite real unless you're there. Take flooding, for instance. When parts of Cumbria were submerged underwater in 2011, or during the widespread flooding of England and Wales in 2007, hundreds of businesses were affected, and some were damaged to the point that they were unable to continue after the clear-up. But how many business owners sat there and thought about the consequences for their business if something like that occurred?

In 2007, a business owner in Hull said, 'I just wanted advanced warnings from the authorities.' Although this request is reasonable, fulfilling it is simply not always possible, and so the only way to mitigate uncertainty is to have a plan in place for keeping your business going even when you receive little or no warning of events.

In addition, consider this: instead of the huge national event causing disruption, the situations that stop businesses without a plan in their tracks are the smaller occurrences, such as the burst water main in the car park, the overflowing cistern in the office toilet or the dishwasher water hose giving way. All businesses are surrounded by risks, not all of them grand, but the consequences can often be show-stopping. (We talk more about crises and disruptions in Chapter 10.) Perhaps we should have called this book *On with the Show* — and because the show is yours, so is the choice. Creating a BC plan may well be the most cost-effective and sound decision you ever make for your business.

Read Chapter 2 for more on what BC can offer your business.

Chapter 2

Understanding the Importance of Business Continuity

In This Chapter

- Bringing your business sense into play
- Cashing in with commercial sense
- Employing people sense
- Reaping the benefits of good financial and legal sense

*T*his chapter gets your business continuity (BC) journey well and truly underway, as we take you from where you are, via what's important to your business, to where you want to be going. We show you how initiating and embedding BC into your organisation brings business, commercial, financial and legal benefits and advantages, as well as helping you to support and protect your employees.

BC doesn't need to be complicated. We understand what you want and need as a small- or medium-sized business, and in this chapter we provide the essential information to help you make the necessary decisions. Whatever the size of your organisation, BC can work for you.

Appreciating the Benefits of Business Continuity

Getting straight down to the important stuff, here are some of the key benefits that an effective BC system can produce:

✔ Understand what's important to your organisation and in turn facilitate better, more confident decision-making (turn to Chapter 4 for more on how to do this).

✔ Bring assurance and protection to your staff (which we discuss further in the later section 'Developing Your People Sense' and Chapter 17).

✔ Increase your company's reputation (check out the later section 'Enhancing and supporting the reputation of your business').

✔ Show that you're serious about the resilience of your business (see Chapter 6 for details on demonstrating your business continuity to your customers and suppliers).

✔ Ensure that you have measures in place to fulfil your obligations as a supplier (flip to 'Supporting Financial and Legal Aspects', later in this chapter, for more info).

✔ Introduce testing and exercising of your BC strategies, which helps your team bond, raises staff awareness and ultimately strengthens your firm's resilience (we describe testing in Chapter 11).

Answering the following questions should indicate how introducing BC into your organisation is a must:

✔ How would a failure affect your legal and contractual obligations?

✔ Would your brand and reputation suffer in the event of a failure?

✔ How are your customers, suppliers and backers going to react to a real or perceived fall in your business's service?

✔ Can you afford to fail, or do people (including you!) rely on your business for their livelihoods?

Having effective BC doesn't turn a bad business into a good one or a failing business into a successful one, but it does help you when things go wrong – small or big time.

Business continuity is about knowing what you need to have to hand during a disruption, thus allowing you to keep calm and carry on.

Here are three more positive points to take on board:

✔ **Not expensive:** BC doesn't have to cost the earth.

✔ **Not technical:** BC involves no science.

✔ **Not complicated:** BC certainly involves no rockets!

No one can get around the fact that BC just makes plain good sense.

Making Business Sense

Business continuity makes good business sense for any size of organisation operating in any sector. Of course, the main purpose is to keep your business running when disaster strikes or disruption hits and to bounce back, but BC features much more good stuff besides.

Small- and medium-sized businesses build up over time, growing gradually and carefully and not necessarily following a grand plan that the business owner lays out from the start. As a result of this common situation – and generally because of the lack of hours in the working day – you seldom (if ever) have time to pause, take stock and get to understand what your business has become, and what really matters.

You can therefore have difficulty understanding properly the risks that your business faces. In addition, addressing the risks that threaten your business's critical activities – the ones that are vital to your business continuing – becomes almost impossible (check out Chapter 4 for all about identifying your critical activities).

Business continuity provides you with a logical and simple system to uncover those aspects without wasting that precious commodity of time on irrelevant things and without spending a lot of that other precious commodity: money.

A central theme of BC is that you don't do anything that isn't necessary. In addition, you receive some immediate benefits as well as, in the event of a disaster, having a lifeline for your business.

In this section, we describe four ways in which BC makes good business sense: maintaining stability, protecting your reputation, meeting your obligations and achieving your objectives.

Stabilising your organisation

A great deal of uncertainty permeates the business world. An ever-changing environment makes for an exciting working life and creates opportunities, but with these conditions comes instability that can have a detrimental effect on businesses.

Having BC gives those at the top of your organisation the understanding and confidence to make decisions, secure in the knowledge that they've got critical activities covered in the event of a disruption. Perhaps most important of all: you can lose your business without BC.

Enhancing and supporting the reputation of your business

In any business, your reputation plays a key part in how successful you are. Globalisation and the reduction of trade barriers have opened up greater opportunities for businesses, allowing you to do business more easily across continents. But this advantage creates an even greater need for you to guard against failed deliveries, which can so easily lead to customers going elsewhere. We touch again on the importance of your reputation in Chapters 15 and 19.

Being able to demonstrate resilience and having BC in place can mean that you win and keep customers ahead of your competitors.

Fulfilling your obligations

Business continuity can help you fulfil your obligations in two areas:

✔ BC is a good way of trying to avoid situations that end in a legal wrangle but also of demonstrating diligence in the event of something going wrong. The structured process for putting a BC system in place means looking at the risks that your business faces; one of these is likely to be the consequence of legal neglect.

✔ BC helps you to make contractual commitments to deliver goods or services because your organisation has planned what needs to happen to ensure you achieve your commitments.

Ultimately, whoever's in charge of the firm is liable if found to be negligent in the operation of the business and may face criminal proceedings. BC encourages the smooth running and resilience of your organisation to prevent this unpleasant event from happening. In Chapter 5 we encourage you to consider any obligations that your organisation has and, for specific sectors such as manufacturing (Chapter 13) and professional firms (Chapter 15), discuss what these might be.

Achieving your objectives

Business continuity isn't useful only in times of crisis. Although it certainly safeguards you against a disruptive event, it's also an effective way of helping you to meet your business objectives. For instance, if the overarching objective of a firm is to increase its market share, BC allows the organisation to understand and protect the resources it needs to deliver this objective. For example, say a bakery wants to increase its market share and has the opportunity to buy out another firm and move into larger premises. BC helps the bakery to understand what this action will mean for the combined organisation, and therefore BC improves decision-making.

If nothing else, the process of analysis and insight that the BC process gives you is invaluable. Forming a business impact analysis (BIA), as we discuss in Chapter 4, requires you to look at your resources, risks, staff, premises and supply chain. Doing so helps you understand exactly what's going on in your business, right down to the individual processes and activities. This level of insight enables you to pinpoint the weak areas in your business, break down the everyday motions of your business into understandable chunks and work to improve them.

Helping You to Profit from Commercial Sense

In this book, we work on the assumption that your business is profit-maximising. An important aspect of this aim is cost-minimisation, and BC most certainly plays its part here. If you sit on your organisation's board, you may well take a particular interest in this section. After all, unless this aspect of BC makes financial and commercial sense, you aren't going to want to implement it. If you aren't at board level but are going to need to gain the support of the board to get the green light for BC, this section helps you make your business case.

We break down commercial sense into three areas: we discuss customers and business opportunities in this section, and give the financial and legal side of things their own section later in the chapter: 'Supporting Financial and Legal Aspects'.

Considering your customers

Businesses are nowhere without customers – the organisations and individuals that give you money. Therefore, anything you can do to please and retain your customers must be a good thing.

BC is a valuable tool in this area because it helps businesses retain their existing customers by:

✔ Providing reassurance that the business will make deliveries and meet orders.

✔ Demonstrating diligence by being able to explain how things will keep running in the event of a disruption.

✔ Allowing you to deliver a service when other companies may be failing.

But BC also provides you with a competitive edge in another way. Approximately 20 years ago, customers and suppliers increasingly talked about quality management, with more customers wanting reassurance that the orders they were placing would be delivered to their requested specifications. Today, customers are demanding more than ever. At one time having a BC policy wasn't a prerequisite, or even a consideration, when doing business, but now we're seeing more and more organisations asking companies what BC arrangements they have in place, before signing or re-signing contracts.

If you can say that you have BC arrangements embedded into your organisation and can satisfactorily answer pertinent questions about those arrangements, you're a step nearer to retaining existing contracts and winning new ones.

In this book, we arm you with all the information you need to fulfil your potential to meet new or existing customer needs and protect your organisation and its reputation.

Recognising opportunities

Having BC embedded into your business demonstrates that you take the reliability of your service seriously, which you can use as a competitive selling point when pitching for new business. Firms that are able to keep operating when all around them are grinding to a halt have an opportunity to fill the shortfall for those customers that have been left short.

When disruptions hit a particular geographical area, such as flooding and major industrial accidents, almost always some businesses keep going while others are unable to do so. Think how much effort your business has put into winning and retaining customers – and the value that's at risk if you let them down. Ask yourself whether you really can afford not to have BC in your firm.

'Yes, we can do that for you' is one of the most satisfying things to tell a customer, and BC can give your organisation the ability to say these seven words – and mean them. The business world is, of course, not just about protecting what you have and shouting 'Steady as she goes!' from the helm, whether you're in choppy waters or not. It's about looking for, creating and responding to opportunities when they arise and being in a position to grasp and hold on to them. Although nobody likes to take advantage of other people's misfortune, in reality business misfortune is rarely simply unlucky. When a business fails one of its customers the reason may well be that it didn't have a continuity, alternative or backup plan in place – which enables your business to step in.

At the point when the customer is desperately ringing round to fulfil an order – having been let down by a supplier and not expecting to get a positive response because the incident that affected the regular supplier also affected others in the area – you step forward and say, 'Yes, we can do that for you. I'll put you through to Sales to take the order.'

How satisfying and what a great position to be in: you're one step closer to a new customer and a little bit nearer to your sales target for that month.

So, how were you able to say that with such confidence, when so many other suppliers couldn't help? Well, most likely because of one of these two scenarios and one or both of these reasons:

- ✔ Your business has been able to recover more quickly and continue after the recent flood, flu epidemic/pandemic, industrial fire, road closure and so on (delete as appropriate).

- ✔ Your organisation has a lean, flexible management structure and operational capacity, and your staff understands the business and is focused on the things that really matter.

  because . . .

- ✔ Your business has a business continuity system in place. You were able to access your plans quickly and efficiently from suppliers who adopt the same BC outlook as you.

- ✔ You just got lucky: you happened to have over-ordered that particular item last month.

If your answer in the 'because' section is the second one, in this book we support you in moving to the first option – helping you to get a BC system in place. However, if your answer was the first option, we're going to help you test and review the quality of your BC arrangements.

In most cases, your actual plans aren't what save you, but the planning that goes into creating them. To paraphrase General Eisenhower: *Planning is everything, the plan is nothing.*

By investing in BC and making it part of your business you're putting your business into a position where it can take advantage of opportunities when they arise, which enables you to say, 'Yes, we can do that for you'.

Developing Your People Sense

Your business is about people. Your staff members are the difference between making a delivery or missing it, getting that contract or not, enjoying being at work or hating every minute, and between success and failure.

BC is one of the most cost-effective ways of:

- ✔ Protecting your employees and their livelihoods.
- ✔ Providing peace of mind for you and your staff.
- ✔ Building team camaraderie within your firm.

In this section, we look at these three areas in a bit more detail.

Protecting your staff

Every organisation needs people and some need quite a few. But because people are human, they make mistakes that can cost you and them dearly. However, employing human beings also brings a vast wave of skills and endearing qualities that you just don't get with machines and equipment. So, accepting that everyone makes mistakes, BC is a useful way of protecting your organisation from the impact of these errors and your employees from losing their jobs.

Ensuring peace of mind for you and your staff

Peace of mind stems from knowledge, shared understanding and confidence in your organisation and its ability to continue 'whatever the weather'. Most of you can say that you've lived through a recession, and so you're acutely aware of the anxiety that lean times cause where job security is at the forefront of every employee's mind. Now, we aren't pretending that BC is the panacea for all your business's ills and woes, but it *is* a useful way of protecting your organisation from the impact of mistakes and disruptions.

How many times have you seen a seemingly minor disruption turn rapidly into a major crisis because the business failed to control the disruption at the start? BC can nip such situations in the bud by recognising the signs and helping you put measures in place to keep delivering your critical activities (we describe critical activities in Chapter 4). BC enables you to keep trading and equips your staff to deal with business-as-usual even when all may not be going so well. The knowledge that staff members build up when dealing with exercises (more on this in the following section) and real-life situations gives them confidence in the organisation and an understanding of what's important, which would be difficult to achieve with anything other than BC.

People feel insecure when they fear the unknown. BC reduces this fear by arming staff with knowledge and skills to deal with disruptive events. Employees understand what's critical to the organisation and how the part that they play in day-to-day business and during a disruption can have a major effect down the line. This knowledge and familiarity translates into a sense of job security that encourages people to focus on the things that matter and discourages your greatest asset from looking elsewhere. As a result, you retain staff and avoid the dreaded cost of recruitment.

Building team camaraderie within your firm

Even in a market where jobs are scarce and applications are plentiful, the situation doesn't fundamentally change: good people are hard to get and keep hold of. Finding people with the requisite level of skills and experience to fit seamlessly into your organisation's structure and culture is hard. You're sure to spend time and money replacing them and your expertise is diluted if a 'gap' appears. When valued staff members leave, your firm experiences direct and indirect implications, and rectifying these can cost you. Here are just a few of the potential costs involved:

- ✔ Time spent covering for the member of staff who needs replacing.
- ✔ Direct recruitment costs.
- ✔ The possibility of having to pay a higher salary.
- ✔ Indirect costs, such as internal training and induction.
- ✔ The interviewing and selection process.
- ✔ Setting up new employees in your firm's systems.
- ✔ The time for a new staff member to develop the required knowledge.

Staff retention is important and BC assists by overtly showing an investment in employees and instilling confidence and resilience. We discuss this point further in Chapters 9 and 17. Investing in measures that protect people in the event of problems is a sound investment that encourages co-operative working, thus enabling your business to flourish.

BC fosters co-operative working within your staff through the continual improvement process that it embeds into an organisation. The initial stage of understanding what's important to your business empowers staff members to look at the things they do in the context of the entire process. This wider viewpoint allows staff to identify dependencies by speaking to other colleagues, which in itself can open up ideas for new and better ways of working.

When you have BC in place, one of the most useful elements is to regularly test your recovery capability through the use of exercises. We look at testing, exercises and scenario-creation in Chapter 11.

A BC plan isn't really a plan until you've tested it. Exercises provide you with reassurance, de-briefing, opportunities for discussion and lessons to take on board. In addition, a BC exercise:

- ✔ Enables your staff to know what to do in a disrupting event, which can even save lives!

- ✔ Acts as a team-building day, at the same time as being of real value to the business in other ways.

- ✔ Provides feedback in a realistic situation that would be difficult to get in any other way.

You can hold an exercise anywhere that suits your business, on any scenario that you choose, and can involve anything that you want. As long as the scenario is feasible and allows you to test the assumptions you make in your plans and the associated arrangements, testing becomes very worthwhile. Another achievement is your staff acting confidently in a positive way at a time of disruption. And testing provides the opportunity for you to empower staff to take leadership roles that can assist in their development.

By investing in BC arrangements, you're directly investing in your business and your staff.

Supporting Financial and Legal Aspects

As well as making great business and commercial sense (subjects we cover in the earlier sections 'Making Business Sense' and 'Helping You Profit from Commercial Sense'), BC features other advantages too, some of which you may not have considered. In this section we discuss how introducing BC brings benefits relating to insurance, contractual obligations and profit margins.

What the insurance industry says about BC

The 2011 Business Continuity planning survey produced by the British Insurance Brokers' Association (BIBA) and the Cabinet Office contains the following valuable information:

- Sixty-two per cent of respondents said that those businesses with a Business Continuity Plan (BCP) will benefit from doors opening to new markets, a premium discount or a reduced excess.

- Forty-four per cent of respondents said that business interruption insurance would benefit from improved terms or discounted premiums if a robust BCP was in place.

- Of the insurer partners that responded, 83 per cent said that they would give a discount or improve terms to a business interruption policy if a BCP was in place.

- Various respondents stated that a tangible benefit of a BCP was turning what would probably be an unacceptable risk into one that insurers would underwrite.

- Ninety-six per cent of respondents with sufficient information on BC felt that having a BCP in place kept businesses trading when they would have otherwise likely failed, or that it seemed to reduce the cost of disruption significantly.

- The emergencies/disruptions that respondents most frequently had to deal with were flood or escape of water at 41 per cent and fire at 33 per cent.

- Some respondents stated that a BCP could be a condition of cover for high-risk business interruption exposures instead of giving a discounted premium.

- Forty-eight per cent of respondents said that insurers always suggest that customers arrange a BCP or suggest adoption of a BCP if asked what an organisation can do to be more resilient.

Covering what your insurance doesn't

When disruption hits, many businesses assume that their insurance policies are going to cover it. Although insurance policies can help businesses recover, and in a lot of cases the policies are mandatory, insurance alone just doesn't cut the mustard (whether your business is supplying condiments or not!). Here are the reasons:

- **Insurance doesn't cover your firm's reputation.** Insurance policies may well pay out in most cases, but remember that you need to carry on delivering to your customers the day that the disruption hits.

- **Insurance claims take time to settle.** Unless you have contingency plans to keep trading, you can be waiting weeks or even months before receiving payment and being able to buy more stock.

> ✔ **Insurance final settlement figures don't cover all your losses if an excess applies, if you're underinsured or an uninsured area is involved.** Therefore, you may well have a shortfall in what your business has lost and what your insurance company actually pays out. By having BC arrangements in place, you're more likely to be able to keep cash coming in and lessen the effect of your policy payout not matching your actual losses.

We provide a list of insurance tips in Chapter 16.

Helping you adhere to contracts

Contracts are an inevitable part of any business. They exist to protect yourself and the other party in delivering on your agreement. But with a contract comes commitments. You consider both contractual and legal obligations at the early stage of setting up BC: identifying the key products and services that your business delivers. Therefore, when trouble hits you've considered, and most likely put in place, contingency plans to ensure that delivery happens.

In the event that you're unable to deliver, because your contingency measure also fails or you decide to accept the risk of the failure occurring, you're at least able to demonstrate that you were diligent in ensuring that your business didn't breach the terms of the contract. Taking this precaution can assist in convincing your customer that legal action would be troublesome or, in the event of civil proceedings, that you took reasonable steps to avoid the failure.

Protecting profit

As a small business, making a profit and maintaining cash flow are priorities; after all, cash flow enables you to pay your bills. A high turnover can make the business appear to be doing well but can lead to cash flow problems and relentless pressure to maintain high sales volumes.

The profit that higher-margin products generate can be important to a business's survival. Usually, products and services have high margins for one of the following reasons:

> ✔ They have a unique selling point that distinguishes them from competitors.

> ✔ They're scarce and therefore demand is high (perhaps because a patent is in place).

> ✔ The production costs are low, usually brought about by volume (economies of scale).

> ✔ The supplier consistently delivers a quality product.

If your business has a product that accounts for a significant amount of its sales and delivers a higher margin, any reduction of this margin can have a significant impact on your business's profit. High-margin products can be threatened for a number of reasons:

✔ A competitor brings out a 'me too' product at a lower price.

✔ A patent expires or a product is developed by competitors that does the same job but doesn't infringe on the patent.

✔ Demand decreases through substitution or tastes changing.

✔ The cost of sales increases due to commodity price rises, existing supplier price increases or your having to turn to a more expensive supplier.

✔ You're unable to maintain quality or deliver consistently.

All these problems can result in your having to reduce the margin of products, just to be able to compete in the changed environment. Although BC can't protect your business against all these issues, it can help your business avoid times when you're forced to reduce your margin because of quality and/or delivery failings. BC can also provide some protection from supplier-driven price increases, because BC strategies encourage the use of alternative suppliers.

Making the Case: BC is Common Sense

Common sense is not so common.

— Voltaire, philosopher

Francois-Marie Arouet, who used the pen name 'Voltaire', perhaps knew a thing or two when it came to BC: it's common sense and yet not commonly used by small- and medium-sized businesses. In this section, we take a quick look at some possible objections to introducing BC.

Although the case for introducing BC into your business is, and perhaps always has been, compelling, we appreciate that other apparently more important things always seem to push BC back down the list of priorities. To help, in this book we make BC simple: simple to understand, simple to undertake and simple to make work for your business.

An objection may be that BC requires time and cost to introduce, and so we break it down into manageable chunks, none of which are costly or take a great deal of time to undertake.

In addition, as we describe in the earlier section 'Covering what your insurance doesn't', don't fall prey to the misconception that at a time of disruption your insurance is going to cover everything or that the emergency services are going to save the day. Although your insurance policy will, in most cases, pay out, your business is vulnerable while you're trying to get back up and running. Of course, the emergency services do a wonderful job of saving lives and regaining calm, but they can't save your business and regain your customers.

The mindset that says 'our business doesn't need a plan; *we're good at dealing with crises when they happen*' just doesn't work. By not having contingency strategies in place, you're leaving your business's survival to chance and frantic activity when things go wrong. Also, no one's immune to disruption and disaster: no business can influence or control everything.

BC provides a way to manage large disruptions and minimise the effect on your business, and can prevent an incident turning into a crisis. But BC's not just there for the big things – it also functions to keep things going smoothly during minor hiccups and whatever life throws at you.

Business continuity can give you (especially if you're kept awake at night because of personal guarantees you gave) and your staff the confidence and peace of mind to get on with what matters: doing business.

But, above all, BC is just common sense!

Chapter 3

Achieving Rapid Results and Quick Wins

In This Chapter

▷ Assessing the resilience of your business

▷ Making immediate progress with the 'Seven Ps'

*H*uman nature dictates that you believe your business to be more resilient than it actually is. And because staff members take their lead from you, when you give them the impression that all is hunky-dory, they aren't going to be alert to risks. The buck stops with a firm's owner as regards business survival, and if you always do what you've always done, you always get what you always got . . . which means that lightning – metaphorically – can strike in the same place twice, or even three, four or five times.

So you want to begin introducing business continuity (BC) in your organisation without delay. For this reason, we design this chapter to get you off to a flying start by offering a host of inexpensive and simple ways to begin building resilience quickly within your business.

This chapter describes some straightforward measures that don't take long or cost much, but do encourage the resilience of your business. We take you through some great tips and quick wins – under an easy-to-remember framework of the 'Seven Ps' covering everything from People and Premises to Publicity and Public Infrastructure. Although following the tips in this chapter doesn't mean that your business has full BC in place, these actions can make a big difference when you need help the most.

Giving Your Business a Resilience Health Check with The Seven Ps

Approaching something as large as building resilience in your whole business can raise the question: 'Where on earth do I start?' Well, to help you we split the simple tips in this chapter into seven useful areas that influence or form part of your business:

- ✔ **People:** HR and skills.
- ✔ **Premises:** Property/locations.
- ✔ **Processes and information technology (IT):** Activity/functions/technology.
- ✔ **Priorities:** Your customers and suppliers.
- ✔ **Publicity:** Internal and external communications.
- ✔ **Public infrastructure:** Local authority, environment and community.
- ✔ **Phone numbers:** From your nearest and dearest to emergency experts.

The precise way in which you use this chapter is up to you. You can start where you like, leave and come back when you choose, or work through each list in turn and in doing so give your business a bit of a resilience health check.

The lists in this chapter contain inexpensive actions that you really need to take and precautions you need to have in place. Although not as comprehensive as a car MOT, by developing a few simple ideas your business can become resilience roadworthy. The quick wins in this chapter are all about implementing now some basic things that can make a big difference later on.

You can use the lists in this chapter as checklists and tick off each item as you complete it. Or simply cross out the aspects that aren't relevant to your firm. Those that do apply are simple to use and cost little or nothing. All the tips get you thinking about the sort of things that you could do to make your business more resilient.

A good early quick win is to look only at the components of your organisation that we describe in this section in the context of your business's *critical activities:* the things that you have to perform in order to deliver your most important products and services. These activities enable your business to meet its most important and time-critical objectives that you can't manage without. We look into critical activities in more detail in Chapter 4.

People: Keeping Staff Members Safe and Accounted For

Your staff members aren't called your business's human resources for nothing. Their training, skills and expertise are the supporting backbone of your firm. In this section what cover some initial measures that you can take to protect and look after them:

✔ **Produce an emergency contacts sheet.** Include telephone numbers and contact names for all the people you need to speak to in an emergency.

To help compile this information, imagine that you've just received a call on a Sunday night from the fire brigade telling you that your firm's building has been caught in a fire and razed to the ground. The question to ask is: 'Who ya gonna call?'

We show a simple example of a contacts sheet in Figure 3-1.

Management Team			
Maureen Bonn	General Manager	0207 568 7895	07986 8
John Ansell	Operation Manager	0207 687 7865	07272 8
Peter Wright	Quality Manager	0118 789 8383	07777 8
Geoff Winfield	Head of Sales	01987 839622	07898 9
Matthew Chris	Finance Director	0211 3873 933	07902 9
Production Team			
Steve Creed	Shift Manager	0218 221 2247	0754
Warehouse			
Pauline Barclay	Cambridge	0208 215 8963	07
Jim Spriggs	Doncaster	01398 454457	
Maintenance			
Willie Johnson	Production	0208 456974	
Tim Squires	General Duties	0258 46846	
Key Suppliers			
Cogs and Turns Ltd	Jim Reeve (Sales)	0800	
	Peter Windrush (Ops)	018	
Trim and Bumper Ltd	Angela Main (GM)	02	
	Pete Connolly (Ops)		
Oil and Grease Plc	Colin Candahour (Sale		
	Margaret Timms (On		
Key Customers			
Oxbox auto	Janet V·		

Figure 3-1:
A simple contacts sheet.

The contact information needs to be simple and done on a spreadsheet (as in Figure 3-1) or by hand. Emergency contact names and numbers change frequently, which causes expense and difficulty in printing updated cards. Mobile phones are useful for storing numbers; even without a signal, the numbers are still available.

Another useful tip is to list numbers and other information that doesn't change on a thin piece of card that you fold in a zigzag shape down to credit card size and keep in a wallet or purse. You can keep staff up to date with changes through text messages or 'V' cards – such as electronic business cards adapted for this purpose.

The key points to remember when you're finished with your contacts sheet are:

- Give a copy to all members of staff who may find it helpful.

- Print off hard copies, in case an emergency affects your IT.

- Ensure that you have a copy easily accessible and, most importantly, in a safe place off-site.

- Make sure that the sheet is updated regularly; a good approach is to make updating the contacts sheet part of someone's role and link it to that person's appraisal objectives.

- Emphasise to staff the importance of keeping this information safe.

✔ **Account for your staff and visitors.** Create and maintain an in/out register at reception that you can carry during an evacuation and use to ensure that everyone's safely outside.

If you have a large workforce or members of the general public are inside your premises, pass a pen and a pad around during an evacuation for everyone to write down their names and a person (and telephone number) to contact on their behalf. Doing so confirms people's safety to the emergency services and gives you the details to reassure invariably concerned relatives who may try to call them, you or the emergency services to check people are okay. Having a list helps prevent any confusion, reduce anxiety and cut down the number of unnecessary phone calls.

✔ **Create a set of roles and responsibilities.** Communicate it to all staff detailing who'll take control of an incident and who'll step in if that person is absent.

✔ **Set up a skills register.** You and your staff may have skills, such as languages, first aid, accountancy qualifications and IT or DIY skills, that aren't always apparent until you ask. These abilities can become really useful at a time of disruption. Also, consider maintaining contact with staff who retire by offering to pay them a monthly retainer and refresher training, so that in the event of a disruption you have additional resources to call upon.

Make sure that your insurance covers retired or temporary staff while they're working for you (read more about insurance in Chapter 16).

✔ **Cross-train and multi-skill-train your staff.** You want your staff to be able to replace or reinforce each other (plus multi-training adds a bit of variety, which is of course the spice of life; and you thought this was going to be dull!).

Why not make the cross-training a topsy-turvy day in which people do each other's roles? Doing so may well uncover single points of failure you didn't know you had. You may even be a single point of failure yourself, and so ask yourself: 'What happens if I'm away or caught up in the incident itself?' Managers and owners aren't exempt from being the cause of problems!

✔ **Create an emergency number for staff to call.** The most cost-effective way to do this is to buy a pay-as-you-go mobile and follow these steps. Before an incident:

- Give staff the number in advance and ask them to call it in an emergency and listen for instructions.

  Explain that during an emergency they need to call the number regularly because you'll endeavour to update the message on the hour.

- Test the number at least once a month.

- Keep the mobile telephone off-site, or have two: one off- and one on-site.

At the time of an emergency:

- Record a voicemail message that provides the information you need to give.

- Test it.

- Ensure all calls are diverted to this recorded voicemail.

By recording a message in this way, callers can listen to the message, which you can update regularly on the hour every hour. Therefore you can brief many people at the same time without having to call each person individually.

✔ **Have hand sanitisers ready for use during a flu epidemic or pandemic.** In the 2009 flu pandemic, retail stocks ran down very quickly and suppliers were unable to meet rising demand. The upshot was that businesses were unable to provide a low-cost way to avoid the spread of germs and help prevent their staff getting the virus.

Premises and Assets: Preparing and Taking Precautions

This section contains some easy measures to take to protect your business buildings (and the people inside them) and keep your assets safe:

- ✔ **Plan the evacuation of your building.** Consider how you're going to evacuate the building and how you can ensure that everyone gets out safely, taking into consideration those with less mobility. Plan where you're going to evacuate to and assemble.

  Now, imagine that the exit you intend to use is blocked and the congregation area you select is cordoned off. Plan your contingency arrangements to deal with these problems. Also consider:

  - **Your way of alerting people to an evacuation.** Shouting or blowing a whistle may be the quickest and easiest method. But make sure that staff are aware of the plans in advance and that you test them . . . while you have the chance. An evacuation situation is not one where you want to be relying on lessons learned for the next time during a real event. You need an effective way of communicating to people.

  - **Your routes of escape.** Even if you or staff members are working from home, ensure that you can open an upstairs window and throw a mattress out to soften your landing, in case you have to climb out, hang from the window ledge and drop onto the mattress. In an office you can test the effectiveness of your safe route by timing you and your team.

  Panic and other potential difficulties, such as heat and smoke, mean that these tasks may well take two or three times longer in a real-life situation than during a test scenario. If appropriate, mark exit routes along walls or on the floor.

  - **How you or your staff are going to dial 999.** If everyone makes it safely out of the building but nobody has a mobile phone, or no signal is available, where are you going to go to raise the alarm? Check for premises nearby and public call boxes.

- ✔ **Consider 'invacuation' (taking shelter where you are).** *Invacuation* is a relatively new word and pretty much means remain where you are, identify the safest place to be and stay inside. This place may be the cupboard under the stairs if you work from home or the core of the building in offices.

Basements and cellars are often cited as being the best place (if you have one and flooding isn't a problem), but check that you can get a mobile phone signal to notify people that you're safe and whether the basement is big enough for everyone to fit into.

Write a list of what you'd want in the basement if you had to stay for a couple of hours and then get these items in. Although situations in which you and your staff need to invacuate may be uncommon, they do occur – for example, during bomb threats or following a contamination – so this precaution is worth taking.

✔ **Identify muster points, assembly areas and take care of immediate business.** Of course you need to identify and communicate where everyone should meet up outside – such as the car park or the end of the road – to carry out a roll-call. But in addition to this initial muster point, for more prolonged periods, think of alternatives such as a cafe, pub or hotel that would be more comfortable. Wherever this alternative is, perform a roll-call of all who were in the building, remembering to account for any staff and visitors, and let the police know if anyone's missing.

Later you could meet at your home or look to have a reciprocal agreement with another business premises to plan things in the immediate term. As time ticks by and minutes appear about to turn to hours, you need to keep your business activities going. Here are the key considerations connected to your temporary, alternative place of working:

- Does this place have Internet access?

- Do you have means of accessing the Internet, such as a laptop?

- Do you know what business needs to be done today, such as orders that need to be dispatched or invoices that need to be sent out?

- Can you get access to files through the Internet; for example, through *cloud computing*, where your business can hire storage areas held on remote machines to keep files and software applications, which means you can access files wherever you have a computer with an Internet connection.

If you realise when asking these questions that your business would be unable to carry on without access to your permanent site, consider how you can store information so that you can access it away from the office. Store any company property and information securely, such as in a box with a numerical padlock to which only relevant members of the firm know the code.

✔ **Don't dispose of old equipment unless you have to.** This particularly applies to specialist equipment that your business has replaced with newer items. Reconditioning the old equipment is worthwhile (if the cost is acceptable); hold it in reserve at another location or in storage.

Even common equipment such as printers and fax machines, if they're still working, is worth keeping as a standby along with ink cartridges. In the case of reusing old computer equipment, ensure that your IT team fixes them up regularly and downloads all relevant software patches.

✔ **Take digital photos of your office.** This way you have evidence of what it looked like before it was burned down, ransacked, flooded or contaminated with toxic waste. The photos are useful for insurance purposes and to jog memories about what's lost.

✔ **Identify any localised risks to your business premises.** Who are your neighbours and what do they do? Carry out a quick search online against your postcode to see who works close by and the type of businesses they run. Take five minutes to walk around your local area, looking to see who does what and where. Think about potential risks within the environment or associated with the business; a business doesn't have to be a multi-national petrol chemical plant to hold hazardous or inflammable substances.

Ask yourself: if something happened here, would my business's

- Premises be affected (for example, from fire or fallout)?

- Buildings still be accessible?

- Stocks become contaminated with no contingency stocks available?

✔ **Make arrangements for a backup location.** Use your local business network to find an alternative location for use during a crisis or disruption until recovery allows you back into your premises. The most cost-effective way is to find a business with spare capacity, within a similar sector to yours, in an adjoining district (near, but not too near) and not in direct competition with you. Speak with the owner about putting in place a reciprocal arrangement whereby in the event of a disruption your staff can work from those premises to carry out your firm's critical business functions.

Serviced offices are another option. Provided the information and communication technology (ICT) is covered, a business can be up and running in hours. Some services provide access to PCs, printers and faxes at a moment's notice. Cloud servers make an ideal alternative to physical storage and are likely to work out less expensive than buying backup hardware.

✔ **Find an alternative location that can receive your deliveries.** So you've had a disruption and can't get access to your site. All's still well, however, because your staff are carrying out critical activities (taking orders, sending out invoices and so on) at a pre-arranged backup location. The trouble is that you need to receive some more goods and you have nowhere to receive them. In this situation, find a local warehousing firm that has suitable accommodation for your goods (dry, correct ambient temperature and so on). Ensure that the firm is likely to be able to receive a short-notice call to receive goods. Alternatively, use your business contacts to work out who you'd call in the event of needing some short-term space. Arrange this now and you've one less thing to worry about if the time comes.

✔ **Contact a local vehicle hire company.** You need a vehicle, suitable for your business needs, and delivered to your door. If your business relies on a van to deliver goods, find a local rental firm that can replace it if yours is stolen or involved in an accident. An alternative is to use a reciprocal arrangement with another business or arrange to borrow a vehicle from friends or family.

In this latter case, make sure that you have the appropriate insurances in place.

Processes and IT: Keeping Data Safe and Your Business Trading

In this section we provide some useful advice relating to computing and technical system processes, and we also describe a few simple measures for keeping your general business processes up and running.

To protect that most valuable but intangible resource – your business data – here are a few tips:

✔ **Copy your data regularly onto a memory stick, DVD, portable hard-disk drive or backup tape and take it off-site.** Whatever option you choose, test it to make sure that you can retrieve all the files on another PC.

One of the most common mistakes that a business makes is conscientiously backing up its data every day, but not checking that the backup is working and that staff can retrieve the data when necessary. You don't want to discover this problem during an incident. Also make sure that another person has permission and access to get to the backup files so that in your absence someone else can restore your data or recover a lost file.

✔ **Print off copies of documents that you can't afford to lose.** Invest in storing important paper copies off-site or scan documents and hold them electronically on a memory stick that you can easily access.

✔ **Prioritise your electronic files so you can back up and protect the most important ones.** Do the same with your company's documents: scan them in and save them so they're backed-up off-site.

✔ **Train someone to navigate your data.** In an emergency, that person needs to be able to find the files that you need urgently.

✔ **Establish levels of authority.** Ensure that support companies, particularly IT, finance and other key departments, have a chain of command set up. No point having someone authorised to make important departmental decisions if that person's on holiday when an important decision needs to be made.

✔ **Create an asset register of your hardware, with photographs of each item.** See whether your accounting software has a built-in asset register for depreciation of more expensive and durable items.

✔ **Design a user policy.** Explain the dangers of information security to your information (and IT) users. This policy can be as simple as not downloading anything from the Internet and not opening attachments from unknown sources. Choose the best option for your firm based on your staff and business culture.

✔ **Remember the impact that social media can have during an incident.** Ensure that staff members are familiar with the rules and make sure that your user policy (see the preceding bullet point) includes references to how employees should be cautious of what they publish on their social media accounts. Inappropriate messages can have a detrimental effect on your organisation and its reputation.

✔ **Keep servers and other crucial bits of equipment out of the basement if any chance exists that it may flood.** The basement is a tempting place to store these sorts of items and in some cases can be a good solution, but a possibility of flooding means the risk that you have to carry wet equipment upstairs in a hurry. Best to move any equipment now in your own time, while it (and you) are dry.

In the following list, we give you some easy ideas for keeping your business processes up and running in an emergency:

✔ **Identify your business's main profit-earning product or service.** Consider carefully all the processes that need to happen to keep delivering this product or service (see Chapter 4 for more on this aspect). Now, with this list of activities in mind, work out what you'd do if the processes failed. Here are some solutions:

   • **Dual-source vital component suppliers.** Although doing so may have a cost in terms of losing a better price by not committing to a higher volume with a single supplier (an economy of scale), it may make all the difference if your supplier lets you down.

Dual-sourcing also provides a hidden benefit in that the two suppliers don't want to be outdone by the rival on quality or delivery reliability. A single supplier that you rely on and has had your business for years may take it for granted and get complacent, whereas a supplier that knows it's not unique tends to raise its game and pay better attention to your account.

- **Maintain a contingency stock at a separate location to your main site.** The best and cheapest way is to negotiate this extra stock as part of the existing contract with your supplier, so that it always has one month's worth of supply in stock at its location and cost.

  Also, carry one month's stock based on your current forecast. So if you forecast to sell 112 pallets in February, ensure that you have 224 in your warehouse at the start of the month and that the level doesn't fall significantly below the original 112 figure. Although predictable seasonal spikes in sales are easy to recognise and prepare for, businesses can get caught out with the unexpected spikes in demand caused by external events (an example is the run on antibacterial products during the swine flu scare).

- **Know what happens during a week in the life of your business.** Sit down with a colleague or two and write down all the processes that take place in a normal week in the life of your business. Then identify the things that must happen for those processes not to threaten the business's survival. If you don't have the answers now, Chapters 4 and 7 provide you with options to consider for some of these items. Often, the simplest and most common-sense solutions are the best.

- **Keep an eye on the news.** Look at how events can affect your business and the wider business environment. Not only can you steal a march on your competitors, but also you may even create a few new business opportunities.

- **Carry out a regular quality check on your stock received.** If one of your suppliers changes the specification of a component or produces something to a lower than expected standard, make sure that you find out first, before one of your customers.

✔ **Create a mini Business Continuity Plan (BCP).** Just to get you started, imagine an incident befalls your business premises: say a fire has ripped through and nothing appears salvageable. Take ten minutes with a pen and paper to work through the scenario as you imagine it playing out. How would you recover from something like this? How would you keep going during the worst of it? What are your considerations? Write them down and produce a simple two-page plan for what you'd do. We provide much more of your full BCP in Chapter 8.

Prioritising Your Customers and Suppliers

Of course, all businesses need to maintain good relations with their customers and suppliers, and no doubt you spend considerable time and effort doing so. Therefore, the last thing you want to happen is for a disruption to put these carefully nurtured relationships at risk. In this section, we discuss a few precautions you can take to mitigate that possibility:

✔ **Think about your critical suppliers and customers so that you know which to concentrate on when a disruption hits.** A very simple approach is to get hold of a list of all your suppliers and plot them on a matrix that shows the criticality of the things that they supply and the amount you spend with them. Carry out a similar process with your customers to show how much they spend with you and any onerous contractual penalties. Figure 3-2 shows an example of this kind of matrix.

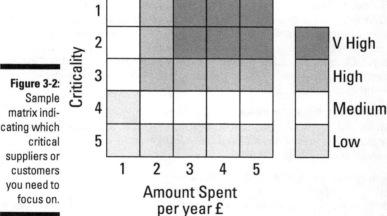

Figure 3-2:
Sample matrix indicating which critical suppliers or customers you need to focus on.

A graph like the one in Figure 3-2 can identify those suppliers that supply critical products (they're plotted higher up on the vertical axis), and those suppliers that your business spends a lot of money with (plotted further to the right on the horizontal axis). So you see the suppliers that deliver critical components and that you spend the most with. (However, bear in mind that the volume of goods purchased with a supplier, not cost, may be the most important factor to your business.)

✔ **Find out what continuity measures your suppliers have in place.** For the suppliers that you identify in Figure 3-3's matrix as being critical and/or high volume, ask them whether they have BCPs in place and if you can see a copy. If they're that critical to your firm but don't have any continuity plans in place, find another supplier or work with the existing one to help it put something in place.

Even when you have the most secure BCPs in place, if your sole supplier doesn't then the danger of failure somewhere along the line remains high. An investment, such as working with your key suppliers to help them put BC in place, not only makes your supply chain a bit more resilient, but also may reveal other frailties that you need to address – the sorts of things that you wouldn't be aware of until your expected delivery of raw materials fails to arrive.

✔ **Ask your customers what service level they expect from you while your business is suffering a disaster and afterwards.** Putting a Service Level Agreement (SLA) in place is a good idea so that in the event of difficulty you know exactly what suppliers expect of you and can work this into your BC considerations.

✔ **Come up with other ways to influence the resilience in your supply chain.** In the bath one evening – you need to be relaxed – think about your suppliers and their suppliers and their supplier's suppliers and see whether you have any influence on the chain that enables your business to function. The key is to focus on the suppliers that are crucial to your core business functions. If your stationery supplier lets you down, you simply run to the local retail park and get the things that you need. But if your sole oohjamiwotsit cog supplier lets you down in supplying the cog that keeps 'line 1' running, life may be very different.

✔ **Question your professional services vendors about what help you can expect from them if you have a disaster.** Accountants, lawyers, doctors, bankers and consultants may offer you advice, special terms, office space at their premises and/or back office help. If you don't ask, you don't get (of course, sometimes you ask and still don't get, but you know what we mean). Also, look into what plans and procedures they have to keep you going if they have a disaster.

✔ **Use your supplier contacts for advice and support.** This point may sound obvious but you can be surprised at how far suppliers may go to support a customer. Use this support to ensure that you can keep your business running when disaster strikes. Your suppliers have a wealth of experience in dealing with all sorts of disruptive events and may be able to advise you on the best course of action or even provide support through offering the use of their premises or hauliers, for example.

✔ **Get to know your suppliers.** Whether you've not ordered enough to meet the demand of your customers or your supplier has had a disruption at its end and is below usual capacity, the relationship with your supplier can be crucial. If the supplier is that important to your business and supplies goods that form part of your business's critical activities (the ones we focus on in Chapter 4), building up a good relationship is an essential investment. Doing so may mean a face-to-face meeting each month and doing your bit by providing regular forecast updates for orders, or even inviting your contact to the firm's Christmas do – simple stuff that can make all the difference when push comes to shove.

✔ **Discover how important you are to your supplier.** If you're a big customer, you can expect a higher priority than a small customer, and vice versa. If you discover that you're of low priority then it's time to start looking at ways to increase your firm's importance with the supplier through additional orders or face-to-face discussions. If this isn't feasible, seek out alternative suppliers while you have time on your side. The worst time to find out that you're not on the priority list of one of your key suppliers is during a disruption!

Publicity: Keeping People Informed

In an emergency, you need to get information to the right people quickly, concisely and accurately. The following list provides some ideas relating to your business's internal and external communications:

✔ **Warn and inform.** Write a template for what you may want to communicate and tape it to the side of a megaphone or keep it in the boot of your car. You then don't have to struggle to recall what to say when you're briefing your staff.

✔ **Set up an all-staff text message so that you can send a text broadcast from your phone.** Do the same with an email group so you can email everyone you want to notify; it saves wasting time selecting the group. Test this broadcast, so that recipients know what to expect and what action they need to take; for example, acknowledging by email or texting back that they're safe.

✔ **Use a conference bridge facility.** Many vendors offer this service for free. To discover the companies that do in your area, type 'conference bridge facility' into your Internet search engine. The service works by simply telling your staff to call into a pre-existing number with a personal identification number (PIN). All callers are then able to talk together on the same call, which can help avoid confusion with people passing messages on incorrectly (such as 'everything is all right' becoming 'everything is alight'!).

Have a structured agenda ready for these calls because during tense times of disruption people forget the normally observed protocol that only one person can effectively speak at a time.

Rehearse these calls, if only to check that the number still works.

✔ **Appoint a single point of contact for the emergency services.** This arrangement ensures that one person handles any questions and answers effectively and only once. Preferably, this person is level-headed and able to think rationally in a crisis. The person should be able to provide maps or floor plans of your premises that show hazards and the locations of stopcocks, mains switches, shut-off valves and so on. Also, appoint an informed deputy to cover when this person is out of the office.

✔ **Keep an eye on what's going on in the world.** Some people see 24-hour news as intrusive and/or boring, but for the small business, being able to see what's going on in the world in near real time can be a plus. Check what's happening internationally, regionally and locally, and assess the impact that these events may have on your business. For example, if a major road traffic accident affects one of your supply routes then early notice of this can give you the time to make alternative arrangements, such as using other routes or transport options.

Public Infrastructure: Liaising with People in Your Community

Maintain a list of contacts for reporting an emergency to, such as your utility providers, local authorities and other businesses within your area, and keep it safely off-site so you can access it quickly. Other useful numbers are those commonly referred to as 'In Case of Emergencies' (ICE) contacts such as 101, 999, Crimestoppers (0800 555111) and the Counter-terrorism Hotline (0800 78932).

You can add all these numbers to your staff contact list (which we discuss in the earlier section 'People: Keeping staff members safe and accounted for'). Also, ensure that staff enter numbers they're likely to need in an emergency into mobile phones as easily identifiable contacts.

Here are some more preparations that you can make in this area:

✔ **Book yourself and your staff onto a Project Argus (Area Reinforcement Gained Using Scenarios) course with your local police or local council.** These courses aim to simulate terrorist attacks in order to teach businesses how to deal with different situations and reactions. They can provide you with solutions for dealing with and recovering from an act of terrorism, if such an incident strikes your business.

✔ **Enrol your security or reception staff members onto a Project Griffin course.** Again run by local authorities nationwide, Project Griffin encourages relations between the police and local businesses in order to communicate with each other and share information about any terrorist activity or crime in the area. Both Project Argus and Griffin courses are free to attend and are particularly relevant if your business is situated near or in a city. They provide invaluable advice to make your business more resilient.

✔ **Ask your local council whether it offers free advice and assistance on BC.** Make contact and check whether it has a BC or resilience forum that you can join. These groups can offer a good introduction to business continuity and local authority BC managers are a good sources of reference for putting BC in place in your business.

✔ **Download your local area's Community Risk Register.** You can find it through an Internet search engine. Have a look and see what risks your particular area faces, or indeed the area that your key suppliers operate from – just to give you something else to worry about (we write more on risk in Chapter 5).

✔ **Speak to your local fire station about fire safety for your business.** Arrange a PAT (Portable Appliance Test) for your electrical appliances, get a D certificate on your power circuit and a free smoke detector/alarm from the Fire Brigade, and buy a fire extinguisher. Ask your neighbours what fire prevention they have in place.

✔ **Look around your locality and spot potential hazards.** A petrol station, a pub, a back alley, a jeweller's or a doctor's surgery may present risks to your business.

✔ **Download your flood risk map from the Environment Agency.** Be pleased with what you see . . . or start carrying items upstairs.

✔ **Contact your local crime prevention officer or neighbourhood watch scheme.** Ask about crime in the area and assess your crime prevention measures. You can check your local area for crime rates by searching the Internet.

Phone Numbers: Keeping Essential Contact Info Handy

Having up-to-date contact details is crucial if you find your business in a tight spot. Here are a few people and organisations to consider contacting if things start to go awry:

✔ **Next of kin:** Keep a record of the designated next-of-kin details for your staff. Police require this info because they have the awful job of notifying relatives in the event of an injury or death.

✔ **Skilled trades-people and responders:** Store details for people and companies that you may need to call upon such as emergency services, local authority, taxis, vehicle, accommodation, locksmiths, landlord, plumbers, electricians, carpenters (for boarding up), glaziers, IT service providers (helpdesk), utilities and professional services (doctor, accountant, solicitor, bank manager, insurer, loss adjuster and so on).

Some areas distribute locally produced directories where local firms can advertise their services. These are posted through the doors of local businesses and houses or may be available at the local library or on the internet.

✔ **Customers and suppliers:** Realistically, you aren't going to be able to call all your customers or clients immediately following a disruption, and so you may want to prioritise these contact details: those that depend on you as a supplier and would be unable to survive without your business's output.

✔ **Your friends and family:** Murphy's Law says that your mobile phone battery won't be charged at the time you need it most. Call your nearest and dearest and ask him or her to call everyone on your Christmas card list (oh yes, make a Christmas card list!) to let them know you're fine but not to call because you're busy with incident management. You could suggest that they can call your partner for an update later on at, say, 6 p.m. You then ring your partner at 5:50 p.m. to give an update. Doing so means you have to make only one call and you manage the inevitable call volume during a newsworthy incident in your area.

✔ **Recruitment agencies:** Firms you can call for casual labour or interim special skills to reinforce or replace your workforce.

✔ **Salvage and restoration specialists:** Companies that specialise in document recovery, data recovery, underpinning, drying/de-humidifying, fire/ smoke damage, flood damage, structural engineers and pest control.

✔ **The media:** Create your own contacts within the local press; call them and introduce yourself before they need to get hold of you during a crisis. This approach encourages good relations and gives the impression that you're working with rather than against the media.

Part II

Starting Out on Your Business Continuity Journey

The 5th Wave   By Rich Tennant

"It's the crew, Captain Columbus — they want to know what our flat-world contingency plan is."

In this part . . .

*W*e launch you into the world of business continuity, showing you how to identify what's important to your business and the risks to watch out for, as well as building resilience in your supply chain. We also cover designing and constructing your business continuity framework and turning it into a plan that's practical and useable.

Chapter 4

Focusing on What's Important: Business Impact Analysis

*A*lthough every aspect of your business is important, some things are absolutely essential for the running of your firm and others fulfil lesser roles. If you can't fix everything at once and 'something's gotta give' when disruption hits, you're better off already knowing which parts of your business you can afford to put on hold and what gets priority treatment – you certainly don't want to be making these decisions in the middle of an incident.

After deciding on these key products and services, you need to determine and prioritise the activities that are critical to delivering them. In this chapter, we help you identify these critical activities and look at their time sensitivity to help ensure that you don't miss any when the pressure is really on.

We call this whole process *Business Impact Analysis* (BIA). By analysing your business in this way you can work out exactly what activities are critical and by when you need to recover them. In this chapter, we use the example of a bakery to illustrate the various stages of performing a BIA.

Although the idea of carrying out a BIA may appear pretty daunting and involved, in fact it's less confusing (but possibly more important) than it sounds. When done well, a BIA lays the foundations for good business continuity (BC) arrangements for your organisation.

Understanding What Matters Most

Your *key products and services* are the ones that are truly essential to your business's survival. Even if a disruption stops you performing in some sectors, these areas are the ones that you need to prioritise and can't allow to fail. These products or services are supported by a number of activities, and we call the most important and time-critical of these your *critical activities*. Without them you have no product or service to offer, and in due course, perhaps no business.

Identifying your key products and services and associated critical activities is about deciding what's in and what's out (of scope). In general, small or medium businesses focus solely on what they need to do to achieve their goals anyway, and if this sounds like you, you're already halfway towards having a BIA.

The initial stage in the process is to write down a list of all the products and services that your business produces or delivers. (We assume that your aim is to make a profit by selling products or providing a service, or if you're a charity or not-for-profit firm that you aim to do what you do for the best value.)

The next step is to decide on the relative importance of the products and services by thinking about what would happen if you weren't able to produce all your usual outputs. How would your customers deal with this situation and how long would you take to get the organisation back on its feet?

Your business has an existing strategy or certainly plans to meet its objectives and aims. Supporting these are your products and services, and in turn supporting them are activities or processes. The loss of each of these activities or processes has a different impact within hours, sometimes even minutes. Your priority is to restore the activities that have the greatest impact in the shortest timescale: that is, your critical activities.

Identifying your key products and services

You may be able to write down a list of your key products or services right now. In which case, you may ask, what's this section for? Well, this section:

- Checks your assumptions about what your key product and services are.

- Shows you how to rank them in order of importance.

- Highlights any assumptions you need to include but didn't, or vice versa.

- Allows you to demonstrate the reasons behind your decisions.

The Business Continuity Institute's Good Practice Guidelines offer some useful guidance: a business should review its products and services against its strategy, objectives, culture, ethical policy and legal and regulatory requirements. In addition, the Guidelines list the following relevant factors to take into account:

- ✔ Customer requirements.

- ✔ Regulatory or statutory requirements.

- ✔ Perceived high-risk location due to proximity to other industrial premises or physical threats such as flooding.

- ✔ One product providing an overwhelming proportion of the organisation's income.

To help with this task, we focus on a few vital areas in which trouble can arise and we identify them with the mnemonic 'FORCES' (Financial, Operational, Reputation, Customers and suppliers, Environment and Staff; flip to the later section 'Protecting Against the FORCES of Disruption' for much more detail on each of these areas). You use these six factors to determine your key products or services by attributing scores to each one on a grid (check out the later Figure 4-2).

A simple way of deciding the importance of something is to consider what happens if it isn't in place. In terms of your business, what would happen if you couldn't send out a product or you couldn't provide a service? What would be the impact on your business as a whole and on other aspects of your organisation? In BC terms: what would be the business impact of failing to deliver the product?

A *business impact* is the consequence that an event or incident has for your business. This impact is any level of disruption on your organisation from loss of revenue to damaged reputation. You measure the time taken for an impact to have a severe effect on your business to give an indication of how soon the important activities affected by the impact have to get back up and running.

Putting it into context: If I were a baker . . .

In this section, we apply the process of assessing the impact of a disruption to your critical activities in an example scenario.

Say you run a bakery and you've built up a reputation selling fresh cakes and biscuits through your shop and a weekly shipment to a national chain of coffee shops. Imagine what happens if one day you have a power failure and you can't bake anything.

No doubt some shop customers are upset if you run out of their favourite cake, but most are probably reasonable and accept the problem as a one-off, without it affecting their custom. However, if they arrive the following day to see no products again, they may well begin to look elsewhere. Perhaps your good reputation gives you a period of grace, certainly with your regular customers, but how long does that situation last before you lose them?

In addition, would the large chain of coffee shops be so forgiving if you miss a large order? After a while, both big and small companies start shopping around for an alternative supplier.

If we look at the impacts of this problem, you can probably see where we're going:

✔ You suffer financial loss in the short term through loss of sales revenue and perhaps worse – the cash flow may dry up.

✔ Your orders with the national chain are affected, causing your cash flow problems to continue into the longer term.

✔ Your loyal customers at the shop are impacted, soon leading them to try other bakeries nearby.

✔ Your orders of raw materials from the local farm slow right down too. Without being able to produce the products, you have no need for the fresh supply; cancelling may have a knock-on impact on the farm's business.

The longer the problem persists, the more likely you are to lose market share, reputation and custom.

Using this bakery example, we assume a simple scenario in which you provide three products for the shop: cakes, biscuits and pastries. You also sell the same products to the national coffee chain. You want to know which of these items are your key products and services. (Obviously your business may have any number of products and services, but for this simple example we stick to three.)

To help with considerations within the financial element, your bakery produces a report to show profitability by product based on the last 12 months' numbers (see Figure 4-1).

Product	Cost per Unit	Unit Sale Price (Wholesale and Retail Average)	Margin	Sales Figures for past 12 Months				
				Sales in Shop	Sales to Trade	Total Revenue	Total Profit	% of Sales
Cakes	0.57	1.80	68%	12,600	148,720	161,320	109,697	65%
Biscuits	0.14	0.28	50%	8,200	65,520	73,720	36,860	29%
Pastries	0.23	0.25	8%	5,700	14,976	20,676	1654	7%
				26,500	229,216	255,716	148,211	100%

Figure 4-1: Bakery's profitability by product.

We can draw the following conclusions from Figure 4-1:

- ✔ Your most important product is the cakes, because it accounts for 65 per cent of your sales and has a 68 per cent margin.

- ✔ Your biscuits are also a significant contributor at 29 per cent of sales.

- ✔ Your pastries are a low-margin product that accounts for only 7 per cent of your sales.

On this basis, you can reasonably conclude that your business's key products are cakes and biscuits, and that if your bakery is subjected to a disruptive event, not being able to produce pastries isn't going to threaten your business's survival. Yet if you can't produce and deliver your cakes, you're in trouble.

You can now use the FORCES mnemonic (Financial, Operational, Reputation, Customers and suppliers, Environment and Staffing) to produce a high-level analysis of the impact on each of these factors for each product.

In Table 4-1, we use a simple star rating, giving 1 star for the lowest impact and 3 stars for the highest impact. However, you can use a numbered rating or put a specific weighting on certain impact factors if you choose. The objective is that you gain an idea of what's most important to your business.

This process doesn't have to, and probably won't, be an exact science, but it's a good exercise to challenge your assumptions on what's really important to your business.

Table 4-1	The Impact on the Bakery's FORCES Sectors for Each Product					
	Cakes		Biscuits		Pastries	
	In Shop	Wholesale	In Shop	Wholesale	In Shop	Wholesale
Financial	*	***	*	**	—	*
Operational	*	***	*	*	—	*
Reputation	***	***	*	*	—	*
Customers and suppliers	**	***	***	**	—	*
Environment	***	***	*	*	—	*
Staffing	*	***	*	**	—	*
Total	11	18	8	9	0	6

*Minimum Impact; ** Some Impact; *** Maximum Impact*

Use the template of the impact grid in Table 4-1 to create one that's relevant to your business, placing your products and services across the top.

Using the FORCES categories and the impact grid simplifies the process of identifying the products or services that are going to have the highest impact on your business if disrupted. You can then decide which of them are key and which aren't. You may decide to have a cut-off point on the scoring grid or simply take the top five products. Whichever method you decide is best for your business, you have a rationale to support the action that you subsequently take.

Protecting Against the FORCES of Disruption

Good mnemonics are invaluable because they make remembering things so easy, helping to ensure that you don't leave out important areas. Take the six FORCES sectors that we introduce in the preceding section: Financial, Operational, Reputation, Customers and suppliers, Environment and Staff. These areas are ones on which a disruption in product delivery can have an adverse effect.

We take a closer look at the sectors in this section and suggest questions you need to ask to identify the aspects that score highest on your business's version of the impact grid in Table 4-1 (that is, the products and/or services posing the greatest risk to your business).

Financial: Asking, 'Where's the money?'

This area is the most obvious and probably the first one that springs to mind when you think of a business disruption. If you aren't producing key products, your sales revenue is most certainly going to be adversely affected. You still have to pay your fixed payments and overheads and you may well face extra ones in order to pay to fix the problem. In addition, contractual penalties may also arise because you miss deadlines and lose sponsors.

Ask the following key questions:

- ✔ Do you know your profitability by product? The products that account for the most revenue cause most trouble for you if they're out of action.

- ✔ Do you face any financial penalties in your contractual obligations if you don't deliver these products?

An important aspect of any business is the profit that it makes from the key products and services. Make sure that you know which ones make you the most money, and where, because the main money-making sources are likely to be the first thing you notice missing if a disruption occurs.

Operational: Anticipating production problems

Failure to deliver key products usually creates operational difficulties as you re-organise processes to compensate. During a disruption, you may need to replace well-thought-out systems that almost 'run themselves' with work-arounds, which can have a knock-on effect: a malfunction in one area results in a chain of operational disruptions farther down the line.

The key questions you need to ask are:

- ✔ Which products or services, if not delivered, would cause the most disruption to your processes and business?
- ✔ Would you suffer a knock-on effect to other parts of your business if you didn't deliver these products or services?

The products and/or services that score the highest on the Table 4-1 grid cause you the biggest headaches.

Reputation: Maintaining your business's good name

Unless you can contain the impact of a disruption internally, or can be seen to be managing it effectively, your business's reputation suffers. The effect can be gradual – with productivity declining over a few weeks as you struggle to keep up with a backlog – or it can be instantaneous, with the loss of several key clients. In addition, if you attract the attention of the media, any negative opinion is likely to be heightened and so even more difficult to recover from.

The key questions to ask to raise your awareness in this area are:

- ✔ Which products or services would, if lost, cause reputational damage to your business?
- ✔ Which products and services would, if lost, result in people saying negative things about your business?

> ✔ Which of your customers are most likely to complain the loudest – thereby causing reputational damage?
>
> ✔ What's the profile of your product(s) and is it likely to be of media interest? For example, baby foods would be; standard nuts and bolts wouldn't be.

Those points that would cause widespread bad publicity or make the newspapers score highest on the reputational impact grid.

Within the small business world, word-of-mouth can be very powerful as a marketing tool and, in this case, as a barrier to people using your business.

Customers and suppliers: Considering others in your supply chain

Clients, customers and anyone else who relies on your business are going to be inconvenienced by an incident, albeit to varying extents. Depending on the severity of your disruption and the time you take to recover, they may look to alternative organisations or demand financial compensation from you.

If you're involved in manufacturing, your demand for suppliers and orders is going to change. You may need to cancel or delay orders because you can't deal with incoming raw materials and they go to waste.

Winning new customers is a lot harder, and costs a lot more, than retaining existing ones.

The key questions here are:

> ✔ Which of your customers and suppliers are most important to your business?
>
> ✔ Are any of them so small that they rely on you for a large proportion of their business, in which case they may fail if you can't place orders, and are any of them so big that your business may be viewed as being less significant than others? In this case a failure to place orders for any prolonged period may result in them not supplying you.

The suppliers and customers of those products and services that generate the most revenue or have the highest margin – the ones you identify in the earlier section 'Financial: Asking, 'Where's the money?'' – score highest on the impact grid.

Environment: Staying competitive

A disruption can certainly affect your organisation's position within the business environment (the marketplace) and among your competitors. Opponent businesses are unlikely to overlook the opportunity that your misfortune provides to them. Remember that even if your local competitors are affected by the same problem as you, if they have more efficient resilience measures in place, they can shake off the impact and win business.

The key questions to ask in this context are:

- ✔ Which products and services are unique to your business; which are your flagship products?

- ✔ If you're unable to provide one of your key products or services, would the opportunity be lost or severely diminished for the future?

- ✔ Are any of your key products competing in a highly competitive market, in which losing ground to competitors is going to have a high impact on your business?

The products and/or services that you identify score highest on the impact grid as regards your business environment.

Staffing: Keeping staff employed

During a disruption, some of your staff involved in product delivery may be underemployed while you fix the problem. Furthermore, you may need to call in additional staff while you're trying to catch up. You may have to borrow staff from other areas of your company, which can then have an adverse effect somewhere else.

Ask the following key questions to gain information about the staffing sector:

- ✔ Who are your key staff and what backup is available if they aren't available?

- ✔ Which products and services, if lost, would mean that some of or all your staff aren't gainfully employed?

- ✔ Which products and services, if lost, would result in uncertainty in the business and cause staff to begin to leave your business for more secure employment?

The products and/or services that fall into the staffing category score the highest on the impact grid.

Drawing conclusions from this process

We now consider again the example of the bakery from the earlier section 'Putting it into context: If I were a baker . . .'. Using the grid in Table 4-1, the bakery selects as its key products the cakes for the shop and the wholesale market and the biscuits for just the wholesale market; it rules out the pastries entirely.

In this section, we investigate the underlying factors in making this decision:

- ✔ **Financial:** Fulfilling the weekly wholesale shipment is most important because it generates most revenue. The financial impact of losing the pastries would be minor.

- ✔ **Operational:** Operations would be unable to function effectively if the business couldn't produce cakes, and yet the pastries use so little capacity that the difference would be minimal.

- ✔ **Reputation:** The brand of the cakes, built up over many years, is important. In contrast, customers don't see the pastries as being different to any others available and so their popularity is less. However, the sales of the cakes in the shop are important for the company's reputation because the sales won them the coffee shop contract in the first place.

- ✔ **Customers and suppliers:** If the cakes are lost, the company can't continue for long with just the remaining products. The other consideration is that the supplier of the biscuit mix is a very small family firm that relies on the bakery for a significant part of its revenue. If the bakery doesn't place orders, can't attract the customers into the shop and can't maintain the profit, the likelihood is that it would cease trading.

- ✔ **Environment:** If the coffee shop contract were lost then the market position that the bakery enjoys would be irretrievably damaged. If customers stopped buying the pastries, it would have very little impact because the margin of that product is so low.

- ✔ **Staffing:** Most of the staff's time is used in the production of the cakes for the coffee shop.

You need to consider all the FORCES elements, but in simple terms the products and services that bring in the most money for your business are likely to be your key ones.

Identifying and Prioritising Your Critical Activities through a BIA

A Business Impact Analysis is a method of understanding your business – a scheme to collect information on your key products and services and prioritise them and the critical activities that support them. A common way to go about doing this is to use a questionnaire and follow up with face-to-face meetings with your staff. You can then measure the impact to your business of your critical activities being disrupted by working out the time that your business can survive without them, along with the level to which you need to restore them.

The BIA may sound very grand but don't be put off! We show you how to work out your key products and services in the earlier section 'Protecting Against the FORCES of Disruption' and we help you with your critical activities in this one.

Although many of your key products and services are no doubt obvious to you, the critical activities upon which they depend may not be so clear. A BIA helps you understand the crucial activities so that you can deal with the most important things first when disruption hits.

Time is an important factor here because you're hunting for the answer to the following question: 'What's going to have the greatest impact on your business in the shortest amount of time?'

Another advantage is that people sometimes get distracted by recent events or their particular interests and prioritise the wrong things. A BIA can help you to convince others what matters most and where the real risks lie.

Tailoring the BIA to your business

The fact is that you may not necessarily be the best-equipped person to carry out the BIA. Ask yourself how much involvement you have in the everyday running of the business and whether you deal with the customers, suppliers and basic functions of the organisation.

Perhaps someone else in the organisation understands the everyday processes and systems of your business better than you, and if so entrust that person with the task.

Also, the scope and detail of your BIA is going to vary according to the size of your business. Very small businesses supplying only one product should find it comparatively easy to identify their critical activities, important business functions and maximum tolerable period of disruption (MTPD, which we define in Chapter 1). For bigger businesses this may mean breaking items down by department or product type for example, to make the identifying process more manageable before bringing it all together. As always, BC is dependent on your organisation and you need to adapt your plan accordingly.

Considering your critical activities

Armed with your key products and services (from 'Protecting Against the FORCES of Disruption', earlier in this chapter), the next step is to work out the critical activities for each one, and ascertain which activities, across all your key products, you need to do within a certain time to avoid failure during a disruption.

To do so, you pull information from your business's different areas so you can gain an understanding of the processes and resources needed to make the critical activities happen. You look at how urgent a process is, what it depends on and the resources required to keep it going. You then organise this information into a way that allows you to view the overall picture, which enables you to identify your critical activities and gain an understanding of them. You'll find that this process is really helpful when you come to make decisions when determining your business continuity strategies (something we describe in Chapter 7).

Seasonal demands affect your key products and critical activities. If you're a bakery, you probably produce hot cross buns or simnel cake before Easter but not any other time. You may have more deliveries around Christmas time or sell more wedding cakes in the summer months.

Each process is likely to have a number of *dependencies* – those things that the process needs in order to work; for example, power, people, information and communication technology and raw materials. Look at the impact on each critical process of being without its dependencies, which allows you to prioritise recovery of the dependency as well as understanding how it all fits together.

Carrying out your BIA

Follow each step that we describe in this section and you have a BIA, and a relatively painless one at that (take a look at Figure 4-2).

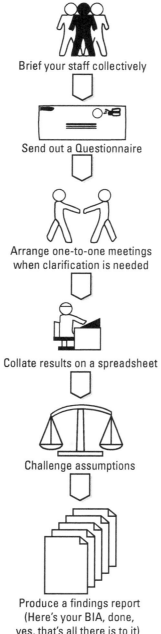

Brief your staff collectively

Send out a Questionnaire

Arrange one-to-one meetings
when clarification is needed

Collate results on a spreadsheet

Challenge assumptions

Figure 4-2:
Stages of
creating
a BIA.

Produce a findings report
(Here's your BIA, done,
yes, that's all there is to it)

Briefing your staff collectively

Collect your staff together and explain that you're looking to work out all the things that keep the business going. Describe the key products and services that you've identified: depending on your business, you may want to explain the rationale behind the selection of them.

Avoid anxiety by making clear that this process isn't a test.

You can obtain the information for a BIA in a number of ways. Each method has advantages and disadvantages but can provide information. Tell staff that they may be asked to complete a questionnaire, answer questions, attend a one-to-one workshop or take part in a discussion about their work area. Talking of questions, invite them to ask any at this early point.

Sending out a questionnaire to each staff area

Devise questions to investigate issues such as:

- The activities that staff carry out for each of your key products.

- The maximum period that each activity can be out of operation, before it becomes irretrievable (the MTPD).

- The ideal time period for recovering these activities (called the *recovery time objective* or RTO).

- Whether the process for the activity is continuous or follows a calendar cycle.

- The point (usually relating to data) to which you'd need to resume the activity. Your *maximum tolerable data loss* (MTDL) is the amount of data that your business can tolerate losing before the survival of your business is threatened. Confusingly, you measure MTDL in time rather than the amount of data, so for example you may be able to lose two hours' worth of data.

  An example is the loss of IT systems: is it essential that when you regain access it's to the same position at the point of loss, or is yesterday's backup sufficient? This is the *recovery point objective* (RPO), and it needs to be a shorter time than the MTDL figure to offer a bit of leeway to deal with other unexpected things that arise.

- The things and people on which the activities and processes depend.

- The resource requirements for an activity (for example, minimum staff numbers).

- The equipment people need to carry out these activities, including IT.

- Whether any contingency plans are currently in place.

We say more about the concepts of MTPD, RTO and RPO in Chapter 1.

Arranging one-to-one meetings

Consult individually with staff to discuss any answers provided in the questionnaires for which you want extra clarity or more information.

Look at the results that staff members provide through the lens of their perspectives, needs and assumptions. Naturally, people view the things that they carry out as being vital to the business and make assumptions of urgency that reflect this view. They may well be right, but when you place results in the context of the entire organisation, the overall result may temper some of these assumptions (check out the later sidebar 'Challenging maximum periods of disruption').

Here are some issues with questionnaires to bear in mind:

- ✔ The information can be inconsistent.
- ✔ Response rates may be low and some people go into greater detail than others in their answers.

Initial informal workshops and discussions are also valid means of obtaining information: use whatever methods work best for you and your business.

Collating the results on a spreadsheet

Begin to draw together the overall picture for all your critical activities. Figure 4-3 gives an idea of how this spreadsheet may look, but of course the detail is very much dependent on your type of business, and how many key products and/or services you have. Lay the spreadsheet out in a way that makes most sense to your business.

Cakes	MTPD	RTO	Calendar/Continuous	RPO	Dependencies	Resources Req'd	Equip Needed	Existing Plans
Order process: componenets	2 weeks	1 week	Every two weeks	N/a	Electricity	Order processing system trained staff member	Computer with Order Processing Software	Nil
					Sales orders		Printer	
							Email	
Delivery	3 days	2 days	Every 3 days average	N/a	Warehouse	Warehouse Operative	Computer with Goods Received Software	Nil
Warehouse	6 hours	3 hours	Continuous	N/a	Electricity	Warehouse Manager	Forklift	Nil
					Access Roads			Nil
					Electricity	1 Ops Manager/5 Production Operatives	Filler/capper/packaging machine/labeller/computer with software	Spare parts for machines kept
Production	6 hours	3 hours	Daily	N/a				
Packaging	6 hours	3 hours	Daily					
Dispatch	6 hours	3 hours	Daily					
Transport	12 hours	6 hours	Daily					
Retail outlet	24 hours	12 hours	Daily					
Sales and marketing	48 hours	24 hours	Daily					
Product Deveopment	~	10 days						
Product Testing	2 weeks	2 weeks	Monthly					

Figure 4-3: An example of a spreadsheet collating the BIA questionnaire results.

Challenging maximum periods of disruption

In a motor-parts business based in the heart of Northamptonshire, the general manager conducted a BIA using the process that we outline in this chapter. Drawing together the results of the questionnaires into a spreadsheet, it became clear that some of the maximum tolerable periods provided by staff were questionable. The head of sales had put down on the questionnaire that he needed his entire team of five sales reps up and running with access to the server within six hours. The management team could see only one way in which it was able to achieve this demand: to have three of his team working from the Northamptonshire office and the other three working almost 100 miles away at their Doncaster office. When told, the head of sales realised that actually they could survive for 24 hours and also that three members of the team was enough to keep the critical activities going.

The spreadsheet needs to include all your key products and services and show the factors that we cover in the earlier section 'Sending out a questionnaire to each staff area' so that you can view them together. In essence, you're looking to see which critical activities you need to recover first, and to what level, and to understand the things on which they depend.

From the information contained within the spreadsheet you want to start drawing some conclusions about which activities you need to look at first. You may well find that you see a lot of competition at the priority end of your spreadsheet, but don't let this deter you. What you're left with when you've collated this information is a basis upon which to start making some decisions.

Expect quite a few queries to come to the fore. To give you an idea, here are some examples of the type of common questions that arise at this stage:

- ✔ 'Does he really need to have that up and running within 45 minutes?'
- ✔ 'Is there really no flexibility on switching that off for even an hour?'
- ✔ 'Is that really so important that we need to get it back within 24 hours?'

Challenging your results

You want to you pull together all the questions that you had from the preceding section and search for more. A good idea is to draw together a small group of managers to question the results and assumptions that the different areas of the business have given you. With the results from this group you need to go back to those who initially provided you with the information and put the challenges to them. This exercise is about seeing which MTPDs stand up to rigour and which were cautiously set by the area from which they originated.

When challenging the results, consider asking the managers specifying the MTPD the cost of meeting their requirement. When they find that amount out, they often discover that the MTPD isn't as short as they originally stated (see the nearby sidebar 'Challenging maximum periods of disruption').

Producing a findings report

After you complete the challenge phase in the preceding section, your spreadsheet is likely to look slightly different to before you began. This altered spreadsheet allows you to work out the following:

- ✔ Your business's critical activities.
- ✔ The order in which you need to carry out critical activities.
- ✔ Recovery time objective for each one.
- ✔ Whether these activities are continuous or on a calendar cycle.
- ✔ Things on which each activity depends.
- ✔ Resources, staffing and equipment needed to support each activity.

This spreadsheet also shows you what current contingency plans your business has in place for each one. From this information you can produce a findings report detailing the information in a way that provides a firm foundation on which to base your resilience strategies and a way to support the need for these strategies to others.

Deciding on your continuity requirements

Your critical activities don't all necessarily need to be functioning at 100 per cent by their RTO. In the bakery example that we use throughout this chapter, the cake production line and the biscuit line depend on staffing and procurement among other things. But if the business can tolerate the shop being closed for longer than it can tolerate the biscuit production line being closed, initially the business needs enough staff and procurement activity only to support the biscuit line. This aspect is called the *continuity requirement* for the activity.

When thinking about the continuity requirements, you also need to consider the resources that you require. This includes the information and communications technology or factory production that keeps your product going, and your staff and the teams that fulfil vital roles in your organisation. During a disruption you may need extra resources, particularly staff, in order to get yourself back on track. You may face a backlog to deal with, if not necessarily in terms of product then at least in dealing with suppliers or customers.

Also, most small businesses depend on some form of data in their everyday working, in electronic form or as original documents, including things such as contacts, contract lists and sales reports. You need to recognise the extent of data that your business can realistically survive without. Basically, when you decide this figure you need to plan to recover this amount of data.

Recovering everything in one go after a disaster is rarely possible and so most recoveries are phased. Finding the MTPD and RTO, and the MTDL and RPO, lets you know what you have to bring back in what timescales.

Chapter 5

Considering the Risks to Your Business

*T*aking the occasional risk is fine – everyone does from time to time – but risking the safety of your business is a bit different to taking a chance and going out without an umbrella on an ominously cloudy day. Of course, you know this, and one risk you certainly don't want to take is to risk neglecting the risks facing your company. But perhaps you also think:

> *I just want to keep my business going if we get hit by something. I don't want to be an expert in risk management.*

We hope so anyway, because then this chapter is the one for you. Here we demonstrate that risk assessment and management don't have to be complicated.

Building an understanding of risk in your business allows you to develop plans and strategies to protect your key products and services and the critical activities supporting them (which we discuss in Chapter 4). Through business continuity (BC) you can mitigate significantly or even eliminate threats to your business just through understanding what they are and where they originate.

In this chapter we look at how risk fits into BC and show you how to:

✔ Select the right way to deal with risk in a BC context.

✔ Identify the potential risks that your organisation faces.

✔ Evaluate risks in terms of their likelihood and impact on your critical activities.

✔ Record risks in a clear way that helps you respond to them.

✔ Respond with appropriate strategies to your identified risks and so reduce the severity of any disruption and its financial impact.

We design this chapter so that even if you have no experience in dealing with risk, you can easily put practical measures in place to build resilience within your business.

Looking at Risk in a Business Continuity Context

Risks surround you every day. You take a risk when crossing the road that you may be struck by a car, cyclist or bus. But you take precautions to manage the risk, such as checking the road is clear first or using the underpass as an alternative.

The precautions that you take to deal with a risk are based on the likelihood of it happening. For example, you may do lots of things to deal with the likely risk of your old, but only, car breaking down – particularly if you need it to take the children to school. You service it regularly, buy breakdown cover, change the oil and so on. But for other risks, such as being struck by lightning while dashing home in a thunderstorm, you may do nothing. This different approach is because the likelihood of these two risks happening is very different.

You may well ask: isn't there a way for me to avoid risk entirely? The quick answer is no; organisations have to take risks because otherwise they'd fail to meet their objectives. Standing still and doing nothing in itself runs a different risk – that of being overtaken and put out of business by competitors. Therefore, risk is an inherent part of being in business and you have only one option: deal with it through effective risk management.

Good risk management allows your organisation to:

✔ Have increased confidence about achieving its desired outcomes.

✔ Constrain threats effectively to an acceptable level.

✔ Take informed decisions about exploiting opportunities.

✔ Provide confidence to customers, suppliers, stakeholders and staff by showing a good understanding of your business.

Effective risk management also allows stakeholders to have increased confidence in your organisation's corporate governance and ability to deliver.

Often BC experts look at risk management in the context of an organisation's strategic objectives, but this is a wide area to cover, thus making the subject time consuming and complicated. Identifying the risks that your organisation faces is difficult and putting a system in place that orders them and provides remedies, so that the remaining risk is acceptable, understandably fills many people with dread.

For this reason, we take a simpler approach, as we describe in the next section.

Selecting the Right Risk Approach for Your Business

You can approach risk within a BC context in a number of different ways, and in this chapter we offer two:

- ✔ **Simple risk approach:** A very simple way to deal with risks that deliberately looks *only* at the impact of them occurring.

- ✔ **Risk-management approach:** A more detailed (though uncomplicated) method if you also want an idea of the things that can affect your business and to gauge and assess how likely they are to happen.

We suggest that you read the next 'Looking at the simple risk approach' section first. Then, if you're uncomfortable with not exploring where the likely disruptions can come from, or you simply want to know more about the risks that your organisation may face, continue to the risk-management approach in 'Understanding risk management'.

Looking at the simple risk approach

Taking this simple approach may mean that you're able to skip through most of this chapter, but only if you feel comfortable doing so.

Generally, the key to risk is understanding it. After all, risks aren't always obvious and for the most part, unless you go searching for them, they stay hidden. However, in BC you want to focus on the impact of disruption on your critical activities, and therefore one school of thought says that you don't have to know anything about the risks that cause the disruption, just their impact. For example, if you can't get access to your building, you don't care whether the road closure is due to a major accident or a flood from a burst utilities pipe. Both are very different risks, but as far as you're concerned, the impact of being unable to access your building is the same.

In this vein, the following is all that you need to know to do. Think about which of your business's key products and services you can't survive without and how long you can manage without them. This allows you to think about which ones you need to resume if any of them suffer a disruption. In general your main concerns here focus around loss of:

- Premises
- Technology or data
- Key staff
- A business process
- Corporate management control

Then consider the different and varying levels of impact that the disruption may cause to any of these areas. The impact can be financial, operational, political or reputational – or a mixture of any, or all, of these aspects.

If you deem the level of impact to be significantly high, the chances are you need to do something about it. Unless the likelihood is almost impossible, you need some sort of response to try to avoid the risk from happening. This response may include spending money to reduce the risk, such as replacing that dodgy boiler, or devising ways to cope if the risk manifests; that is, when the boiler does give up.

For the simple risk approach within the world of BC, that's all you need to consider. If you're content at this point, and want to keep things as simple as possible and avoid the need to look at the precise nature of the risk that causes the disruption, you need go no further in this chapter. If you're interested in the risks that may cause you trouble, however, read on.

Understanding risk management

If you're reading this section, you're quite understandably concerned by and/or interested in the risks that your business may face. Or maybe you just feel more confident understanding the sort of events that may cause disruption. If so, this section and the rest of this chapter are for you.

We look at four steps to take by using a simple mnemonic IERR – as in 'IERR on the side of caution':

1. **Identify the risks that your organisation faces.**

2. **Evaluate those risks.**

3. **Record those risks into a risk register.**

4. **Respond so you can keep on top of new and emerging risks.**

BC narrows down the huge world of risk to 'your world of risk'. In a BC context, risk is manageable because the risk assessment focuses only on your critical activities and their dependencies (which we define in Chapter 4). BC is all about keeping your business going during, and bouncing back after, a disruption. To do this the focus is on the things that must continue in order to keep your company alive; or to look at it another way, BC doesn't look at things that you don't need to continue in order for your business's survival. You're then free to spend time and resources on the areas that you must maintain during a disruption. Therefore, you need to think only about the most important bits of your business.

To manage the risk to your business's critical activities effectively, you need to have a system that helps you by examining factors such as the likelihood of the risk occurring and the impact on your organisation if it does happen. By combining these elements, you have a basic risk assessment process that helps you to evaluate threats, prioritise risk and create strategies to deal with them.

BC recognises that protecting your business against every risk is simply impossible. Even if possible, it would be prohibitively expensive anyway. Therefore, never try to list all known threats or hazards in your BC plans, because you'll never finish (in fact, never even start) your plan.

Identifying, Evaluating, Recording and Responding to Your Risks (IERR)

The first step to managing risk is to identify the risks to your business and then evaluate them. You then record and report on them and finally respond by developing appropriate strategies to address the threats they pose in a structured way. Using this 'IERR' process, you can judge how risks impact on your business.

As you may have spotted, the process of risk assessment is closely linked to the Business Impact Analysis (BIA) that we discuss in Chapter 4, which is where we also help you identify your critical activities and assess the maximum period for which they can potentially be disrupted before the disruption proves threatening to your entire business.

A *risk strategy* is simply deciding how you're going to address a risk or a group of risks. You may decide that for specific risks you need insurance. For others you may choose to invest to reduce the risk. For still others, you may choose to do very little or even nothing because of a low impact or slight chance. You can blend risk strategies to optimise the benefits, reduce costs or create more effective solutions.

This process may seem like a lot of work initially, but it's all manageable. And when the systems are in place and you've trawled the risk-infested waters in which your organisation swims and assessed what you've found, ongoing maintenance is fairly plain sailing. The stormy waters that catch businesses unawares are the problem.

In the rest of this section, we show you how to build a risk register you can use as a basis for your business to make decisions and as a useful way to monitor risks.

IERR Stage 1: Identifying your business's risks

Risks to your organisation abound far beyond your own building or systems, and also lie in services you depend on – telephones, power supplies, water, technology, suppliers and transport systems – out in the wider environment. Failures in these areas are common and have a domino effect that means your business can be seriously affected even though the event didn't happen to you directly.

Risk environment

When you think of risks, you need to consider not only your organisation, but also the environments in which it operates. In this section we split the risk environment into three areas (see Figure 5-1):

- ✔ **Wider environment:** Risks over which you have little control but can militate against, such as major transport disruptions.

- ✔ **Immediate environment:** Risks that you have more control over, such as not having a contract with one of your key suppliers.

- ✔ **Internal business environment:** Risks on your doorstep that you can control the most.

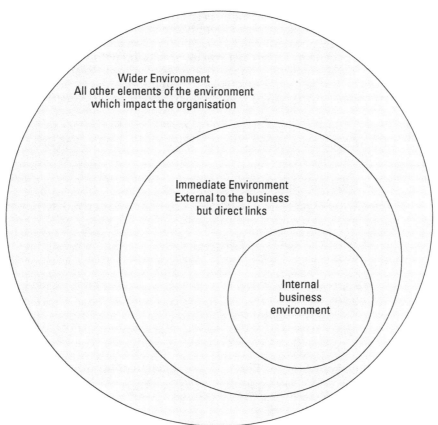

Wider Environment
All other elements of the environment
which impact the organisation

Immediate Environment
External to the business
but direct links

Internal
business
environment

Figure 5-1:
The risk
environment.

This way of thinking about your risk environment provides you with an overview of all the type of risks that your business faces.

Your organisation has resources and uses processes that it depends on to operate. For a one-person plumbing business, say, these may be tools, a mobile phone and a van, but don't forget all the materials you use, the insurance and licences to operate and a whole host of other things that you need for your business to work. Even with the smallest business, the risks of disruption exist and can have a serious impact pretty quickly.

You may find that identifying risks arising from the wider environment is easier than detecting those right under your nose. This is because most of the wider risks are the sort of things that you read about in the newspapers or see on the evening news: flooding, flu pandemics, extreme weather, terrorist atrocities and so on.

Despite this, you (or an appropriately experienced person within your company) are best equipped to identify the internal business environment risks to your organisation. You know it better than anyone else and probably have seen some near-misses that you need to bring onto your risk radar. Or if you've been unlucky, you may have been involved in some real-life disruptions that themselves offer lessons and information for making sure that they don't occur again. Or, if they do, that you can at least continue trading.

As you work through this section, draw up a table similar to the one in Figure 5-2, which allows you to jot down the risks as you think of them. The columns to fill in here are:

✔ Brief description for the risk.

✔ Where you identified it – that is, as part of your wider, immediate or internal business environment.

✔ Which grouping it seems to fall under – for example, staff, premises and so on.

Use a spreadsheet package if possible so that the information is easier to group and read later on.

Number	Risk	Environment	Grouping	Owner	Dependency Linked Risks
Example	Loss of Main Server	Business	IT	J. Clare	4,7,9
1					
2					
3					
4					
5					
6					
7					
8					
9					
10					
11					
12					
13					
14					
15					
16					

Figure 5-2:
An example of a risk register.

The detail is unimportant here and so don't spend loads of time thinking about the likelihood or severity of the risks that you identify; you do that in the later section 'Looking at a scoring system', which is also where you complete the 'Owner' and 'Dependency linked risks' columns.

Wider environment

This area includes all elements of the environment that impact on your organisation's critical activities but with which your business doesn't have direct contact. A good, effective and simple starting place is to look at the National Risk Register (NRR; check out the nearby sidebar 'Consulting the National Risk Register' for more details). This government publication sets out a range of risks that the UK faces and that may have a major impact on all or significant parts of it. The NRR is freely available and updated on a regular basis. It tells you which risks are relevant nationally and gives you an indication of their potential likelihood and national impact. Take a look at www.cabinetoffice.gov.uk/resource-library/national-risk-register.

You may be thinking that this information is all about civil emergencies and isn't likely to affect your plumbing business in Kettering. However, these situations are precisely where considering the wider environment is so important, because although a flood may affect everything within, say, Cambridge, your suppliers may be caught up, leaving you unable to carry on and so cost you money.

Consulting the National Risk Register

The NRR provides information on the most serious national risks and provides an illustration of the relative impact and likelihood of the threat. The Register is valuable to you as a business because it sets out the consequences of these risks. Although much of the information in the NRR may be unsurprising, it's useful to your business because it brings together a great deal of risks that are relevant and consistent in presentation, allowing you to compare them on a broadly like-for-like basis. And with so many possible kinds of emergency, it helps in making decisions about which risks to plan for and what the consequences are likely to be. It also provides useful information for businesses on specific risks with some key considerations in dealing with them.

The NRR risk assessment process involves assessing the likelihood of these risks occurring.

The NRR treats hazards and malicious attacks differently. For hazards, the Register uses historical and scientific data to take into account known or probable developments over the next five years. For malicious attacks, the assessment is more subjective. The willingness of individuals and groups to carry out the threat balances against an objective assessment of their capacity and the vulnerability of potential targets.

In assessing the impact of these threats, the NRR takes account of the following factors: number of fatalities, human illness or injury, social disruption, economic damage and psychological impact. The NRR gives these factors a rating that dictates where overall the risk sits on the impact axis (see Figure 5-3).

Figure 5-3 shows the 2012 NRR risk matrix and gives an idea of the likelihood and impact for each risk along with its relationship to other identified risks.

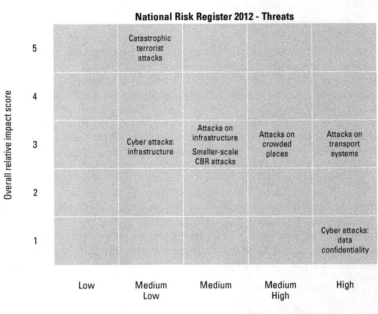

National Risk Register 2012 - Threats

National Risk Register 2012 - Hazards

Figure 5-3: The 2012 National Risk Register: An illustration of the high-consequence risks facing the UK.

Immediate environment

This area covers the risks contained within the running of your business, such as ones connected to partners, competitors, suppliers, distributors, customers and other entities that have direct contact with your organisation. If they come to pass, these risks are likely to impact your critical activities, including the production and sale of products, the preparation and delivery of services, or a number of other things depending on the type of business you have.

Factors to consider here are:

- ✔ What happened to your business in the past?
- ✔ Have you had any near-misses?
- ✔ Have other similar companies to yours sustained a disruption or crisis?
- ✔ Have other businesses within your geographical area been subjected to any problems that may affect you?
- ✔ Do your staff know of anything within their areas that's causing them concern, such as something that they keep sticking a plaster over to get by?

A good starting point when looking at your immediate environment is to get hold of a copy of your local Community Risk Register (CRR; see Figure 5-4 for an example). These registers are in the same family as the NRR from the preceding section, but look only at risks and hazards within a specific area. Risks vary in different geographic locations and for areas with different demographics. The CRR gives you a good idea of any larger risks to your critical activities that you need to be aware of; for example, being situated near to a hazardous site.

You can find more information on community resilience on the Cabinet Office website: www.cabinetoffice.gov.uk/content/community-resilience.

To demonstrate this risk area, we use the example of a business selling products to supermarkets (the principles are the same for all businesses).

Your business Shine Cleaning Co. sells four products that you produce in a number of different ways as follows, including the percentage of revenue generation for each product:

- ✔ **Oven cleaner:** Outsourced to a manufacturing firm in Coventry. Accounts for 80 per cent of revenue.
- ✔ **Disinfectant:** Outsourced to a small firm outside London. Accounts for 5 per cent of revenue.
- ✔ **Hand soap:** Outsourced to a firm in China. Accounts for 12 per cent of revenue.
- ✔ **Sponge cleaner:** Produced in-house from components ordered in. Accounts for 3 per cent of revenue.

Risk ref.	Hazard category	Hazard sub-category	Outcome Description/ Variation and Further Information	Likelihood	Impact	Risk rating	Lead responsibility
INDUSTRIAL ACCIDENTS AND ENVIRONMENTAL POLLUTION							
H1	Industrial Accident & Environmental Pollution	Fire or explosion at a gas terminal as well as LPG, LNG and other gas onshore feedstock pipeline and flammable gas storage sites	**Outcome Description** Up to 3km around site causing up to 3000 fatalities and up to 1500 casualties. Gas terminal event likely to be of short duration once feed lines are isolated; event at a storage site could last for days if the explosion damaged control equipment. **Variation and further information.** Risk is based on a large industrial complex, gas processing site or gas storage site near to a populated (i.e. urban) area. Impact on environment, including persistent/widespread impact on air quality.	Negligible (1)	Significant (4)	Medium	LFB
HL25	Industrial Accident & Environmental Pollution	Fire or explosion at a flammable gas including LPG/LNG storage sites.	**Outcome Description** Up to 1km around site, causing up to 50 fatalities and 150 casualties. **Variation & Further Information** Event at a storage site could last for days if the explosion damaged control equipment. Impact on environment, including persistent/ widespread impact on air quality.	Negligible (1)	Moderate (3)	Medium	LFB

Figure 5-4: An example of a Community Risk Register.

Based on the revenue percentage, you identify your critical activities to be those associated with the production and sale of your key product – the oven cleaner. If a disruption hit your own business, it would cause problems, but any sustained failure by your supplier to produce the oven cleaner threatens closure of your company.

Setting aside the other products, you can break down the activities into the following categories:

✔ **Partners:** The risks in this category include the following: a partner with your business not having sufficient components to make up orders; machinery defects resulting in loss of production capacity; labelling not meeting your customers' standards; quality of product falling below acceptable standard of your customers; and delivery unable to take place.

In the example, although an outside firm produces the oven cleaner, you view the firm as your partner because it purchases components for the product on your behalf. Your business relies on this manufacturing firm to order in the components and be able to produce the products, pack them and ship them to your warehouse.

✔ **Competitors:** The threats that arise from your competitors include things such as the threat of substitution, the ease with which a new competitor can enter your market and releasing a rival product onto the market.

You're already in the cleaning industry, so you have a good idea of the level of competitive rivalry within it and the bargaining power that suppliers and customers have. These factors combined give you a good idea of the risks from competitors and the things that are at the back of your mind as worries. You now need to bring them out and record them as not just worries but risks to address.

✔ **Suppliers:** The obvious risk here is that your suppliers can't supply you with your product – in this example, the oven cleaner. But other risks apply as well, such as under-delivery of quantities needed or delivering poor-quality products. Here you see clear links with the wider environment risks (check out the preceding section) in such areas as transport disruption from extreme weather or major accidents.

✔ **Distributors:** The risks here are interwoven with other areas but worth making plain. We are, of course, talking about transport and warehousing. These are integral parts of the supply chain because everything else going without a hitch is all for nothing if the goods don't reach the customer due to problems with transport or road problems.

✔ **Customers:** The risks that arise from your customers are generally centred around them no longer using your firm for their products and services; in this case, oven cleaner. You need to record this risk because failure to address it may leave your business lost when a significant customer that you rely on stops ordering. Nobody wants to consider losing customers, but you're more likely to survive if you think about it and are prepared.

✔ **Others with direct contact with your organisation:** You look at all other aspects that you haven't captured in the preceding categories. In the oven cleaner example, you need to be aware of a couple of additional players: regulatory bodies; in this case trading standards and the health and safety executive. Your oven cleaner is corrosive, and so you need to produce and register a medical safety datasheet with the relevant authorities. Failure to have a safety datasheet means that you can't sell the product.

Ask yourself whether any regulatory obligations are associated with your business.

Figure 5-5 illustrates that this process doesn't need to be complicated or a beautifully crafted piece of work; it's simply about looking at the risks that you face by breaking down your key products and services. In Figure 5-5, we show the product at the centre with the suggested risk areas coming from it, spreading into risks that may materialise. In the figure, we stop there, but for your business, you may want to go a step further in breaking these risks down.

Internal business environment

This area covers the aspects within your business, the ones you know the most: staff, premises, IT systems, machinery, equipment, heldstock and vehicles.

Examine these areas through the lens of your critical activities. To get you thinking, we stick with the Shine Cleaning Co. example from the preceding section and work through each of the elements:

- ✔ **Staff:** Your aim is to continue producing and selling your key product, here the oven cleaner. Although you rely heavily on outside parties such as suppliers and haulers, your staff need to manage these contacts. The risks include not having the staff available to invoice customers or send over dispatch paperwork to the transport company.

Look at staff members you know contribute to your critical activities and identify the associated risks such as illness; being unable to get into work through bad weather or school closures; leaving your organisation after winning the lottery; or getting stuck in a foreign country after a holiday because a volcano is blowing ash over the continent.

- ✔ **Premises:** Risks to your premises are likely to be that you can't get access to it, perhaps because it's flooded, and yet you store essential equipment and information there. Start to look at how you'd handle this situation. So, if you think, 'We don't really need an office, just a broadband connection,' hold that thought because it may form part of your response strategy.

Know your local area and building so that you can recognise when something begins to go wrong. You can easily discover some things for yourself if you take a bit of time. For example, walk around the outside of your building and look out for any frayed wires, a slight leak, a pipe that you don't know the purpose of and all the things you don't notice as you hurry past every day.

- ✔ **IT and other systems:** We could write pages here, but you know the risks – so scribble them down. Threats include viruses, denial of access attacks, hackers, the air-conditioning units in the ceiling leaking all over your server and causing a power failure – and that's just the beginning.

- ✔ **Machinery and equipment:** Equipment can be anything from the forklift for getting the pallets onto the truck to the printer ink cartridges for printing off your invoices. If you have equipment, you also have risks in that it can stop working (or stop working effectively). In the oven cleaner example, you outsource your manufacturing, but this doesn't mean that you outsource the risk. Just because you aren't carrying out preventative maintenance yourself, doesn't mean that you don't need to see the schedules from your supplier.

- ✔ **Held stock:** If you hold stock and it's part of your critical functions, look at the risks to it. Damage, theft and too little to meet immediate orders are the obvious risks, but plenty of others apply too, if this is an important area to you.

- ✔ **Vehicles:** Having identified the vehicles that you use when carrying out your critical activities, now is the time to look at the associated risks. These can range from failure to start, to being written off in an accident or not having suitable staff around to drive them.

Write down the risks that you're aware of, because they're the sort that become reality just at the wrong moment. Urgent deliveries seem to attract road closures and tyre blowouts. You've seen the shredded rubber from tyres on the side of the motorway; likely as not, that happened on an urgent delivery to a customer.

If you find yourself thinking, 'But what about such and such . . .' put it in; our example is just to give you an idea.

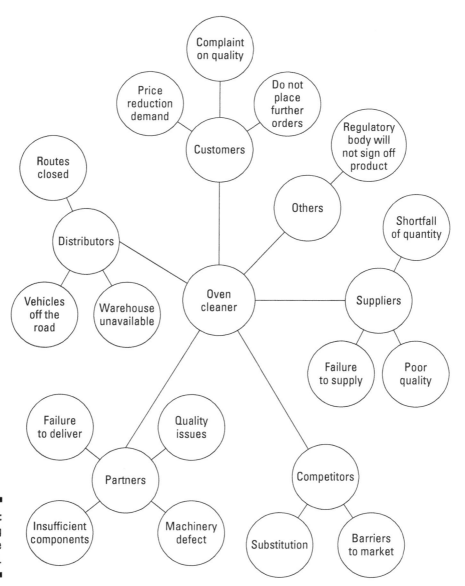

Figure 5-5:
Breaking down the risks.

Completing your risk register

The activities that you carry out to produce your risk register give you a structured way of identifying a large number of the risks facing your business. How you write them down precisely is less important than physically recording them. Your aim is to have a risk-management process in place that you can build upon as you think of and discover new risks. Nothing stays the same, including your risk environment, which means that your risk register can't either.

IERR Stage 2: Evaluating your businesses risks

From IERR Stage 1 (in the preceding section) you have your risks, at least the ones that you've identified anyway. The next step is to take these rough jottings, now bursting at the seams, and evaluate them and turn them into something that you can present as a risk register. In a lot of ways, Stage 2 is the most tricky because you have to assess the likelihood and impact of these things occurring. At times, you may have to make a best guess, though at others you may have a fairly clear idea, certainly on the impact factor.

As we work through the chapter we build towards providing a clear visual representation of the risks you've identified on a grid. We plot these on the grid using your assessment of the likelihood of these risks occurring and your judgement of the impact they'd have on your business.

The methodology of the NRR (from the 'Wider environment' section, earlier in the chapter) is worth remembering because we use an adapted version to guide you through the next stages.

Creating a risk matrix

The risk picture that you've started to build up can be difficult to absorb, because single pieces of the puzzle aren't enough to enable you to rely on them in making decisions. For this reason, you need a risk matrix that puts these pieces together to form your organisation's all-important risk picture. This picture is the overall view that allows prioritisation: where to act and provide support in rationalising why you aren't spending money in certain areas. The risk picture also enables you to communicate this information clearly to colleagues, owners, shareholders and, if required, customers and suppliers.

After you've evaluated your identified risks, you can see which ones are more likely to happen than others. And then which of these are going to have the most impact on your business. But before you can do this, you need to calculate these ratings. So to evaluate the risks that you've identified, you need to work out a scoring system based on factors that make sense to you. Of course, the system needn't and can't be perfect.

You're looking for an idea of the risks that are going to have an impact on your critical activities, how much of a problem they may cause and whether they're worth worrying about or are never likely to happen. So forget, say, about the 1-in-every-200-years flooding event – you really want to know about the likelihood of your premises being flooded (again) by that faulty dishwasher hose that you've never put right and how to stop it happening. Or the likelihood that the whole accounts department is going to be off at the same time with flu and you can't get your invoices out.

Looking at a scoring system

We present a simple 1–5 scale that you can use for both risk impact and likelihood, with 1 being the most minor and 5 being red alert; you get the picture, we're sure.

Here's the risk-impact scoring scale:

> 1 = Limited
>
> 2 = Minor
>
> 3 = Moderate
>
> 4 = Significant
>
> 5 = Company crushing

Table 5-1 shows the risk-likelihood scoring scale.

Table 5-1	Simple Risk-Likelihood Scoring Scale		
Score	*Descriptor*	*Likelihood Over 5 Years*	*Likelihood Over 5 Years*
1	Low	> 0.005%	> 1 in 20,000 chance
2	Medium Low	> 0.05%	> 1 in 2,000 chance
3	Medium	> 0.5%	> 1 in 200 chance
4	Medium High	> 5%	> 1 in 20 chance
5	High	> 50%	> 1 in 2 chance

This scoring system is just a very simple example. But to get you started in this area, the simpler the better. For each risk that you identify on your risk register, you need to allocate a score for its impact on your business and the likelihood of it occurring.

These scores are only ever going to be a best guess because not even the largest organisations can accurately rate each risk; even with the most expensive systems. The likelihood columns just give you an idea of the chance ratings that may be associated with your scoring system, but if you find them confusing then ignore them.

The key to this exercise is that at the end you can relationally compare your risks.

When you begin attributing scores to your risks, you may need to return to some and have a re-think; this is the benefit of considering all your risks as they crop up and not just one in isolation. Also, examine the risks that are linked and put the risk number in the 'dependency linked risks' column of your risk register from Figure 5-2, which then looks something like Figure 5-6. Doing so enables you to put strategies in place for dealing with multiple events that relate to each other.

Figure 5-6:
Risk register with impact and likelihood columns.

Number	Risk	Environment	Grouping	Owner	Dependency Linked Risks	Impact Scoring	Likelihood Scoring
Example	Loss of Main Server	Business	IT	J. Clare	4, 7, 9	4	3
1							
2							
3							
4							
5							
6							

Of course, you can describe the risks that your business faces to staff using words that give a flavour for the severity or likelihood. A staff member who doesn't frequently deal with risk may respond better to being told that something is 'highly likely' rather than 'a 5 on the scale'. Use whatever works best for you, but being consistent throughout your workforce makes communication easier in a stressful situation.

This evaluation stage is about starting to look at your risks in relation to each other and leads you nicely on to the next section, which covers plotting your risks onto a relational matrix. Contain your excitement!

IERR Stage 3: Recording what you discover

After you've identified and evaluated the risks facing your business to help protect your critical activities, you arrive at the recording and reporting stage. The initial questions that you need to ask here are:

✔ Do you have any regulatory needs in terms of reporting?

✔ What information should you be reporting to the board on risk?

✔ What do your other stakeholders, such as shareholders, need to know about risk?

For the last two questions in this list, such risk reporting enables people to make strategic decisions up to and including ceasing ventures and projects or investing in them in ways that reduce the risks.

Knowing and understanding your risks isn't going to take them away, but it is going to help you deal with them. Clear reporting provides a sound footing on which to do so and good risk information can be pure gold to your organisation.

Creating your relational matrix

One of the most common ways to show clearly your risks is to plot them on a relational matrix. This matrix has the benefit of easily showing the following:

✔ Impact scorings

✔ Likelihood scorings

✔ Relationship of these factors to other risks

The scorings that you have on your risk register (from the preceding section) are all you need to create a relational risk matrix. Figure 5-7 shows a grid with the vertical axis representing impact and the horizontal one representing likelihood.

The grid is split in the same 1-to-5 way as the scoring system in the earlier section 'Looking at a scoring system'. Now you're going to create a similar grid, using a spreadsheet package, to plot the risks using the numbers that you allocated in the risk register; in the example diagram we label our risks R1, R2, R3 and so on for simplicity. You can do this, or if you have different types of risk, prefix them with a letter, such as O1 (for operations risk 1) and A1 (for administrative risk 1); whatever makes sense to you and your business.

Figure 5-7:
Example of a relational risk matrix.

	Low (1)	Med Low (2)	Medium (3)	Med High (4)	High (5)
Catastrophic (5)	R14, R15				
Significant (4)		R1		R6, R21	
Moderate (3)		R5, R7, R25	R9, R22, R23		
Minor (2)	R4, R20	R9, R24		R12, R19	
Limited (1)	R2, R3, R8, R10, R17, R18				R11, R13, R16

Your completed grid then provides a clear visual aid to spotting those risks that you need to tackle and deal with now (the darkest shading in Figure 5-7 indicates the most serious and likely risk combinations), those that you can begin to prepare for (medium shading) and those that you simply ignore at this time and monitor (lightest shading).

IERR Stage 4: Responding

After you've produced your risk register and displayed your findings in a risk matrix, you immediately have a better understanding of the ones that you ought to be looking at soonest. The question now is what to do. A lot depends on how much resource your business has at its disposal and the attitude that your board or senior management has regarding risk (we explain risk appetite a little further on). Although your business's spare cash may be low and its appetite for risk high, you may have highlighted that some risks exist that you can't afford *not* to do anything about. This section looks at some of the broad options that you have in dealing with risks, and also provides some guidance on other things that you can do to ensure that you keep on top of new and emerging risks.

Strategies for dealing with risk

Your organisation's *risk appetite* is the amount of risk that you're prepared to tolerate before you consider action is necessary to reduce or remove the threat. For each risk to your critical activities, you need to draw up a strategy to bring it within your business's risk appetite. Unless, of course, it's already within it. We show five strategic types of response in Table 5-2 to start you thinking.

Table 5-2	Five Strategic Types of Response
Strategic Type	*Response Description*
Prevention	Terminate the risk by doing things differently and removing the risk. Put measures in place that stop the threat or problem from occurring or prevent it having any impact on your critical activities.
Reduction	Treat the risk by taking action to control it in some way that reduces the likelihood of the risk developing or limits the impact on your critical activities to an acceptable level.
Transference	This is a form of risk reduction where the management of that risk is passed to a third party via, for instance, an insurance policy or penalty clause. Nonetheless, if your critical activities come to a halt and your insurance is unable to help you recover, the risk is still yours and your critical activities have still come to a halt. The same applies if your supplier fails to deliver; you may get paid later but you're still at a standstill for now. And you remain the business that fails to supply your customer.
Acceptance	Tolerate the risk, perhaps because you can't do anything at a reasonable cost to mitigate it, or the likelihood and impact of the risk occurring are at an acceptable level.
Contingency	These are actions planned and organised to come into force as and when the risk occurs.

© OGC

You can select many different ways to respond to the risks that you've identified, and listing all the options here would be almost impossible. The response very much depends on the type of business you have.

Residual risk

The level of risk remaining after you employ your strategies is the exposure in respect of that risk. This *residual risk* needs to be acceptable and justifiable; essentially, it should be within your business's agreed risk appetite.

Monitoring and Reviewing Your Risks

When you've completed the four stages of the IERR process and produced your risk register (as in the earlier section 'Identifying, Evaluating, Recording and Responding to Your Risks (IERR)'), congrats! You now have an overall understanding of the sort of risks that your business faces to its critical activities. Your work isn't finished (sorry), but you can be satisfied that the time-consuming part is behind you. You can't ever say that the next part is complete, because you're continuous monitoring and reviewing the risks.

But like the other stages, this process doesn't have to be painful. Here are eight simple steps to keep your risk world under control (well, as much as anyone can):

1. **Make somebody within your organisation the risk co-ordinator.** This person keeps overall track of all risks and has responsibility for the risk register and reporting on it to the board or senior management team. The risk co-ordinator may be you or not, as long the person can pull together information, assess it, and report and recommend to top management.

2. **Add a column to your risk register (see the earlier Figures 5-2 and 5-6) entitled 'owner' and allocate each risk to the most appropriate person in your company.** This step is about monitoring, and that 'owner' reports any changes and updates the risk co-ordinator on a frequent basis.

3. **Get confirmation from top management on your company's risk appetite.** If that's you, no problem because you already know how much risk you're willing to accept. If not, you need to find out what the decision makers in your business are comfortable with. This may mean presenting them with the options open to them alongside the risk matrix to demonstrate the level of impact that risks may have on your business. An easy way to initially decide which risks you're going to deal with is to use the risk matrix (from Figure 5-7) and draw a line around the boxes that you're willing to leave and those that you aren't. This approach can certainly form part of your presentation to the board or senior managers in making the case for doing something about your identified risks.

4. **Attribute a RAG rating (Red, Amber, Green) to each risk, derived from a combination of where the risk sits on the matrix and how far the response strategy is down the line.** For example, a high-level risk that needs work doing that was agreed in the strategy may have a red rating, whereas a high-level risk where everything that was agreed to be done has been done may attract a green rating and just need to be reviewed for change. This system allows management to track progress of risk-response processes.

5. **Encourage and introduce into your organisation a culture of identifying and reporting new risks as people discover them.**

6. **Provide a monthly report to top management on the risk register, in particular:**

    - Risks that are changing

    - Newly identified risks

    - RAG ratings

7. **Encourage decisions from management on risks and action points to be taken up within your business.** Make sure people carry out the actions in a timely way and report back on these in the following month. Unless of course it was your action to complete and you forgot all about it. In this instance we find that starting your sentence with 'This one was rather complicated and may require some additional work; it may be beneficial if I give a full update next month' is useful.Or, if you're feeling brave, 'I'll give a full update in a couple of months when we have a better picture of what we're dealing with here.'

8. **Conduct a yearly review of your risk environment.** Scan for anything that you may have missed to pick up on any risks that don't seem to be a problem but that you need to record on a separate register called 'risks under review'. Look at these items for any changes that mean that they've fallen outside your agreed tolerances and so you need to take a close look at them.

Chapter 6

Building Resilience in Your Supply Chain

*Y*our business doesn't work in isolation. Like all firms, you're part of a chain of suppliers, with businesses that rely on you and others on which you depend. For the purposes of this chapter, we define a *supply chain* as:

> *a chain of suppliers that cuts across borders, drawing firms and contractors into the process of making and delivering a single product or service.*

So, for every product and service that you produce, you more than likely rely on others: for example, to supply you with components so that you can assemble your product. Your business then continues this chain of supply by delivering a completed product, boxed, on a pallet, to your customers.

This definition doesn't necessarily mean that your supply chain *has* to cut across national borders, but even if you're ordering items from the other side of town, the principle remains the same. Your supply chain is essentially about pulling together all the things you need from their various locations to produce and then deliver your end product or service.

People have employed numerous methods to make the concept – and indeed the reality – of supply chains very complicated and therefore of little or no practical use to you as a small business. But in this chapter we aim to do exactly the opposite. We're interested in giving you an understanding of what a supply chain is and its relevance to business continuity (BC), highlighting the potential problems that you may encounter and looking at the measures you can take to manage your supply chain vulnerabilities. We also cover the flip side and show you how you can give reassurance to your suppliers and customers. Doing so not only helps you to keep your key activities going by avoiding being substituted for another supplier, but also gives you that all-important competitive edge when going after new business.

Defining a Supply Chain

The clearest way to describe supply chains is through an example. We imagine that you run a business supplying lemonade to a major supermarket chain, and we show you step by step how the supply chain is made up. Of course, different supply chains contain different elements; this example aims to give you a basic understanding to work from.

Take a look at Figure 6-1. That's you, standing outside your factory, which contains machinery to produce lemonade and staff ready to operate it.

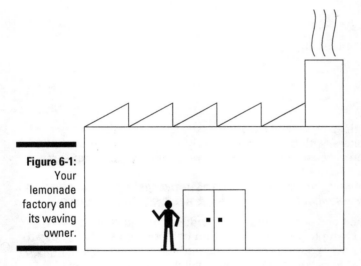

Figure 6-1:
Your
lemonade
factory and
its waving
owner.

Assume that you receive an order for ten pallets of lemonade from a large supermarket chain. To fulfil this order you need some other items to produce your lemonade, and so you place your own orders as follows:

- ✔ Bottles from Supplier A.
- ✔ Caps for the bottles from Supplier B.
- ✔ Labels for the bottles from Supplier C.
- ✔ Outer trays and shrink wrap from Supplier D.

You're now part of a supply chain. You have suppliers delivering goods to you so that you can produce your lemonade and deliver it to your customer, the major supermarket, thus fulfilling its order (check out Figure 6-2; you're still waving so things must be under control).

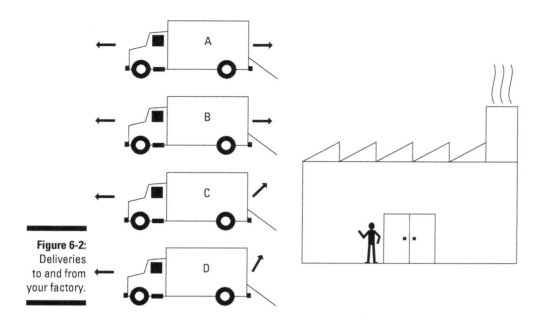

Figure 6-2:
Deliveries
to and from
your factory.

In Figure 6-3, your components have been delivered and you're able to produce the ten pallets of lemonade. Having done so, you contact your haulage company so that it can deliver the pallets to the supermarket.

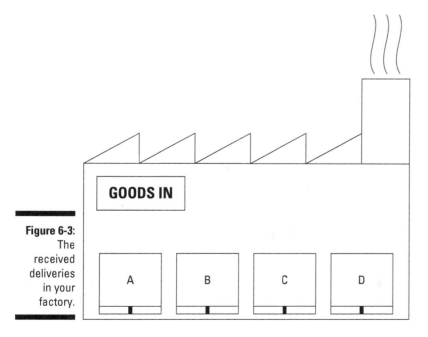

Figure 6-3:
The
received
deliveries
in your
factory.

And, as Figure 6-4 shows, that's it: a supply chain in its simplest, and we do mean most simple, form.

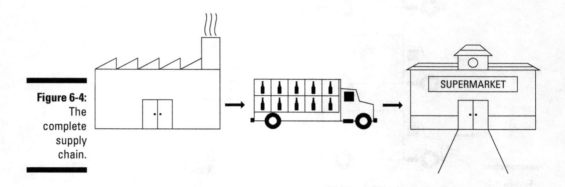

Figure 6-4:
The complete supply chain.

Focusing Your Actions for the Most Benefit

Looking at the simple supply chain in the preceding section, you may wonder what can possibly go wrong. Well, how about your supplier's supplier failing to deliver components to it, and your supplier's supplier's supplier not delivering as well? You can go on and on in this way until you chase your components right back to their raw source, such as oil being extracted from the ground to produce shrink wrap.

But we're keeping things simple and practical, and our focus is on getting a good return for the time you spend examining your supply chain.

Here are four key principles to bear in mind when striving to encourage the resilience of your supply chain – these measures bring the most benefit for the least effort:

- ✔ Concentrate on your pre-identified key products and services and the critical activities that provide them (which is part of your Business Impact Analysis from Chapter 4).

- ✔ You can only do so much with any single supplier and receive only so much reassurance. Where the activities are critical to producing your key products and services, consider a secondary supplier.

- ✔ Single points of failure exist in every supply chain; those pinch points where if that supplier fails, the entire chain collapses and can go no farther. When you recognise the points of failure you can support them, giving you a second option if things go wrong.

✔ Be prepared to reassure those that you supply, in the same way you'd expect your suppliers to reassure you.

Using the CHAIN Mnemonic to Manage Your Suppliers

Business continuity is all about ensuring that you can keep delivering your key products and services when disruption hits, and one of the areas from which disruption can originate is of course your supply chain. You want to avoid trouble arising initially if possible, but when it does, stop the problem from threatening your business's critical activities.

Managing the resilience of your suppliers may sound a little difficult to do because they aren't under your direct control. In one sense that's absolutely right, in as much as you can only influence and try to gain reassurance in what they do. In other ways, however, you can take control and protect yourself against suppliers failing, such as having a backup, or secondary, supplier that can continue to supply you if the other one fails.

Most of the actions that we suggest taking are simple measures you can put in place immediately, to work towards a safer business. All our suggestions aren't going to suit you and your business, and so select the ones that work for you.

We split the measures into five easy-to-remember aspects, based around the mnemonic 'CHAIN':

✔ Contracts and relationships

✔ Hierarchies

✔ Assurance

✔ Initiative

✔ Needs

Considering contracts and relationships

Clearly, good relationships between businesses are crucial to maintaining a mutually beneficial supply chain. Establishing a feeling of trust with your suppliers can only serve to be an advantage if something goes wrong and you're left wondering when the next delivery of those bottle caps will be. In addition, contracts can give both sides a certain level of assurance and protection when faced with a tricky situation. A combination of trust and contractual agreement is probably the best way to approach relations with your supplier, and here are a few ways you can achieve this end.

Service Level Agreements

Nothing is more likely to cause friction between you and your suppliers than when something goes wrong, which can certainly happen when expectations on both sides are different. Putting in place an agreed Service Level Agreement (SLA) can make things easier to correct when they do go wrong, and even avoid them going wrong in the first place.

A SLA is a document that sets out the agreed level of service that you can expect as a customer in terms of communication, quality and how things are going to be rectified if problems arise. Not only does this document ensure that both sides are on the same wavelength, but it also highlights clearly to you any vulnerabilities that exist with receiving goods from that supplier. A SLA can also provide some assistance in legal recourse . . . not that, we hope, you ever get to a point where that's necessary.

Although SLAs can be very useful in setting standards of expectation, a clause appears frequently in SLAs known as *force majeure* ('superior force'). This contractual clause frees both parties from liability or obligation if you can attribute a breach to an extraordinary event or circumstance beyond the control of the would-be liable party. We're talking about things such as extreme weather, a disruptive volcanic eruption or even war. Most force majeure clauses don't excuse a liable party's failure entirely, but are more likely to suspend it for the duration of the extraordinary act.

Watch out for attempts by suppliers to excuse poor performance or defend negligence by calling upon the force majeure clause even when no significant causal effect applies. Seek legal advice if you're unsure.

Relationships

Having a good working relationship with your supplier greatly improves the resilience of your supply chain. Take the time and effort to get to know new suppliers; even as your relationship develops, consider inviting them to social events, such as the office Christmas party. You may think that inviting the person who supplies, say, your printing ink to the office bash is overkill, but establishing and maintaining contacts is important.

For particularly critical suppliers, hold a monthly face-to-face meeting to maintain communication and discuss any issues.

When you're on friendly terms with your suppliers, you're more likely to be one of the first customers they call when something goes wrong their end (as opposed to being a small organisation they deliver to every now and then and have only spoken to once over the phone). Forming a solid relationship gives your business more chance of being told when something is wrong, instead of components just failing to turn up for the delivery.

A solid relationship involving regular contact also means that you're more likely to spot early warning signs if something starts to slip at a supplier. For example, if the company that supplies your lemonade bottle labels usually replies immediately to your email confirming an order, alarm bells should start ringing if no one gets back to you one afternoon.

Timing is essential in business recovery, and having that extra bit of notice on a supply failure gives you more time to make alternative arrangements, thus minimising the risk of loss to your business.

'Buddying up'

Speak to other businesses in a similar line as you and suggest a mutually beneficial plan to support each other in times of supply failure. Ensure that they aren't one of your direct competitors, though, otherwise what affects you may well also affect them, and be certain to gain assurance that, in the event of a disruption, they'll help.

If a disruption occurs you can give each other a hand by sharing spare stock, offering the details of alternative reliable suppliers or lending staff for temporary recovery work. Mutual agreements like these can benefit both parties and build resilience through alliance.

Understanding supplier chain hierarchies

Just as you assess how important various suppliers are to you, they've probably done the same about your organisation. Even if the supplier has a business continuity plan and is certified against a business continuity standard, you may be but a small consideration on its long list of customers.

Your standing is most likely to relate to how much stock you order from the supplier and how much money you invest in the company. Clearly, suppliers are more likely to prioritise high-profile businesses than your smaller firm that spends only £50 a week with them. Yet that £50 of stock may be fundamental to the continuation of your business's critical activities, in which case recognising this fact and putting alternative options in place is even more important in case that supplier does let you down.

Take a look at the priority matrix in Chapter 3 of your most important suppliers, which reveals the relative importance of your suppliers and their deliveries. Now consider things from the other side: how may *your* business rate on *their* priority systems? If the answer is 'not very highly', you need to take action to improve your standing (see the earlier section on building a relationship with your suppliers).

Reassess regularly where your supplier priorities lie, as well as your position in other suppliers' hierarchies, because these aspects are going to change. Seasonality affects supplier priorities (both theirs and yours) and fluctuations naturally occur according to environmental factors. Supply chains and suppliers themselves change and you need to keep your reviews up to date.

Your prime objective is to understand how a disruption to your supply chain partner is going to affect your resilience and where you fit within its recovery priorities.

Seeking and providing assurance

Identifying your supply chain and building relationships with your key suppliers provides you with assurance and security. Instead of leaving your destiny in the hands of suppliers, you're taking control of your own future and doing whatever is possible to improve the resilience of your business. By prioritising and planning, you recognise the element of risk and so can minimise the extent to which this imposes danger on your company. In addition, showing your suppliers that you're making plans and preparing alternative options gives them assurance that your business is resilient and durable. Where they're convinced of the longevity of your organisation, they're more willing to support your business, because they're assured of your ability to pay them regularly and uphold your end of the agreement.

Your efforts to strengthen the resilience of your supply chain usually gain the support of your critical suppliers. Although asking to see contracts, BC plans and the priority rankings of your supplier may seem demanding, in fact it shows that you're looking after them in the same way that you expect them to look after you. By explaining to potential and existing suppliers the rationale behind your exercises, they can only be convinced of you as a reliable and resilient organisation.

Your important suppliers should be able to provide you with details of their BCP (business continuity plan – if they have one), and in fact many firms are keen to demonstrate their programme to potential customers in order to prove their planning and strategies. If, however, your supplier refuses, for sound security reasons, to provide you with a copy of its plans, don't be put off. Accept the refusal, and perhaps even take it as a demonstration of a supplier who's keen to preserve its resilience. Instead, request a 'body of evidence' that the plans exist.

This body of evidence needs to include:

- ✔ Evidence of an overarching business continuity policy and outlook
- ✔ Evidence that BC plans are current

✔ Evidence of regular testing and exercising, showing that the supplier is identifying, correcting and closing issues

✔ Evidence that the BC plans have been created and maintained by a person competent in BC

✔ Evidence of board oversight in the area of business continuity

Here's an example list of a body of evidence:

✔ A copy of the supplier's BC policy.

✔ A copy of the page in the plan or plans that clearly demonstrates version control and sign-off (approval) of the plan.

A plan dated 12 months or more previous to its examination has little current value.

✔ A copy of an exercise schedule, past and future. Don't waste time asking to see lots of promises and documents if they haven't been tested to see whether they actually work in an emergency situation. As with your own BCP, testing through exercises and workshops is the most effective way of assessing a BC programme.

✔ Evidence – possibly a document with confidential issues blanked out – of how the supplier captures and corrects issues found during exercises or workshops. Expect such actions to be dated.

✔ Qualification of the BC plan creator, for example, member of the Business Continuity Institute or appropriate training in business continuity.

✔ Name of the responsible board member.

Depending upon the nature of your relationship with the supplier, asking to observe its next exercise may be prudent. You can then use the participation, or possible lack of, by the members of any incident management team to assist in your assessment of the supplier's resilience. Where clearly successful, you can even invite the supplier to conduct a joint exercise with you for the benefit of both businesses.

After you identify the person responsible for the creation and/or maintenance of the supplier's BC plans, keep in contact and build a relationship of trust. In this way, if the supplier suffers a disaster, you're notified in good time and not when an order fails to arrive!

The information in this section covers those suppliers who have plans, of course, but what of those firms that don't? Well, much depends on how important you are as a customer to them. If the product or service they supply is of low value to them, no matter how important it is to you, their motivation to co-operate in this area is likely to be limited.

Responding appropriately

Proportionate response is about assessing the risk and deciding how to deal with it in an appropriate way according to the likelihood of it happening. For example, if you buy a train ticket and shove the return part of the ticket in your bag, the risk of losing it before you make your journey next week is fairly high. Therefore, you buy a card holder and keep it in a specific pocket of your bag. This is a proportionate response. A disproportionate and inappropriate response would be to buy ten return train tickets just in case you lose the other nine.

Taking the initiative

If a supplier doesn't have a BCP or arrangements in place, you need to consider the threat posed to your business by it failing and, if possible, take action. The threat posed to the continuity of your business isn't automatically substantial enough to change suppliers. You need to make a proportionate response (check out the nearby sidebar 'Responding appropriately').

If, say, your supplier provides you with plastic bottles, an essential aspect of your lemonade-producing business, and is one of four competitively priced bottle suppliers in your local area, you may not need to dismiss the firm just because it doesn't have a BC plan in place. Instead, choose a backup supplier that you know is willing to deliver locally at short notice.

Having a backup supplier (also called *dual sourcing*) is useful to consider regardless of the size of the supplier and the existence (or not) of its BCP. Things can always go wrong, and having an alternative option in place means that your business can avoid suffering from the failure of another organisation.

You can also protect the continuity of your business from the failure of your supplier by carrying contingency stock, so as to buy you extra time if you're forced to miss a delivery of raw materials.

If your supplier doesn't have a BCP, you have two general options:

- ✔ Accept the risk. If you do, you may want to think about dual sourcing or taking out business insurance to cover the potential loss of profit.

- ✔ Work with your supplier to establish or improve its BCP. Supporting your provider in this way encourages good relations and strengthens the resilience of your supply chain.

Some suppliers may well exist over which you have no influence. For example, if National Grid supplies gas to your office, you can't really do anything to work with it on a BCP or persuade it to prioritise you as a business. Here, you need to think about developing recovery strategies independent of your supplier. For example, if the hot water in your office isn't working, having the contact details of a local plumber to hand is independent of the supplier and provides quick recovery.

Fulfilling your business's needs

When looking at strengthening the resilience of your supply chain, you need to consider whether the BC policies of your main suppliers suit the continuity requirements of your business. For example, if your supplier decides that its maximum tolerable period of disruption (something we define in Chapter 1) is 5 hours for getting back to full functioning capacity, this hardly suits you if yours is only 30 minutes. Your expectations and requirements need to match to ensure that you can deliver your critical activities.

In considering the recovery of your business following a disruption, ask whether your supplier can provide you with extra stock at short notice. Does it have the capacity to be flexible on delivery times if you require stock immediately in order to get your firm back up and running?

To deal with any disruption in your supply chain you have to understand it first. If you're unaware of the position of your suppliers, in terms of what arrangements and plans they have in place and what they rely upon, you can't plan from your end. Therefore the key is communication and understanding each other's expectations.

You don't want to be involved in a disruption to have to find out what level of service you may get from your suppliers. Instead, you need to know this level of service in advance to make sure that you can keep your critical activities going in the event of a disruption.

Chapter 7

Selecting the Right Continuity Strategies

In This Chapter

▶ Getting the necessary information together

▶ Preparing properly

▶ Deciding on appropriate business continuity strategies

*I*n this chapter, we lead you through the process of constructing a coherent business continuity (BC) strategy. A *BC strategy* is the response that your business puts in place to make sure that pre-identified critical activities continue functioning even during a disruption. (To identify your critical activities, flip to Chapter 4.)

We talk you through collecting the various elements that you glean from Chapters 4 to 6 and help you decide on the right continuity strategy. The process that we use in this chapter also suggests two separate sets of considerations – tactical and general – as well as a check before finalising your decisions.

Choosing the strategy that's right for your business is vital, and so in this chapter we introduce some different types that can support your critical activities. You can decide what's most appropriate for your business (also check out the nearby sidebar 'BC should never stand still').

 The BC strategies (plural because you ideally need one for each of your critical activities) that you decide upon don't have to be, and in fact in most cases won't be, complicated. But thinking ahead, predicting what may go wrong and doing your best to prevent adverse events from happening gives you the best chance of continuing to deliver your key products and services during a crisis.

BC should never stand still

You choose BC strategies based on your particular business. We can't advise on the right specific strategies for you, but we do advise that you put something in place. BC is never completed, but instead needs to evolve and mature with your business. Something that's beyond your reach today and seems not worth protecting may very well be within your grasp in 12 months' time and essential to protect against disruption.

The real value in examining your options in keeping your critical activities going is that you develop a far greater understanding of the risks that you're taking and an idea of the sort of things that, if they do go wrong, are going to cause real problems.

Gathering Together What You Need

MTPD:
Maximum Tolerable
Period of Disruption

For each of your critical activities, you need to consider and select a continuity and recovery strategy. By that, however, we don't necessarily mean that you have to identify an *action* for each one, because in some instances you may decide to do nothing because that's the only option your business can afford. After all, the business and the consequences of the decisions that you make are yours.

MTDL:
Maximum Tolerable
Data Loss

To identify and select your strategy options, your mission – if you decide to accept it – is to ensure that your selected responses are within the maximum tolerable period of disruption (MTPD) and within the maximum tolerable data loss (MTDL). To accomplish this aim, we use the recovery time objective (RTO) and recovery point objective (RPO), which provide a guiding light when you're discerning the options that work from ones that don't.

RTO:
Recovery Time
Objective

For explanations of the terms MTPD, RTO, MTDL and RPO, check out Chapter 1.

You get the best out of this chapter when you've:

RPO:
Recovery Point
Objective

- ✔ Identified your business's key products and services (check out Chapter 4).

- ✔ Worked out the critical activities required to keep these products and services running (also in Chapter 4).

- ✔ Gained an understanding of the risks to these products and services (as we describe in Chapter 5).

- ✔ Cultivated an awareness of those that you rely on, their processes and dependencies, and on which your key products and services depend (see Chapter 6).

Deciding on the objectives to use

While considering and selecting your continuity and recovery strategies, you also get an opportunity to finalise the RTOs and RPOs for your critical activities, because often you revisit these objectives as you go along to make everything fit. For this reason, you use your *time objectives* (RTOs) rather than the maximum time you have until things are irreversible (MTPD); that way you get a bit of leeway. The factor that can influence these decisions most is, of course, cost. If having something up and running within 12 hours costs twice as much as for 24, you may put the initially set 12-hour RTO back to 24 hours. As long as the RTO is still within the set MTPD, this decision is perfectly reasonable.

Some businesses, however, do revisit their MTPD in light of the continuity strategy options available and the cost. As ever in BC, nothing is set in stone; BC is about making things work for your business and doing the best with what you have. Therefore, if you need to make some tough decisions about what you can and can't do, better to do so while you have time to implement the decisions, as opposed to at the onset of a disruption when the pressure is on and time is tight.

Having to hand your versions of the Business Impact Analysis (BIA) showing your MTPD and RTO (refer to Chapter 4), and your risk register and matrix (refer to Chapter 5), is also useful as you work through this chapter.

If you're yet to identify these components of your business and you decide to work through this chapter without them, a word of caution. Trying to create your continuity strategies without being sure of these components and time objectives may make the process more confusing than it needs to be.

Looking Before You Leap

In this section, we turn to some overarching considerations for you to think about. Many of them may seem common sense, but we want to make sure that you consider everything when making your continuity and recovery strategy decisions:

- ✔ Ensure that your selected strategy options are readily accessible or available for use within a defined timescale.

- ✔ Allow adequate separation when using duplicate resources, such as a backup site or dual-source goods, so that any incident is unlikely to affect them both.

- ✔ Make any decisions regarding your minimum or correct separation distance between duplicate resources in line with your business requirements and identified risks.

Balancing costs

The value of uncovering the risk to your business and understanding the things that are really important is that you begin to ask yourself the important question: 'How can I afford *not* to do anything?' This approach allows you to strike the balance between doing what you need to, making a sound investment in your business and spending vast amounts of money in areas that are going to be of little value when a disruption occurs. The measures that you put in place don't have to be expensive and, in a lot of cases, can be quite simple to implement.

✔ Weigh up the distance that staff may have to travel versus having a backup so close to your primary site that an incident is likely to affect it.

✔ Appraise your selected continuity strategy solution in terms of cost to implement versus benefit or speed of recovery that it offers.

Although the last point sounds obvious, proposing strategies that meet everyone's needs but then turn out to be unrealistic financially is all too easy. The danger is that implementation of BC then stops because people see it as being too expensive. The main challenge when working through this chapter is to put in place effective strategies that are within the financial grasp of your business (see the nearby sidebar 'Balancing costs').

Working Out Your BC Strategy Responses

You need to consider three stages of an incident when looking at your continuity strategy responses. In the following list, we describe these stages and include some examples from an imagined scenario in which a business loses power and the RTO is estimated to be six hours:

1. **Emergency response and incident management stage:** The strategies that form your immediate actions in an emergency, such as implementing your communications plan.

   In the example, this stage may involve calling for a generator that can provide power for 24 hours.

2. **Continuity stage:** The strategies to ensure you can continue to deliver your critical activities and in turn deliver your key products and services during a disruption.

In the example, this stage may consist of moving operations to another site that has power within 24 hours.

3. **Recovery and resumption stage:** The strategies to recover critical activities to a sustainable level leading to resumption of operations to what your business describes as normal.

In the example, this stage would cover the actions involved in transferring back to the original premises.

These stages may require different strategies to ensure that you maintain all your critical activities, and so consider this aspect on a case-by-case basis.

Figure 7-1 depicts a simple six-phase process for identifying strategies in response to the information that you've gathered about your business. The path follows on from identifying your key products and services and the critical activities that make them happen (see Chapter 4) and the risks that they face (Chapter 5).

Six steps may sound a lot, but most are straightforward and though important don't require much in the way of effort. Phase 3 is the major stage.

In this section, we describe these phases from collecting the information to producing a BC response spreadsheet that forms the launch pad for implementing these strategies in your business.

Phase 1: Collecting the necessary information

To start assessing the best strategies to keep your critical activities going, collect together the information that we discuss in the earlier section 'Gathering Together What You Need': that is, your BIA spreadsheet showing the critical activities with the RTOs, your risk analysis and an understanding of your key products and service dependencies.

Phase 2: Creating a continuity response template

The continuity response template is the foundation for arriving at your strategy decisions and acts as a matrix for recording your initial thoughts and testing them against the later consideration and review points.

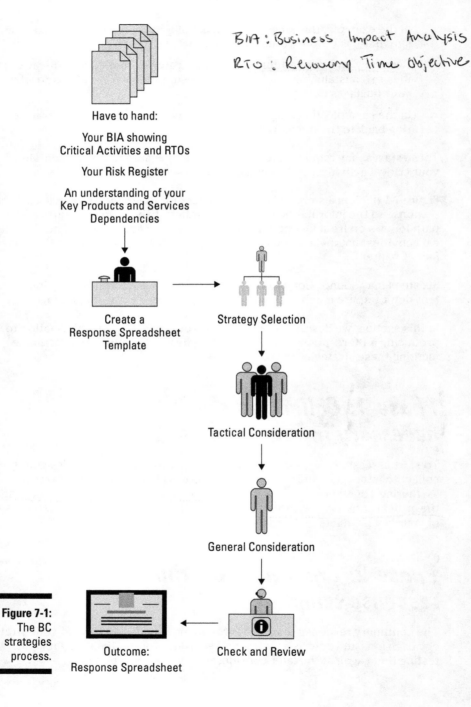

BIA: Business Impact Analysis
RTO: Recovery Time Objective

Have to hand:

Your BIA showing
Critical Activities and RTOs

Your Risk Register

An understanding of your
Key Products and Services
Dependencies

Create a
Response Spreadsheet
Template

Strategy Selection

Tactical Consideration

General Consideration

Outcome:
Response Spreadsheet

Check and Review

Figure 7-1:
The BC
strategies
process.

Pulling this information together on a spreadsheet enables you to see connected areas and links between strategy options for critical activities, as well as where your selected strategies just won't work. In our example of a response template, a number of columns (on the right-hand side) are simply considerations that you check and tick if whatever's in that column heading will work for maintaining the critical activity in question using the proposed strategy. Being unable to tick a column indicates that the strategy has a problem and may not work. The strength of the template is that even though it's simple in construction, it prompts you – as compiler – to consider all the different areas in order for the strategy to work and then shows up the areas that don't work. For example, a strategy may work when you consider people (your staff), premises (your shop) and resources (your components) but not your suppliers. If you can't tick the supplier box in this case, you're likely to need to revisit the strategy option to revise or change it.

Planning for cakes: Bakery example

Sometimes a single spreadsheet can help in working out your strategies. To illustrate, consider the example bakery that we introduce in Chapter 4.

The shop has identified that a critical activity needs an oven to be ready to bake the (key product) cakes within six hours of the current one being out of use. As owner, you've identified a bakery in a different county that has a spare oven and is willing to act as your standby in the event of a disruption. The travelling time is 50 minutes and the oven can be up and running within one hour of you arriving. So far so good. As you work down your critical activities you realise that you also need some preparation space to ice the cakes. The alternative site also has a workspace and therefore offers a solution to keeping this critical activity going too. Things are still looking good at this point.

When you look at the strategy options for *packaging* the cakes, however, the nearest alternative site that you identify is 110 kilometres (some 70 miles) away. This distance means that you'd miss your RTO for getting the cakes boxed and ready to deliver; and it may go beyond your MTPD, which would be disastrous (see Chapter 4 to remind yourself about RTO and MTPD). By using your spreadsheet, however, you can compare the alternatives and select the best fit for your business.

In approaching your critical activities in this way you're working on the basis that you've lost everything and need strategies for all your critical activities. Although doing so is sensible, because life is sometimes cruel, events aren't always like that. If your business just loses power, for example, you can transfer your baking and icing operations to the backup site, and still have your original site to pack and dispatch (providing you have daylight, that is).

Figure 7-2 contains an example of a continuity response template. If you decide on a different format for your business that makes more sense to you, go right ahead. Setting out all your options on one sheet is a good idea, because you can identify crossover, such as strategies that are effective in maintaining more than one critical activity. Doing so also shows up unbridgeable gaps that may require you to consider innovative and perhaps more costly options, which in turn avoids you spending money in areas that you don't need to by focusing on the vulnerable areas that need cover.

Figure 7-2: Sample continuity response template.

Critical Activity	From BIA		From Risk Register		Strategy Option	Considerations										Phase		
	RTO	RPO	Risks	Dependencies		Tactical				General						Incident	Continuity	Recovery
						People	Premises	Resources	Suppliers	Reliability	Cost vs Benefit	Reputation	Customer Needs	Supplier Needs	Emergency Services			

Although much of Figure 7-2 is self-explanatory, some parts may be unclear at this stage. Don't worry, we break each one down as we walk you through the procedure.

The suggested process in this section covers the basics, and you may want or need to tailor the method to record and plan the specific strategies you're going to use.

Phase 3: Selecting a strategy

Although working out the right strategy to fit each critical activity is the most involved task, the approach that we show you in this section helps you break down the job and so lighten the load.

You can write or type the spreadsheet (that we describe in the preceding section) because it's simply a systematic way of working through your list of critical activities and checking them against a series of considerations.

Begin by taking the first critical activity on your list, along with the BC information you have on it, such as the RTO, RPO, risks and dependencies. Now put beside it the best-fit continuity strategy (see the later section 'Continuity strategies') for this information. This process shouldn't be a long calculated exercise but simply a case of placing a potential solution or solutions next to a problem.

Check that the solution meets the key tactical and general considerations for validity. If it doesn't, you either select a different continuity strategy or tailor the existing solution to make it work when checked against the key considerations.

Sounds simple? Well, the process isn't quite as easy as all that, but it is achievable with a little bit of time and a willingness to make changes as you go along. A bit like most things in life really, except that this one can save your business.

Before going any further, we take a look at some of the continuity strategies you can employ to keep your critical activities going during a disruption.

Continuity strategies

The type and number of strategies you can employ to keep producing your key products and services are limited only by the resources at your disposal, such as cash, and the creativity and innovation within your business. No set answers or definitive rigid steps apply when creating resilience. The objective is to be able to continue your critical activities so that you keep pushing products out of the door, and so if you expect your selected strategy option to achieve this object, you have a good strategy for your business.

In most cases you think up the continuity strategies that work within your business, because you know what can work, how much goodwill you have with contacts and the cost restraints that you're operating within. This section highlights some of the strategy options businesses that most frequently use as a way to get you thinking about the specific options you can bring into play for your firm.

The common continuity strategies fall into four general areas: people, premises, resources and suppliers.

People

Most likely, some of your critical activities involve your staff and the tasks that they carry out. If you find yourself without these members of staff, what can you do to ensure that these jobs continue?

In the case of skills that only certain staff members have, you can do several things:

- ✔ **Train people in your business to be able to carry out the roles of others in the event that they aren't available.** A good approach is to get staff members themselves to teach someone else about the key processes that relate to critical activities. Consider using them as cover for leave or to assist during busy periods to maintain capability and confidence.

✔ **Test to see whether other staff can do the job for real.** Every now and again, check that the newly trained member can carry out the role. Doing so irons out any teething problems before an emergency and keeps the skills sharper in the person's mind.

✔ **Maintain documented procedures for these activities.** If both main and backup staff members are off, these documents provide a backup that explains the procedure and enables people to get tasks done, albeit more slowly. In advance, ask someone who's not familiar with the process to try to do the job using the documentation, to ensure that it can clearly be understood. Revise the paperwork if not.

✔ **Enable remote access to systems for key members of staff.** We look at this option in more detail under the later 'Premises' section, but if a staff member can't come into work owing to icy roads, children being ill or a broken leg, critical business can still continue through the employee being able to work from home.

✔ **Keep in contact with retired or seasonal staff who can operate systems.** Remembering any retired or seasonal staff at Christmas is a good idea. Paying for them to attend refresher training once a year costs relatively little compared to these people stepping in to keep everything going during a disruption.

Make sure that your liability insurance covers any staff you bring back into the business.

✔ **Be able to get hold of trained, short-term staff quickly.** Imagine that you're hit by a flu epidemic and 14 of your packers are off ill. At your busiest time with orders needing to go out, this strategy is about having a relationship with a reliable staff provider who can fulfil your needs quickly and professionally.

✔ **Think about how you cope when a key employee is on holiday or off sick.** Can you use the same approach to cover for an absence caused by an incident?

Premises

Your business premises play an important role in your day-to-day trading, especially if you also rely on a factory or warehouse. You can consider a number of different strategies for when your critical activities require your premises to function:

✔ **Have backup premises at an alternative site.** Ensure you can move staff or operations at short notice.

✔ **Store crucial equipment, such as servers, off-site.** Then you can use it when access to your premises is impossible.

✔ **Arrange to be able to use the premises of another business in the event of a disruption – one that isn't in direct competition with your own.** This strategy can be a cost-effective way to keep things going when disruption hits and may be as simple as picking up the telephone to arrange. Consider using partners' or suppliers' premises; after all, supporting the continuity of your business is in their interests.

✔ **Organise a Virtual Private Network that enables staff to log on to systems from home.** You can arrange this facility by speaking to an IT supplier and it can offer a great deal of flexibility. One option is to consider *cloud computing*, which is where you and your employees can access applications, such as emails or databases, through the Internet. Essentially, you can operate your business from anywhere you have access to the Internet. The main benefit is that you only lease the services, which gives you flexibility to scale requirements up or down without the encumbrance of owning the infrastructure. Worth mentioning, however, is that though you can outsource your IT requirements to someone else, the risk stays with you and you must still consider it.

✔ **Install a generator that can kick in almost straight away to support your critical dependencies in case of a power cut, or an uninterruptible power supply.** In this way, you assist in protecting your IT and telephony from loss of power.

✔ **Use third-party suppliers to carry out warehousing on behalf of your business.** Or have a backup warehouse location for outgoing and incoming deliveries of stock.

Resources

Resources is an area over which you can exert some control in as much as it's essentially about holding spares or additional stock. The challenge that you have and the balance you need to strike is not tying up unnecessary cash in stock but retaining sufficient to weather a storm if the winds come blowing. This section provides some strategies for achieving this aim and may in fact show you that your accounts or operations and warehouse staff are already using the calculations you need to be using:

✔ **Hold contingency stock:** This is a simple solution that you can carry out in a couple of ways. You can decide to hold a set number of pallets in reserve, or you can work out how many you need to give you a certain amount of cover; for example, for six weeks. The first option is a little less sophisticated and may give you limited support, especially if you suffer a shortfall at a time of high demand. The second option is more calculated and allows you to hold only the amount of stock that you predict you need. It does, however, require a bit more work.

The first option is useful if you have the warehouse space and can survive with the cash tied up in non-moving stock. Keeping the stock rotated is a good idea, to ensure that you always have fresh goods ready for dispatch and you conduct regular quality checks. No point having to withdraw a quantity of stock from your warehouse because of a leaking bottle-top only to find the same problem with your contingency stock. The number of pallets, goods or components that you hold depends on the lead times for ordering the goods and the number of suppliers to which you can turn if needed.

The second option requires you to forecast how much stock you're going to need for the next four- or six-week period, depending on what you decide is sensible. You may already be doing this in your business for the purpose of ordering components, but if not, consider the following:

- Number of units sold this time last year, to take account of seasonal peaks

- Any promotions you have running or due to run, including any voucher schemes

- The predicted sales volume that sales staff are saying will occur, based on their recent discussions and meetings

A simple approach is to predict a figure that you're likely to sell, or dispatch, during each month and divide this number by four to get an idea of how much you require for each week. You then need to decide how many 'weeks cover' you can sensibly hold, taking into account cash being tied up, warehouse space needed and the likely time that you'd need to get things back up and running. The idea of holding stock to cover sales just in time is a good one and can mean that you don't tie up cash unnecessarily. But you're taking a risk if your suppliers let you down. The decision is yours, but considering this gives you a useful idea of the things that you can do to build your business's resilience.

✔ **Keep hold of refurbished older machines:** An easy option. When your business invests in some new machinery or equipment, consider keeping what it replaces. This approach can be particularly useful if the equipment isn't commonplace or has a long lead time when ordering. You may incur a small cost maintaining the equipment, but this may be well worthwhile if you find yourself unable to produce goods.

✔ **Carry spares:** The simple action to take, which applies mainly to businesses operating any type of machinery. The key is knowing what pieces of equipment are likely to need replacing more frequently than others, what items have a particularly long lead time and which items cause your operations to stop if they go 'pop'.

A simple spreadsheet showing minimum order levels that turn red when reached is a useful way to keep on top of this aspect; as long as each member of staff updates it when they use something, that is.

Suppliers

Your suppliers are always going to be beyond your control to some extent. However, they're also a significant area where problems can arise that call for continuity strategies. The ideas that we suggest in this section aren't exhaustive but do offer some food for thought:

✔ **Dual sourcing:** Nothing's more satisfying than getting a preferential price from a supplier, normally owing to the volume of orders you're placing. But even though cost-saving and profit-generation is the name of the game, you can run the risk of being out of the game if your supplier lets you down. An option that provides you with some resilience is to use two (or more) suppliers for key products, components and services. Although this can mean paying an extra two or three pence a unit, because you're ordering less from a particular supplier, the price may well be worth paying. The benefit of having more than one supplier for your key products and services is that if you get a call from one to say that it's struggling, you can immediately switch to your alternative.

You need to think about several things when considering dual sourcing, and carry out a bit of investigation as well. Only some critical activities require a dual-sourcing option. For example, you may have identified that printer ink may be vital to your business but it doesn't call for a dual-source solution. If your stationer runs out of ink, plenty of options are available from supermarkets to computer shops.

Your key components are the ones that can really benefit from dual sourcing. But when seeking out a secondary supplier, you need to ask the following types of questions:

- Is the quality standard of this supplier up to the levels that you're prepared to accept?

- If your primary supplier is unable to supply you, would this supplier be able to handle the additional orders? Would there be any delay in it being able to accept more orders?

- Does this supplier have any BC plan or arrangements in place?

If you can't satisfy yourself on these three questions, you may be safer staying with your tried-and-tested single supplier; or at least continuing the search for a more suitable secondary one.

If you're happy with these initial checks, though, the next stage is to root out *single points of failure* (ones that if lost or disrupted lead to the failure of the critical activity). This process can be complicated because it entails looking beyond the first tier of supplier. When we refer to *tiers* in a supply chain, we're talking about the different levels of supply: in essence, who's supplying who with what and, in this case, who else they're supplying. Figure 7-3 shows a very simple supply chain, with two tiers, to demonstrate.

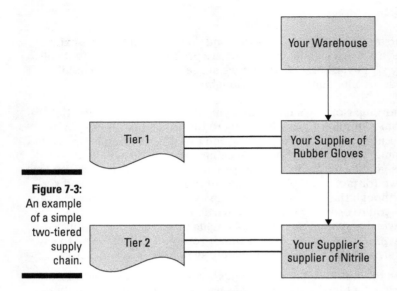

Difficulties arise when you find out what lurks beneath the first tier (Tier 1 in Figure 7-3) of your supply chain, and it's not necessarily obvious (until a problem strikes and you find out what was happening too late to do anything about it).

To discover what you can do to protect against these types of hidden problems, we consider another supply-chain scenario with more than three tiers and a little more complexity (see Figure 7-4).

Although Figure 7-4 may look complicated, in fact it's a simple chain in a lot of ways, albeit laden with risk in parts. We break down what this chain is telling you and identify the single points of failure and areas of concern.

The top of the supply chain in Figure 7-4 is your business and the supply of your flagship product. In the example, you have been diligent in ensuring that two suppliers, A and B, can supply you and therefore you're relaxed in that if one fails, the other can step up. You've put contracts in place with both these suppliers, who've agreed that they have the additional capacity that you require. They've signed up to 'best endeavours' to meet your order demand. Suppliers A and B have demonstrated to you that they use suppliers C and D, and E and F, respectively (Tier 2) and that if they're let down by one of them, the other can step in to meet the demand. On the face of it, this all sounds good, and probably a lot of companies would leave the situation alone, content that if things begin to go wrong, they have cover in place.

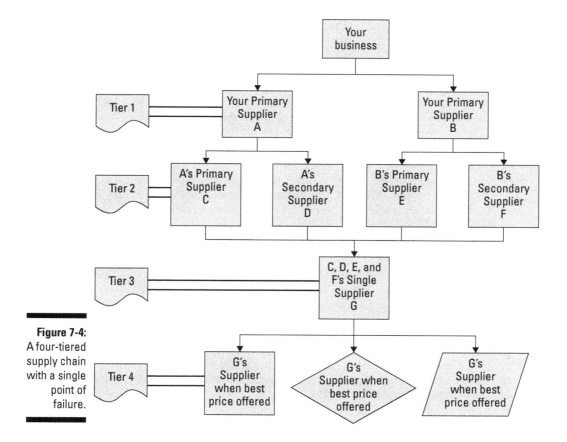

Figure 7-4:
A four-tiered supply chain with a single point of failure.

Doing so would, however, be a mistake, because lurking beneath Tier 2 is Tier 3, a single point of failure lying in wait. As Figure 7-4 shows, suppliers C, D, E and F all rely on supplier G, which of course means that you do too. Worse than that, if supplier G fails, for whatever reason, all above it in the supply chain are going to suffer. The figure also represents the trading activity of supplier G, which has no contract with its suppliers at all, because it buys its raw material from month to month based on which company has the best price. This arrangement now makes the agreements that you've signed with suppliers A and B for 'best endeavours' begin to look a bit frail.

The point of this exercise is to discover this fact *now*, before something happens, instead of when supplier G suffers a factory fire and the only reason you know is because you're left without any goods.

When sourcing suppliers you want to know: what lurks beneath? The farther you can go, the less likely that you'll be the victim of a single point of failure.

✔ **Early warning system:** Nothing that you do can make you totally fireproof. No matter how many checks you carry out, questions you ask or audits you conduct, something can always blindside you and your business – which is where putting in place an early warning system can be so important to picking up a situation quickly and responding to it.

Look at your current situation and see whether you can work out the point at which a problem with one of your key suppliers would become known to you. If this point is very early on, you're already in good shape. If you see, however, that things may rumble on as your stocks start to become depleted, you need to act to give your business that all-important early warning.

Your action can include regular meetings with your supplier to discuss your account and understand any concerns that are on the horizon, or arranging a visit-cum-inspection of your supplier's production line to look for any potential problems.

In addition, get your staff to carry out routine and regular quality checks of goods inwards and record the results. Problems don't generally occur out of the blue; often a build-up of issues or a slow deterioration of service precedes them. Address these concerns with the supplier at the earliest opportunity, and in doing so, check whether anything more serious is wrong. Recording your goods-inward checks allows you to spot clearly any decline in service.

Introduce a culture in your organisation that looks for unusual behaviour within suppliers. An example would be your accountant noticing that a supplier is chasing heavily for a payment before it's due – possibly a sign that all isn't well financially with that business. Anything out of place should have you asking questions.

✔ **Post-incident acquisition:** For the products and components with a longer RTO, and for which you're confident that suppliers are plentiful and able to supply at short notice, you always have the option of buying at the time of a disruption. However, planning this aspect now is preferable, when you have an idea of where you're going to go before dashing for the directories in a panic.

✔ **Insurance:** Insurance can provide compensation for loss of assets and assist with the costs of resumption, but it doesn't respond immediately and can't cover things such as reputational loss. Turn to Chapter 16 to get the most out of your insurance and for help in working out how it can support your business as part of a continuity strategy.

✔ **Do nothing:** This option may surprise you, but in fact it can be the right strategy in certain cases. If the RTO is a long one and other obvious options carry large expenses, doing nothing may be valid as a strategy to recover after the incident occurs.

Phase 4: Assessing progress – tactical considerations

Having selected the strategy option that seems to be the best fit (as we describe in the preceding section), you need to run it through some considerations to check that it's going to do the job. Doing so also allows you to spend less time agonising over the correct strategy.

We use the same four groupings for tactical considerations as we describe when selecting strategies: people, premises, resources and suppliers. Therefore, you look at your chosen strategy for the critical activity in question and check that it covers the people, premises, resources and supplier elements of that activity. The spreadsheet that we suggest in the earlier Figure 7-2 shows these items so that you can simply tick them off.

This tactical consideration may reveal, for example, that your strategy to dual source takes care of the supplier element but not the staff side of things. The process therefore allows you to then look at a different strategy for this element of keeping the critical activity going.

As a result, in order to keep a critical activity going, you may require more than one continuity strategy to cover different elements.

Phase 5: Listing some general considerations

General considerations really speak for themselves and are all the things that you do as a matter of course. However, listing them is useful to be sure that you don't miss them.

The general considerations to use when devising your BC strategies each form a column in the spreadsheet in the earlier Figure 7-2.

Use these areas and add any further ones that make sense to your business. We expand on these consideration areas in the following list, including the type of things you need to be thinking about:

✔ **Reliability:** Is this strategy going to prove reliable when the time comes? If it involves a previously unknown company, ensure that you have the confidence in it being able to deliver. If you have doubts, raise them now, because you don't want them becoming reality when the pressure's on.

✔ **Cost versus benefit:** How much is this continuity strategy going to cost to implement and what may it cost if not implemented? You can turn around this latter cost as a potential benefit if failure costs are high. An expensive, over-engineered option can jeopardise senior management seeing BC as an essential tool, and is rarely likely to be the best solution anyway.

✔ **Reputation:** Consider what the strategy can do to and for your reputation. For example, if your business majors on using recycled and recyclable materials, selecting a continuity option that doesn't align with this ethos can be damaging.

✔ **Customer needs:** Does the strategy meet the needs of your customer? This element is key to the entire process: for example, no point having a continuity strategy that can deliver the replacement component in green, if your customer needs to have it in pink.

✔ **Supplier needs:** Consider not only the supplier that you've chosen as a secondary supplier, but also your existing ones. If, through the implementation of your strategy, you're going to change the dynamic of relationships or beneficial arrangements with your existing suppliers, you may need to reconsider. Or at least work out how you're going to manage the situation.

✔ **Emergency services:** Consider the effect on the roles of the emergency services if a disruption takes place. Are you going to be able to do what you've laid out in your strategy, or are the emergency services going to direct you otherwise? Although the emergency services affect only a few scenarios, they're still worth considering. For example, if you have a fire at your shop, can you still sell cakes from the service window 30 metres down the road?

Phase 6: Checking and reviewing

At the end of the BC strategy responses process, check that what you've decided upon meets the following criteria:

✔ You've aggregated your recovery requirements, to maximise the benefit of the selected continuity strategies.

✔ Your selected strategies are consistent across the organisation and don't conflict with one another.

Also, ensure that you have:

- ✔ Provided top management with an evaluation of your consolidated continuity requirements and the strategies you've identified to deal with them.

- ✔ Obtained agreement from top management for any resources, finance and provisions for implementation.

- ✔ Set in motion work programmes to ensure that your selected continuity strategies are put in place and reviewed on an annual basis and after any events.

Your aim in selecting the right continuity strategy is to ensure that you can keep your critical activities going for your key products and services. The spreadsheet that you create (your version of Figure 7-2) needs to enable you to pick out strategies that cover more than one critical activity and so maximise the strength of your continuity strategies. You need to take some actions straight away to ensure a state of readiness in the event of a disruption, whereas you can do others only at the time of an incident.

You're going to use your spreadsheet to prepare a BC plan (as we describe in Chapter 8) for implementing the agreed strategies, securing the necessary budget and resources, and setting about ensuring that you lay the BC foundations – ready in case a disruption comes your way.

Chapter 8

Developing Your Business Continuity Plan

In This Chapter
- Looking at BC plans
- Planning your own plan
- Bringing your plan to life

*E*ffective planning is vital to staying one step ahead of business competitors and disrupting incidents. At the heart of business continuity (BC) is the BC plan itself, although in most cases what we call your BC plan in fact comprises a series of small plans joined together. In this chapter we look at recording the strategic information that you produce from Chapter 7 in a way that makes things easier during the pressurised time of a disruption. We describe BC plans in detail – including why you need one and how to prepare for it – and we lead you through creating and developing a plan tailored to your business.

Keep your plan simple. For each piece of information that you're considering putting in, ask yourself: 'Is this going to help during a disruption?' If the answer is no, leave that information out. Your BC plan needs to be a useful tool and not exist simply for the sake of saying that you have one.

Examining BC Plans

BC Plan
CHARACTERISTICS :
- Concise
- Accessible
- Easy to read

In this section we take a look at the world of BC plans – what they are, what they provide, what they contain and why you need one.

To paraphrase the Business Continuity Institute's Good Practice Guidelines, a BC plan is

> *a documented collection of procedures and information that has been developed, compiled and maintained in readiness for use in an incident and allows an organisation to maintain the delivery of its key products and services.*

This definition tells you most of what you need to know: a BC plan is a set of plans to aid you in dealing with a disruption. In order to fulfil this role effectively, the plans need to be concise, accessible and easy to read.

All successful BC plans are built upon these three key characteristics: don't veer from them unless an overwhelming reason exists.

Appreciating the advantages of a BC plan

A BC plan is all about making life easier for you and your team at the start of and during a disruption.

At this stage you've done much of the hard work by:

- ✔ Working out your key products and services (check out Chapter 4).
- ✔ Identifying your critical activities (again, flip to Chapter 4 if necessary).
- ✔ Understanding the risks that you face (see Chapter 5).
- ✔ Being aware of your dependencies (which we discuss in Chapter 6).
- ✔ Selecting your continuity strategies to keep things going during a disruption (see Chapter 7).

Creating your BC plan is about collating all this information into a neat set of plans that are useful when trouble hits.

Although you may know all your business's information inside out and see no need to write it all down, consider this: what if something happens that means you can't be present when disaster strikes? In your absence, the plan can guide the business in what needs to be done and how it should be done.

BC plans aren't weighty tomes of text and information, but easy-to-follow, concise instructions that employees can pick up and act upon quickly.

Your BC plan steers your business's emergency response in the right direction by providing a set of previously agreed priority actions that maintain your firm's critical activities. Here's how you want the conversation to go:

'The wheel's come off; what happens now?'

'Let's get the plans and have a look!'

Even if you formulate some of the plan yourself, you can easily forget items over time, especially with the additional pressure of an incident going on around you. Far better to have a written BC plan than to find out during a disruption that you're not as well prepared as you thought; by that time it may well be too late.

Deciding what to include in your plan

The fact is that you need to plan for your plan, but only you know precisely what your business's plan needs to include. In this section, therefore, we can only offer you some areas to consider.

Ask yourself whether what you're thinking about including is going to help during a disruption. Ideally, the plan answers every question that springs into your mind as you pick it up in the heat of an incident. BC plans are an aid, and not an exercise in producing lots of paper and text. If the plan doesn't assist during an incident and takes ten minutes to decipher, you need to think again.

To simplify the task, split your considerations into two distinct areas:

- ✔ **Strategic:** This side allows senior management to maintain an overview of the situation.
- ✔ **Tactical:** This side involves other staff members carrying out the more hands-on roles.

Some overlap between these two areas may exist within your business, and depending on the size of your business you may prefer to add in other levels: your adopted approach should be the best one for your business. Check out the later sections 'Chewing over strategic responsibilities' and 'Thinking about tactical responsibilities' for more on the strategic and tactical aspects of your plan.

Looking at different types of BC plans

When writing a BC plan, consider who it's for and when it's for. In this way you create the right document for the right people and one that's appropriate for your business.

You can create a number of different plans, though they all share the common attribute of being valuable to you at a time of disruption. Some common plans to consider are:

- Bomb Threat Plan
- Building Evacuation Plan
- Continuity of Operations Plan
- Crisis Management Plan
- Escalation Plan
- Human Resources and Welfare Plan
- Individual Activity Resumption Plan
- Internal Communications Plan
- Media Plan
- Pandemic Flu Plan
- Product Recall Plan
- Shelter Plan

Plans aren't meant to cover every eventuality but simply get you started when the pressure is on, and then guide you through the situation as it develops and progresses. Take a look at the three different stages of recovery that we discuss in Chapter 7: emergency response and incident management; continuity; and recovery and resumption. These stages act as a framework for your plans but the precise level of detail is up to you.

A key element of your plans is to produce clear procedures for escalation of response and control. To do so, you may find that arranging your plans under a larger overarching plan is useful, one that details the plans within it and how they fit together. This overall plan is a great place to outline and make clear your general priorities. For example, your business's initial and general priorities are likely to be the safety of your staff, medical attention for the injured and unwell, protection of property and then people needs to do in terms of your critical activities and the strategies that you need.

Your overarching plan can bring these aspects together and pave the way for the smaller plans that will only be invocated, or activated, when you've considered and dealt with your main priorities.

Making a list and checking it twice: Considerations for BC plans

In this section we provide a checklist of the parts that you may want to consider having in your BC plan:

- ✔ **Clear title:** If someone picks up this plan from cold, you want it to do 'exactly what it says on the tin'.

- ✔ **Purpose:** This part says in as few words as possible what the plan sets out to do.

- ✔ **Scope:** This aspect may not be relevant for your business, but if you have more than one site, a 'Scope' section is useful in making clear what the plan covers.

- ✔ **Objectives:** This part consists of a concise line for each objective of the plan. If the plan has one very specific purpose, you may not need this part because you cover it in the 'Purpose' section.

- ✔ **Assumptions:** This part states the assumptions on which you're basing the plan.

Think of these assumptions as weaknesses of the plan, such as: 'We assume that the general manager is available to carry out this task.' Ideally, also answer these assumptions at this point if possible. For example: 'If the general manager is unavailable, someone else assumes these responsibilities.'

- ✔ **Invocation instructions:** These points need to be unambiguous, stating clearly when the plan should and can be invoked and who's authorised to do so.

- ✔ **Team structure:** This part outlines who takes the lead and the roles that other people play. At this point you may decide to separate your plans into strategic and tactical parts because the names and responsibilities may differ between these areas (check out the later section 'Creating Your Own BC Plan'). Include the team mobilisation instructions if necessary in this section – see Chapter 9 for more on organising your team and deciding who needs to be where in the event of an incident.

- ✔ **Locations:** This part of the plan details the locations, such as alternative premises and meeting places, which you plan to use and shows maps and access routes where helpful.

- ✔ **Resources:** This section details the things that you need for this part of the plan. The most useful information is where you can get hold of the resources, whether any access restrictions apply (such as keys or codes) and how you can go about restocking the supply if necessary.

- ✔ **Communications:** This part covers how you plan to maintain communication during the incident.

- ✔ **Contact details:** These sorts of details can frequently change, and so keep them as an annex to the plan.

- ✔ **Action lists:** These contain the nub of each plan. The information that precedes this part is essential, but the action lists detail:

  - What people need to do

  - When they need to do the tasks by

  - How they should do the tasks

You should already have all this information available from your Business Impact Analysis (BIA, see Chapter 4), your risk register from Chapter 5 and your continuity strategy response spreadsheet from Chapter 7. Your BC plans are simply the place to show these findings, but written as specific actions to take during an incident.

The trick is just to put down what people need to do and the information they need to get the job done. In some cases, recording the justification along with the action is sensible, whereas in others putting down what people need to do and who needs to do it is enough.

When laying out your plans, decide on a structure from the start and stick to it where possible. Doing so allows staff members to find the information they need quickly and easily.

Viewing an example plan

BC plans are always going to make more sense and work more efficiently when you tailor them to your business, and so build the plan around the way your business is set up.

As a starting point, however, Figure 8-1 shows what a simple BC plan may look like for evacuating people. By all means use this example as a basis for a template – or devise your own.

BUSINESS CONTINUITY PLAN 1

EVACUATION OF STAFF

Purpose: To document the procedure for safely evacuating and accounting for staff during an incident.

Scope: main site only: Unit 17 Fisher's Yard, Banbury, Staffs ST1 0TR.

Objective: To evacuate safely and account for staff during an incident.

Assumptions: (1) That either the fire escape or main entrances are usable; (2) That the General Manager is present and available; (3) That the Operations Manager is present and available; (4) That the West Car Park shown on the map in annex A is accessible and usable.

Initiation instructions: Any person can call this plan into action upon coming across a fire or other hazard that calls for an evacuation. Its use should become automatic at the sound of the fire alarm or a member of staff raising the alarm verbally.

Team structure: The General Manager (Finance Director if not available) will take charge of the evacuation and accounting for staff at the muster point. The Operations Manager (Marketing Manager if not available) will be responsible for the premises.

Locations: Staff will make their way to the muster point: West Car Park (as shown with a red arrow on the map at Annex A).

Resources: The visitors' book is located on the reception desk. Staff contacts list is held by all managers; building keys held by all managers. First-aid kits can be found by both the main entrance (pink cupboard) and fire exit (blue cupboard).

Communications: Staff are encouraged to keep their mobile telephones about their person. The General Manager (Finance Director if not available) and Operations Manager (Marketing Manager if not available) will communicate clear instructions during and immediately after the evacuation. Any staff member separated from the group should contact either of these managers by mobile telephone, but under no circumstances should they re-enter the building.

Contact details: The contact details for all staff are shown at Annex B of this plan.

Actions to be carried out:

* The General Manager (Finance Director if not available) will take charge of the reception and visitors book and staff contacts sheet.
* The General Manager will communicate that an evacuation is taking place and lead all those in the building through the fire escape.
* The Operations Manager (Marketing Manager if not available) will check each room – only if safe to do so – and ensure that doors are closed before leaving. If safe to do so the Operations Manager will bring the first-aid kit: one is located by the fire escape in the blue cupboard and another in the pink cupboard by the main entrance.
* The group will follow the route (in red ink) shown on the map at Annex A to the West Car Park and remain together while all members are accounted for by the General Manager.
* The General Manager will check for any injuries sustained during the evacuation and seek medical attention where necessary.
* Each group member is responsible for reporting to the General Manager any visitors or other persons who have not been accounted for.
* The Operations Manager will be liaison officer with the Emergency Services.
* If the evacuation is likely to last for more than 30 minutes or render the building unfit to re-enter, the General Manager will decide whether to put in place Business Continuity Plans 2 and 3.

Figure 8-1:
A sample BC plan for evacuating staff.

Creating Your Own BC Plan

In this section we look at the sort of considerations to think about while pulling together your plan. We provide a simple way of taking the information that you have and turning it into a BC plan that is agreed by senior management and validated through testing, so that it's ready for use.

Of course the details are going to be specific to your business, and so what we include are some considerations covering more general responsibilities during the stages of an incident.

Reflecting on roles and responsibilities

You want to make clear who should be doing what when you invoke a BC plan. Working out these responsibilities at this stage is far easier than later on when time is tight.

We split the levels of responsibilities into strategic and tactical areas (as we mention in the earlier section 'Deciding what to include in your plan'). Keeping managers a step back from the actual incident in this way makes sense and allows them to concentrate on the overall picture and get perspective on what people need to do.

Base the precise details (such as what people need to do and where placing staff members is most beneficial) on your continuity strategy (see Chapter 7), the size of your business and the nature of the disruption.

Chewing over strategic responsibilities

A great deal of strategic responsibility is about sound decision-making, anticipating what's going to happen, interpreting the information and assessing the current position. The following considerations all fit within this description, but you may want to reshuffle responsibilities around depending on how your business is structured:

- ✔ **Establish objectives and priorities:** What do you really want, and what do you really need your strategies to support?

- ✔ **Determine the recovery policy:** In most small businesses cost is an issue when determining the scope of your recovery policy. Start thinking about this early on so that you're aware of your possibilities and limitations.

✔ **Set the long-term strategy:** Make this strategy in line with your business's long-term interests.

✔ **Cover communications:** This responsibility needs to take in internal and external communication, including a media liaison role. Ignore this aspect or get it wrong and the reputation of your business can be at risk. Alternatively, a well-managed media situation can be a real plus when dealing with difficult situations.

✔ **Create an emergency services liaison:** This responsibility can easily fall within the tactical responsibilities that we discuss in the next section. The main thing is that you have it covered.

Part of building a strategy and giving it the best chance to be successful is making sure that staff are fully briefed on it, and understand its origins, objectives and what's involved. Briefing your staff when under pressure and in unusual circumstances can mean that you forget something and perhaps leave people feeling uncertain about certain aspects. IIMARC (Information, Intention, Method, Administration, Risk assessment and Communications) is a simple template for briefing staff that you can adopt or adapt for your business (see Figure 8-2).

Briefing Sheet for:

Date:

Information:

Intention:

Method:

Figure 8-2:
IIMARC
guide for
briefing
staff (as
used by the
emergency
services).

Administration:

Risk Assessment:

Communications:

The IIMARC template outlines a common and understood information picture that provides context to the briefing, the intention of the briefing, how it's going to happen, the administration arrangements, an assessment of the risk involved and how you plan to maintain communications. You can break down these component parts and give them to individual staff members to brief them, or just use the template to provide an overview of the entire position.

Thinking about tactical responsibilities

When looking at separating responsibilities, define what the term 'tactical level' means to your business. For example, does it relate to the staff members who are going to be carrying out the actions? Or if you have more than one site, such as a warehouse and office premises, is it the team that's going to direct an operational group at that site?

As a starting point, look at the following considerations when setting the tactical responsibilities:

- ✔ Co-ordinating the tactical level of recovery.
- ✔ Allocating resources.
- ✔ Establishing priorities.
- ✔ Co-ordinating support functions such as ICT, finance, facilities and human resources.
- ✔ Gathering, collating and disseminating information.
- ✔ Organising and mobilising suppliers and external sources.

Building Your BC Plan

Armed with the considerations that we discuss in the preceding section, you can set about developing your plan. In this section, we use a three-stage process – preparation, creation and validation – that helps you produce plans consistently and to a good standard, no matter how many plans you have.

Figure 8-3 lays out the process of developing a BC plan in more detail.

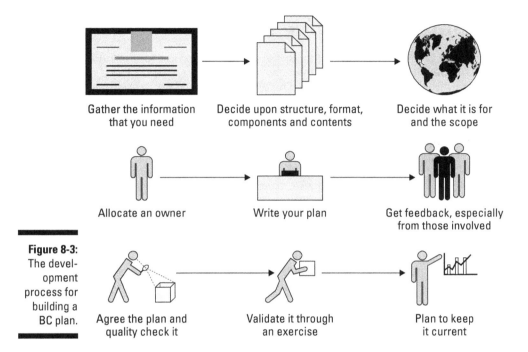

Gather the information that you need

Decide upon structure, format, components and contents

Decide what it is for and the scope

Allocate an owner

Write your plan

Get feedback, especially from those involved

Figure 8-3: The development process for building a BC plan.

Agree the plan and quality check it

Validate it through an exercise

Plan to keep it current

Stage 1: Preparing for your plan

Ensure that you have to hand the information that you need. Collect together your risk register and continuity strategy response spreadsheet (we guide you through creating these items in Chapters 5 and 7 respectively).

Next, decide upon the structure, format, components and contents of your plan. The first elements are, in most cases, the same for all, or most of, your plans and so your risk register and continuity strategy response need only the briefest of revisits if you're happy with them. The next step is also something that may not change much because it sets the scope of your plan.

If you have multiple sites, consider pulling together the plans for each one into groups.

Stage 2: Creating your plan

Start Stage 2 by allocating an owner – someone who's most likely to take the lead on a particular plan because that person is best placed to keep it updated and spot any errors. The owner also needs to write the plan or at least make a significant contribution to its creation.

You can now sit down and draft the plan. This step is a quiet time to draw together all your information and turn it into simple actions that people can pick up and follow.

Afterwards, you need to get feedback on your produced plan. Expect and indeed encourage comments and suggested changes. Doing so not only gives the plan a better chance of working well when needed, but also gets that all-important early 'buy-in' from people who may have to use it.

Stage 3: Validating and embedding

The first step in Stage 3 is to get your plan agreed by the senior management team and encourage them to quality check it. When you have the green light, you undoubtedly want to know whether all your efforts and careful forethought have been useful. After all, a plan isn't an effective plan until it's validated, and the only way to validate a plan is to test it. Testing also gives you further feedback to incorporate and in doing so confirms the plan as being ready for battle (Chapter 11 contains loads of information on testing and exercises).

The best approach to testing is common sense and striking a balance. You can spend your entire working life testing plans and end up making no money at all, and so the amount of testing needs to be proportionate for your business.

Finally, put in place a schedule to keep the plan up to date and current. Depending on your business, this can be as simple as checking details to ensure that they're relevant right through to a more structured annual exercise plan.

Make someone responsible for keeping the details updated. Done with reasonable regularity it takes only a few minutes but can make all the difference when you're standing outside your office at 4 a.m. in the cold and the number you have for the operations manager is out of date – and has been for a while.

The main thing is not to just file your plan away and forget about it.

Storing your plan

You want your BC plan to be accessible wherever you are. If you leave it in the office and have an overnight fire, it's not going to be of use. If you keep it on your shared hard-drive and the server goes down or is stolen, you're also stuck. But if you issue it to everybody you know and sew a copy into your suit jacket, you're going to have immense difficulty keeping people updated and previous versions are bound to pop up just when you don't want them to. In addition, BC plans are likely to contain sensitive company information and staff personal details, and you have a duty to protect them and don't want these falling into the wrong hands.

So, you have to balance the needs of security and version control against utility and accessibility; the plan needs to be secured and well-controlled, but staff members have to be able to use it in a major disruption. The best way to look at this conundrum is to work out where you'll be and what you can access in the event of a disruption. Will you have access to the Internet that allows you to be able to use a cloud computing storage option (see Chapter 7 for more)? Will you have access to a secure car boot or do you have a secure alternative such as a safe? These options are all worth considering, but the important thing is to keep your plans safe and accessible.

Part III
Embedding Business Continuity into Your Company

The 5th Wave   By Rich Tennant

"It's all part of the business continuity plan if e-mail goes down."

In this part . . .

These chapters concern fixing business continuity firmly and successfully into your business. Of course, this aim requires the support of your staff, and so we describe building your business continuity team as well as how to manage disruptions effectively. You also need to be confident that your plans are going to work in a crisis and so we talk you through testing your business continuity plan and running exercises. Running tests offers a great way to get your staff more involved in your business continuity programme.

Chapter 9

Building a Great Business Continuity Team

A great workforce is essential to running any firm. Your team is the foundation of your business and provides the groundwork for your business continuity (BC). Your staff members understand the everyday working of your business, grasp the realities of what you do and appreciate the efforts that go into maintaining the production of your critical business processes and activities. In some respects they probably know your organisation better than you do; they may well have more interaction and stronger relationships with your customers and suppliers on a day-to-day basis.

You need your staff to help maintain the continuity of your business and develop the culture throughout your company so they can be on call and ready to go if things go wrong. To do so, they need to be fully aware and on board with your BC requirements and plans, and know their roles and responsibilities within them.

This chapter is all about achieving a culture of BC within your team and embedding it within your organisation. We look at ways to disperse BC responsibilities through the team, not only to take the pressure off you, but also to encourage participation and enthusiasm.

Ideally, you've undertaken a business impact analysis (BIA) as we describe in Chapter 4 and identified your key products and services. In addition, you know the appropriate BC strategies that comprise your contingency plans (if not, Chapter 7 shows you how to form useful and supportive strategies to ensure the continuation of your critical activities). With these strategies in place, you can recognise the tasks that people need to do on a routine basis and during a disruption, and delegate responsibilities appropriately throughout your team.

Planning and Co-ordinating Your Team

The BC strategies and plans that you select and agree upon are going to direct the roles and responsibilities that you require your staff to take on. Depending on the stage and situation of an incident, you're likely to need different numbers of staff to do different things to different levels of intensity. Planning in advance which people you're going to call upon, for example, at the onset of a disruption, or who's going to be involved in the team that leads the recovery process back to business as usual, helps enormously during an incident. Not only are you better prepared, but also team members know what's expected of them and aren't surprised when you ask them to take on a new role at short notice.

Keep your BC plan updated when you review your strategies so that staff lists and teams remain relevant and up to date. Take into account changes of staff, working patterns and critical activities that may differ according to factors such as seasonality, supplier demands and customer requirements.

Hold a regular review of BC teams and roles with your staff along with the review of your strategies. Doing so ensures that your plans and assessments stay relevant and additionally you involve your staff in greater participation and so generate enthusiasm.

In addition to your review, create a golden rule that you take into account any changes to work patterns or long periods of leave in your BC team planning.

A good starting point, depending on the size of your workforce, is to delegate responsibility for continuity plans to a BC manager. This person needs to know the ins and outs of your business well and appreciate the priorities and critical activities that you must sustain to keep the business going. The BC manager doesn't necessarily have to be the most senior member of staff, but someone experienced in how your organisation functions at different levels to keep the company running smoothly. In smaller businesses the BC manager's role is going to be in addition to this person's normal duties.

BC managers need to be able to lead a team and report back on the successes and failures of firms' BC systems. They need to be creative and flexible enough to come up with new ideas and solutions, and work around any lessons learned that come out of testing BC strategies.

Identifying team skills and capabilities

Staff members need to be aware that business success depends upon the commitment of individuals and the shared understanding of what you want to achieve. The main things to ensure are that everyone's working towards the same goals and that you stir up some enthusiasm.

Look at your team in relation to the BC roles that need to be filled. Ask yourself where people's strengths and weaknesses lie in relation to what needs to be done and maintained. If any necessary abilities aren't available, is someone able and willing to develop a new skill? Staff may be keen to add to their work repertoire and learn something new that they can transfer to other areas of business or project work. If skills are looking a little thin on the ground, you need to provide adequate training in order to equip staff to respond to disruptions and so keep business ticking over.

Here are a few pointers that outline generic skills and capabilities that members of your BC team need:

✔ Understanding of the way your business works so they can identify and assess risks and mitigation options.

✔ Understanding of the contribution they can make and the skills they bring to their BC roles.

✔ Knowledge and understanding of time-critical activities and dependencies of the business.

✔ Understanding of the objectives and benefits of your BC system.

✔ Ability to review their responsibilities and roles to ensure the system remains up to date.

✔ Credibility and authority to promote BC to their colleagues as a primary skill and present it to potential investors and suppliers as an asset of the business.

You or your BC manager retain command of the team, co-ordinate new inputs and respond to any conflicts or concerns, with the focus on leadership and managing events. By delegating as much of the responsibility as possible to your team members, you give them a sense of ownership and stimulate enthusiasm for the BC programme.

Assigning roles and responsibilities

Don't try to take on the whole of the BC system yourself: you'll struggle to manage and anyway, you need your staff on board to integrate the practice into your business's culture. The people to introduce BC into your business (your employees) are already in place; you simply have to use their existing skills and roles to implement BC.

As far as possible put people in BC positions that involve similar capabilities to their usual jobs. For example, the person with responsibility for payments and receipts can cover continuity of finance, and the IT expert is the obvious choice to maintain the backup of your IT system. Make clear to all members of your team the value of their roles and how what they do fits into the structure of the team and the prosperity of the company.

The following list outlines generic roles and responsibilities to consider at this stage of planning. At the most basic level you can use this list to categorise your staff into where you think individual members fall or may be best suited. Doing so enables you to start thinking about forming teams and which combinations of people may work best with each other.

- ✔ **The BC manager:** This person is instrumental to the set-up and maintenance of the BC system, making the key decisions that sell the concept as well as managing the BC team. The manager's duties involve:

  - Making strategic decisions.

  - Discussing major strategic issues with senior staff.

  - Overseeing the BC process.

  - Obtaining a budget.

  - Accessing resources and allocating people's time.

- ✔ **The recovery team:** These people support the business after an incident and recover the dependencies that make the time-critical activities work. Their duties are to:

  - Help develop plans.

  - Co-ordinate and deliver recovery options.

  - Recover those parts of the business to which they've been assigned according to their area of expertise; for example, IT or customer communications.

  - Record progress of the recovery process for future lessons to be learned.

- Ensure that the business recovers at least to a level at which it can remain functioning and doesn't exceed the previously agreed maximum tolerable periods of disruption (which we define in Chapter 1).

✔ **The area champions:** These people work on specific areas of the business to support and maintain the aspects for which they're responsible. They provide information, data and support for their own areas and to others, maintaining communication throughout the organisation. Their duties are to:

  - Support the BC culture.

  - Identify and evaluate risks and continuity options in their areas.

  - Collate data and contacts.

  - Act as representatives for their areas.

  - Support the recovery team as well as the recovery of the business more widely.

Of course, depending on the size of your business, the roles and responsibilities in the list are likely to overlap in places. If you have a limited workforce, the manager is likely to pitch in throughout, and someone in the recovery team may well be an area champion in the finance department too. You can mix and match, have staff double-up on tasks or decide which of the roles are appropriate, depending on the precise situation and what stage of a disruption you're in.

You may need to play around before you find what works best for your organisation and which individuals or teams work best together. However you decide to organise things, though, what's most important is that you clearly define roles and employees understand what their roles are and which people they're working with.

Role is the important factor here, not rank. Make sure that you delegate the people most suitable to their responsibilities objectively based on their individual skills and experience. Your BC goals, roles and responsibilities are inevitably going to develop as business programmes develop or the business environment changes. Your approach needs to balance the conflicting demands of being adaptable enough to cope with change with being stable enough that you don't have to start again from the beginning every time something or someone changes.

To secure that you have the appropriate experience and enthusiasm to cover all roles if something goes wrong, make sure all key people have designated deputies who are suitable and ready to step into the role. Deputies need to have similar knowledge, skills and access to contacts, and be able to contribute at the same level. Include deputies' contact details along with those of other key staff, where all your employees have access to them. Appointing appropriate deputies may be difficult where numbers are small, and so bear in mind planned, or indeed unplanned, leave or holiday.

One essential aspect is that your staff members communicate with each other and keep one another informed of changes in their work patterns. Therefore, pair together people who you know work well together and whose personalities and work habits align appropriately, so that they can support one another in their roles.

Selling BC and Making It Work

When you've decided on your BC team and who's going to help out where (as the preceding section discusses), you can begin the process of getting BC fully embedded into the culture of your organisation. Therefore, you need your BC team members fully committed because they're fundamental to making this happen.

Although all employees don't necessarily need to be directly involved in every detail of your BC system, everyone must be aware of what's going on during these early developments. So you need to persuade staff of the value and benefits of having a BC system in place and avoid a few all-too-easy-to-make errors.

Getting staff members on board

You want to ensure that staff members appreciate that your BC system is designed to:

✔ Register and safeguard all your critical business activities.

✔ Describe all the roles and responsibilities of your staff in everyday business continuity *and* during an incident.

✔ Identify the risks to your business and be able to deal with them.

Keep your goals realistic and achievable at this stage; right now you're just trying to establish knowledge and create confidence in the system, and so start with the basics. You don't have to create a vast amount of extra work for your staff, but simply initiate a learning curve for all. Your aim is for everyone to embrace BC as part of the organisation. If employees get to a stage where they're practising and updating the system without really realising it, you've achieved this objective.

In essence, installing a BC culture among your staff is about retraining the way that your organisation thinks and plans. By promoting it down your line of staff, you soon find that your BC culture develops and is embedded in your company, and after that BC is plain sailing.

To help, share your goals with your BC team members and encourage them to have their own ambitions within the BC system. By now they should understand what they need to do, and that their first tasks are to sell the principles of BC and display evidence of good practice to colleagues. With your help and guidance, their job is to spread the word across your firm. Your BC manager has a front-line role in ensuring that all your senior people are on board and passing down to staff their endorsement of what you're doing. In turn, even those not directly involved in BC in your business need to work closely with each other to achieve what you all want to see in place: an effective, efficient and tried-and-tested BC system.

Try not to make the initiation and maintenance of BC a chore. Minimise the impact on the everyday work of your staff and get them on board by:

- ✔ Alerting them to examples of the risks to your business, and what they therefore need to protect.

- ✔ Inviting them to identify the benefits of BC and what's in it for them.

- ✔ Discussing when and to what extent they're going to be involved, and being equally clear about your own role in the whole process.

In order to make your BC system work in practice you need to remember a number of factors:

- ✔ Make sure that the process is simple, clear and easy to use in order to keep people motivated and focused.

- ✔ Focus on giving clear directions and instructions and avoid reinventing the wheel: where possible, use or build on what already exists.

- ✔ Keep everyone up to date with progress and priorities and adapt to change where appropriate to bring in new roles or combinations of people.

- ✔ Delegate responsibility so as to strike a balance between individual responsibilities and activities and teamwork; in this way, staff members each have their own responsibilities, but also have the support of the team behind them.

Identify, share and give thanks for improvements as they occur and make your staff feel as if they're making a genuine difference. Take time to acknowledge staff input and the effort they're putting into the system. People also have their everyday tasks to be getting on with, and so be considerate to other business areas as regards usual priorities and build this into the timescales for a realistic BC plan.

You can enhance the confidence and effectiveness of your team and the whole workforce through training and opportunities to test and rehearse your capability.

If, as you introduce your system, you find that something is falling short of what you want or just doesn't work in practice, stop and ask your staff why. Discuss the answers you receive with your BC team and, if necessary, agree an alternative approach. You may simply need to increase understanding of a procedure instead of implementing wholesale change. And then tell staff what you propose doing.

The key to a successful BC plan is analysing, testing and reviewing and being seen to do so. If something isn't working for you, change it.

Avoiding common pitfalls

When people try to adapt to new ways of working or new areas of work, the result can be confusion and, perhaps worse, demotivation if they 'fail' to respond as quickly as they should. If you experience issues with the progress of your BC, some problems may exist with how you've organised your staff. Consider the following points:

- ✔ Are too many people involved in these early stages? It may be a case of too many cooks. . . .

- ✔ Do all staff members fully understand their specific roles and are they able to prioritise some time for BC in their normal work schedules?

- ✔ Are some individuals or teams resisting change, or are all staff members on board with the idea?

- ✔ Have you delegated work to an employee who hasn't had the appropriate training to fulfil the role effectively?

Careful coaxing by you with an emphasis on the benefits to the individual and the organisation usually gets things back on track. If problems persist, consult staff to try to get to the root of the problem (as we describe in the preceding section).

Keeping the Enthusiasm Going

After you've introduced your staff to BC and encouraged them through the initial stages, you need to maintain their enthusiasm. The best way is to help them own responsibility for the continuation of the business. Here are some ideas:

- ✔ Instigate a vigilant and engaging review process, to keep staff thinking on their feet and invested in the progress.

- ✔ Make BC considerations an integral part of every new project or enterprise.

- ✔ Get staff to identify for themselves the business assurance measures they'd introduce as a safeguard to any new process or activity.

Don't forget your induction pack for new staff, and make sure that new people introduced to your firm accept all your built-in BC measures as part of the way that the organisation works. Appoint an existing member of staff to mentor new staff in all things BC, and don't dismiss new continuity ideas that newcomers bring with them.

Chapter 10

Managing a Crisis

*A*re you good at managing your business? Although we can't test our assumption, we're prepared to bet that most of you would answer 'yes', 'probably', 'definitely', 'sure' or something positive to this question. And it follows that if you're good at managing your business, you may also believe that you're going to be good at managing a crisis . . . yes? Of course *For Dummies* readers are a superior bunch and perhaps not representative of society as a whole, but logic dictates that not everyone can be better than average (which is our working definition of 'good').

In a classic survey on this human tendency to be overconfident (it's fine, everyone does it), 50 per cent of responding Fortune 500 CEOs during the 1980s had no crisis plan in place, and yet 97 per cent were confident that they'd respond well if a crisis occurred. These numbers just don't stack up. The fact is that being good at leading and managing a business under day-to-day operating conditions is no guarantee of being able to lead or manage a business to survival through a crisis. The good news, however, is that a bit of preparation shortens the odds dramatically.

In this chapter, we explore what makes a crisis (as distinct from an incident or disrupting event), what you can do to head off crises at the pass and what steps you need to take to prepare for the unforeseeable ones that are likely to affect your business. In addition, we cover responding to a crisis and recovering afterwards. Many thousands of pages across dozens of books are devoted to this topic, but the little secret that some crisis management professionals may try to keep from you is that this subject isn't complicated and not even particularly difficult. But it does require you to face up to two facts:

✔ A crisis is more than likely to cause your business to fail.

✔ During a crisis is too late to prepare for it.

So, you have at least two compelling reasons to read on and act on the contents of this chapter.

Looking at What Constitutes a Crisis

The British Standards Institution publication PAS 200 'Crisis management: guidance and good practice' defines a crisis as:

> *An inherently abnormal, unstable and complex situation that represents a threat to the strategic objectives, reputation or existence of an organisation.*

This definition needs a bit of unpicking. Usually, crises are inherently:

- ✔ **Unexpected:** They generally arrive unannounced and/or have unforeseen consequences.

- ✔ **Hard to manage:** If a situation was easy to handle it probably wouldn't be a crisis.

- ✔ **Very serious indeed:** Badly handled crises can drive companies out of business, and they present serious and sustained challenges even for well-prepared ones. Although the language is rather dramatic, crises are events of such severity that they pose a threat to the very existence of your organisation.

Although many textbooks discuss different sorts of crises (and these can be useful in understanding what you may be up against and what you can do about it), to avoid getting hung up on the detail you need to consider the two general dimensions in Figure 10-1: sudden versus slow-onset crises and those originating from inside your firm and ones imposed from outside it.

Although these distinctions are simple and rather neat, note that crises can take many different forms. Some you instantly recognise; for example, an offshore explosion, fire and oil spill is very clearly a crisis for the oil company in addition to a personal tragedy and profound environmental and economic challenge. In contrast, others don't necessarily involve harm or material damage, but can just as effectively damage an organisation's reputation, erode its assets and suppress its prospects for the future; for example, a crisis arising from the illegal behaviour of journalists or pillars of society fiddling their expenses.

One of the defining features of most crises is that they destroy or undermine what your staff, your customers and others with a stake in what your organisation does expect of you – the things they take for granted about your firm. These aspects may be, say, the safety of their family, the security of their property, the value for money you offer, the quality of your products or the continuity of your service. If your reputation rests on these items and you fail (or are seen to fail), you're likely to be facing a crisis.

Sudden crises ◀——————————▶ Slow-onset crises

These happen suddenly and typically without any warning. They tend to escalate rapidly. The effects of the crisis are generally very visible and are likely to attract attention and scrutiny on a scale that is proportionate not just to the size and standing of the affected organisation, but also to other factors such as events in the locality, sector or wider economy to which the crisis may be (or may appear to be) connected.

These are sometimes called 'smoldering' or 'rising tide' crises and they are often hard to spot as indicators of a potential crisis are overlooked, misunderstood or even denied. Typically such crises tend to 'gestate' for potentially quite a long period and then suddenly break, perhaps as a consequence of events in the external environment.

Figure 10-1: Two crucial dimensions of crises: sudden against slow-onset crises and ones originating inside versus those imposed from outside your firm.

Originating from inside ◀——————————▶ Imposed from outside

Many organisations contain the seeds of crises that will affect them within the organisation itself. This is not to suggest that they are entirely independent from external factors. Examples might include the malicious actions of a disgruntled employee or theft, fraud or arson, or more insidious practices that reflect changes in standards and values within the organisation. At the time of writing the crisis affecting various British newspapers and the wider press as a result of phone hacking and media intrusion appears to be an example.

Although some degree of interplay between internal and external factors is typical as crises take hold of an organisation, there are many examples where a crisis has been largely imposed on an organisation from outside, with little that could be done to prevent it. The tampering, sometimes with lethal consequences, of a company's products in supermarkets, or an unforeseen failure in supply chain or supplier quality assurance are good examples; the company may be a victim of circumstances, but if its products, services and brand are implicated then people will be looking to the company to 'do the right thing'.

Crisis management describes the steps that individuals and organisations need to take to prevent crises from occurring (where possible), prepare the organisation to deal with a crisis, respond to a crisis when it happens and recover from the experience. As such, crisis management provides a framework for thinking about risk management, business continuity (BC) and crisis response, as we develop in this section.

Crisis management is much more than just responding to a crisis.

Examining risks and issues

For clarity, we distinguish *risks* from *issues*. We discuss risk in Chapter 5 and you're no doubt aware that things can go wrong and have adverse consequences for your business. For a small to medium-sized enterprise (SME), such risks are likely to include data loss, sustained power or other service outages, supply chain disruptions, loss of staff or denial of access to premises. More precisely, most of these events are in fact first-order consequences of risks, and the *risks* themselves are likely to be potential events such as severe weather, a flu pandemic, a fire, a burglary or criminal damage, fraud or the malicious acts of a disgruntled employee. The simple fact that incidents and emergencies happen isn't in itself a failure of risk management.

However, if your organisation is shown, especially with the benefit of hindsight, to have managed a risk badly – for example, having failed to respond proportionately to a high risk that gave rise to an emergency for which you were manifestly not prepared – you're likely to be facing a crisis.

You can usefully think of an *issue* as a specific type of risk that's less tangible than, say, a fire or a burglary, and is more concerned with matters that can cause reputational damage. The difficulty with issues for an organisation is that their potential to give rise to a crisis is contingent on a range of external factors over which the affected organisation may have very little control.

The case in the nearby sidebar 'When an issue becomes a crisis' illustrates the way in which organisations can have latent issues, with crises potentially lurking within them. No doubt you can think of other instances where the use of child labour, low-paid workers, inadequate data or personnel security measures, or other ethically and operationally questionable practices have caused embarrassment and reputational damage to organisations with the consequent loss of business.

Reflect carefully and honestly on your own organisation. Can you be confident that no such issues are lurking within your firm?

Effective issues management requires you to:

✔ Think long and hard about what issues can bite you, and get different perspectives by asking staff across various areas in your business to do the same.

✔ Implement appropriate measures to address identified issues. Perhaps you're prepared to, or have to, live with the issues for now, but even if that is the case, you need a plan to handle events if they suddenly give rise to a crisis.

✔ Keep looking:

 • Inside, at the issues you identified, to check that you're still comfortable with them.

 • Outside, to check for external events that may trigger attention and the potential spotlight of unwanted publicity.

Distinguishing between incidents and crises

Incidents and crises are different but related things, and for SMEs in particular, focusing on how your preparedness for incidents also applies to crises can be helpful. To start, however, we need to acknowledge that some disruptive events are more serious than others. This may seem like an obvious statement, but spotting when an incident is taking on the characteristics of a crisis is critical.

When an issue becomes a crisis

A few years ago, an environmental organisation very skilfully opposed the disposal of an oil-storage platform. The pressure group used the media to portray the oil company as environmentally irresponsible and bullying, using footage of water cannons harassing small boats to great effect. The response of the oil company was to focus on the scientific rationale for the plan, the consultation measures it had implemented and its adherence to legal process.

The oil company took many weeks to realise that in fact the event wasn't about scientific facts . . . it was about public mood. It was about an issue, and the company's mishandling turned it into a crisis. The oil company ended up doing a U-turn, with its reputation seriously tarnished and at a cost of many millions.

Whereas a crisis can terminate your business, *incidents* are disruptive events of a generally higher frequency but lower severity than crises, and because BC is concerned with the maintenance of business functions and services in the face of such foreseeable disruptions, in general it focuses on incidents. Your BC measures are tested, probably quite frequently, through the natural rhythm of running a business – the power goes off, industrial action or illness keeps many staff away from work, a critical supplier lets you down or key equipment fails. These challenges are incidents; they're undoubtedly disruptive, but you're likely to have foreseen them and put in place measures to mitigate them as part of your business continuity. The objective of your BC, therefore, is to ensure that such incidents don't get out of hand.

In contrast, a crisis is an event, or set of events, in which things look as if they're likely to get out of hand, with the most severe potential consequences for your business. As an example, we look at a crisis arising through an interaction between external factors (the failure of a critical supplier) and internal factors (inadequate quality assurance measures of outsourced components leading to the supply of dangerous products).

Many incidents have the potential to escalate into a crisis, and effective BC needs to intercept these events and contain and mitigate the disruption. This disruption can cascade and escalate to a point that the things people take for granted about your organisation are threatened, which places you on the threshold of a crisis.

Not all incidents give rise to crises but many crises arise from incidents. Additionally, some events are so severe in scale and consequence that BC measures are overwhelmed and they immediately give rise to a crisis.

At this point, you may feel like flicking to another chapter and just hoping for the best, but bear with us. Although a badly handled crisis does represent a threat to the survival of your organisation, one that you handle well can enhance your reputation, credibility, trust and brand value.

Preparing for Crises

Quite appropriately, SMEs prepare for incidents and crises (as we define them in the preceding section) in broadly the same way and look to use many of the same personnel, facilities and ways of working when responding to disruptive events. On the one hand, this approach is entirely proper and reasonable; but remember that in the measures you adopt a point may come while responding to an incident (and possibly arise very quickly) when it takes on the character of a crisis.

In this section, we assist you in preparing for that eventuality. To do so, we need to consider crisis management in the round, focusing on what you and your team need to think about and do before the crisis hits you. That's another way of saying what you and your team need to do *now*.

Crisis preparation is about a number of different things:

✔ Spotting what may cause you trouble, outside and inside your organisation.

✔ Having BC arrangements in place.

✔ Developing a crisis management capability within your organisation that entails:

  • Setting the tone from the top that crisis preparation matters.

  • Defining roles and responsibilities.

  • Writing and maintaining a plan.

✔ Validating your arrangements; that is, testing them.

Remember what Snoopy said: 'Five minutes before a party is not the time to learn how to dance.' In the same vein, crisis management is *not* about 'winging it' on the day when things go wrong. As many organisations have discovered, that approach is the most reliable route to business failure.

To help you avoid succumbing to this serious error, we now describe the measures you need to take.

Scanning the horizon to spot trouble

Horizon scanning is the process of spotting risks and issues (which we discuss and distinguish in the earlier section 'Examining risks and issues') and other potential sources of crisis. The horizon metaphor is useful because it implies that spotting problems isn't primarily about keeping an eye on day-to-day disruptions (though these still have crisis potential if not handled effectively through BC).

Horizon scanning is about looking further ahead, from side to side and inside your organisation as well as outside, and looking for potential problems that may, at some time and in some way, give rise to a crisis or other disruption.

Special interest groups castigate large corporations, institutions and governments (especially with hindsight) for failing to act on warnings and clear evidence of impending crises: for example, of hurricanes, car-safety problems, unsafe level crossings, sex abuse scandals or illegal infringements of privacy. After all, the public view goes, such institutions have the resources to find and fix problems. Hindsight is of course a wonderful thing, but don't assume that interest groups are going to cut SMEs much slack purely on the basis that they have fewer resources to devote to this task.

People are unlikely to forgive any organisation that fails to respond rapidly and effectively to events that cause harm, loss, fear or sustained inconvenience. You need to carry out a balancing act here. On the one hand, horizon scanning can identify risks and issues to address before they become a problem. But on the other hand, you can't root out every risk and issue – risks are a fact of life and some things just appear unseen out of left field, and so trying to plan in detail for every eventuality isn't an option either. Having a crisis management capability, however (as we describe in the next section), can help you tackle both the foreseen and the unforeseen.

Developing a crisis management capability

A *capability* in this context is your organisation's ability to do something effectively – in this case handle all the activities associated with crisis management. Developing such a capability requires you to consider a number of different aspects including:

- ✔ The way you think about risks, issues, your vulnerabilities, strengths and weaknesses as a company.
- ✔ The way in which your business is structured and organised to deal with problems.

✔ The degree to which you and your staff are 'all on the same page' and willing to face up to challenges together.

✔ The practical dimensions such as logistics that ensure that people carry decisions through into (the right sort of) action.

You can prevent or interrupt many potential crises through contingency measures, and so business continuity is a critical tool to any organisation. BC alone, however, can't guarantee that you contain all potential crises, perhaps because they arise from issues that you didn't foresee or were of a severity that overwhelmed existing arrangements. For this reason organisations must give thought to how they would respond strategically to such crises, where a failure to get it right can have terminal consequences for your business.

We elaborate on some of the critical dimensions of a crisis management capability in the next few sections.

Assuming leadership

Leadership is important at the best of times; during the worst of times it becomes vital. Good leaders accept reality quickly, face the harsh facts and lay out the firm's direction. The saying 'management is doing things right, but leadership is about doing the right things' certainly holds true for leadership in a crisis.

Great leadership isn't about asserting detailed control over every aspect, but involves setting the overall direction, communicating that with clarity and then inspiring and motivating people to achieve what you set out.

Defining roles and responsibilities

Because crises are inherently uncertain, you can never be quite sure what you're going to have to deal with. This uncertainty makes it all the more important that you define generic roles and responsibilities – the ones that the organisation is going to need whatever happens.

Many staff members fear that they'll be expected to undertake tasks that they're unable to cope with. Crises are stressful enough without making it even harder for staff, and so stick to the principle of 'broadly normal roles under extraordinary circumstances'.

Ensure that the roles you expect staff to play in a crisis are as close as possible to the ones they carry out under normal business – they know how to do them, so don't complicate matters. For example, information management and log keeping is critical in a crisis, and so aim to use staff with data processing or similar expertise.

Creating a crisis plan

Plans can be a two-edged sword. Not having thought about and developed a plan almost certainly consigns you to failure, and yet many organisations develop plans of impressive length and remarkable detail, only to discover that they don't help much when a crisis erupts.

When this happens, doggedly trying to stick to the plan, or worse, fit the crisis to the plan instead of the other way round, is usually the worst thing you can do.

Incident management and BC plans are likely to be reasonably detailed. This is appropriate because you can foresee and describe the risk impacts to time-critical activities and dependencies with a fair degree of accuracy. Therefore you can set down in detail what people need to do in the event of incidents arising. Crisis plans, in contrast, need to be much shorter and more flexible, reflecting the inherent unpredictability of such events.

Successful crisis responses are fast, well-informed, involve good decisions, communicate appropriately and manage the return to business as usual, sensitively and effectively.

Although no single template exists for a crisis plan, it needs to cover the following points:

- ✔ **People involved:** The plan needs to identify who's authorised to determine that your business is facing a crisis and so activate the plan. Practically, it also needs to include up-to-date contact details and other information such as out-of-hours security, log-on passwords, door codes and so on, which enable people to access the building, log on and get working.

- ✔ **Getting started:** The plan needs to stipulate what people are expected to do from the word go. Getting this clearly written down, perhaps as an aide memoire, is critically important – remember that people are likely to be under stress and that's when mistakes happen.

- ✔ **Information management:** You can't hope to manage events to your advantage if you don't really know what's going on. Information is therefore the lifeblood of crisis management. You have to consider carefully all potential information requirements against all reasonably foreseeable crisis scenarios and practically define how you would:

    - Find the information you think you're likely to need.

    - Get hold of that information in practice.

    - Assess the accuracy, timeliness and relevance of the information.

- Collate and transform raw information into the various briefing and information products required.

- Maintain your awareness of what's going on.

✔ **Agreeing objectives:** The military refer to ends, ways and means:

- *Ends* describe what you're trying to achieve.

- *Ways* are the options for achieving those ends.

- *Means* are the resources at your disposal to achieve the ends.

One of the early priorities for a crisis management team is to produce a statement that defines, agrees and communicates the desired end state that everybody is working to achieve.

✔ **Joining it all together:** To be truly effective, a plan has to ensure that the organisation is acting as a coherent whole. For example, unless you take steps to ensure this, you may well end up in a situation where your senior staff have decided to do one thing, your operational managers are working to achieve another thing and your communications staff are saying that you're doing something completely different. This situation is bad enough at the best of times, but when you're trying to assert control, *and be seen to be in control*, it undermines all your efforts.

Very often business owners and managers assume that people will do things, or that things will happen, in a particular way. The solution is one word: *check!*

✔ **Sustaining the effort:** Responding to a crisis is likely to start with a sprint, as you seek to assert initial control and organise your response, but it turns into a marathon. If you overstretch your staff and yourself, you're going to fail. You need to face up to this reality and set expectations and working practices that are sustainable for weeks and months rather than days.

Training

You train and prepare for most things that you expect your staff to do – customer service, accounting, health and safety, and a range of other skills central to success – and crisis management is no different.

If, after diligently considering your risks and taking steps to develop a crisis capability, you don't train your staff in what's expected of them, you've largely wasted a lot of effort.

Some common misconceptions abound about crisis training, and so we repeat the guiding principle of 'broadly normal roles under extraordinary circumstances'. Of course, you expect employees to operate under different conditions and probably at a higher tempo, but that's where the training comes in. It builds employees' awareness, hones specific skills and above all gives them confidence that they can play their role in any crisis response.

Here are two final points on training to consider:

- ✔ Prepare yourself adequately. Don't fall into the trap of being overconfident. Seek out specialist training from which you think you'd benefit.

- ✔ Don't be tempted to try to conduct training through means of an exercise that's also intended to test your preparedness measures. It may seem like an efficient approach, but you won't achieve either aim properly. You're likely to leave your staff lacking knowledge and confidence and still not have any real idea of whether your plan is up to the job. Train your people for the anticipated roles, and then look at validating your arrangements.

Validating: Are you ready?

Validation is the process of assuring your readiness for a crisis. You can go about this in different ways; some are relatively exploratory and others may feel much more like a test with a pass/fail result. Cutting to the chase, the most important thing is to do something rather than nothing, and then take stock afterwards.

Chapter 11 explains what validation is all about, how to go about it, and what the various options are.

Whichever approach you undertake, don't be too easy on yourself – prepare one that gives you, your team, your systems and your plan a thorough workout.

Observe the following mantra: prepare for the worst, hope for the best – and if that sounds like something the US Marines would say then it probably is, but it's the way to go. Many organisations have made themselves feel really good about their crisis preparedness by validating their arrangements with scenarios that are, frankly, far too tame. The scenarios you choose have to test your organisation; prepare for the reasonably foreseeable worst case, instead of something you reckon you can cope with.

Responding to a Crisis

Traditionally, crisis management is the business of responding to a crisis. The preceding sections help you to set the essential foundations, but you can't neglect the self-evidently critical importance of your *crisis response*: getting things right on the day. We keep this fairly simple and talk about two strands of response:

- **Situational awareness:** Knowing what's going on.
- **Decision-making:** Deciding what to do about it.

Communication is also clearly vitally important – telling people inside and outside your company what's going on and what you're doing about it – and we discuss internal and external communication in Chapters 18 and 19, respectively. These items are inextricably linked. Decision-making without facts is like driving in the dark without lights. If you don't make decisions then the crisis controls you and not the other way round. If you make decisions without communicating, you don't carry anyone with you, stakeholders despair, customers abandon you and the media savage you.

If this sounds a little extreme, recall the last time you were on a train, heading for an important appointment, when it stopped. Nobody told you anything about what was going on, what they were doing about it and what you could expect, and by when. Infuriating, wasn't it? And we imagine the experience caused you to consider using other forms of transport in future.

Developing situational awareness

Situational awareness sounds forbidding, but it just means knowing what's going on around you. In the earlier section 'Creating a crisis plan', we discuss the importance of thinking through how you're going to organise and manage information, get facts in, check them and share your understanding with people inside and outside of your company. Well, you build and sustain situational awareness through those processes.

Situational awareness is about more than just the basic facts of a situation; it also involves getting on top of what they mean and what they may imply for the future. You need to be constantly asking three questions:

✔ **What's happening?** You need to establish and check the facts of the situation, consider them in context so you know the degree to which the events are abnormal and find out what people are saying about it.

Remember that if somebody else thinks you have a problem, you probably do!

✔ **So what?** You need to work through the implications of what's happening to figure out what it means and what the impacts and broader consequences may be.

✔ **What may happen?** Crisis response is about asserting control over a very difficult situation and influencing events to your advantage. You need to see the future as something to be shaped instead of something that's just going to happen to you. To achieve this aim, you need to identify the potential outcomes (from good to bad to worst is a good place to start). (Take real care over this analysis rather than just sketching out something reasonably plausible.) When identified, you can work back to consider the steps you need to take to mitigate risks, make the most of opportunities and influence events towards a more positive outcome.

Here are two important points to consider:

✔ Situational awareness never stands still – you have to keep asking the three questions to check your understanding and stay on top of developments or changes in the wider context.

✔ Just because you see something in a particular way doesn't mean that your colleagues, suppliers, customers, competitors and the media view things the same way. Get other people to challenge your thinking, evidence, conclusions and decisions. A crisis is no time to be precious, and getting different perspectives on a problem can only strengthen your understanding of it.

Making decisions under pressure

Bad decisions can precipitate crises and good decision-making can help to steer an organisation away from, or out of, a crisis. Many people think that they're good decision-makers: reflective when necessary, intuitive and decisive when that's required, prepared to consider alternative perspectives and aware of the mistakes that others have made in the past. The reality, however, may be less flattering.

Decision-making under pressure is a complex field, but take some time to reflect on these key points:

✔ The concept of rational decision-making (gather all the evidence, reflect on it, construct options, evaluate the options in light of all the information and then make an optimal decision) really doesn't reflect reality for the following reasons: people are unlikely to have all the information; they probably don't have the knowledge and skills to comprehensively analyse what they do have; and their actual decision-making is subject to a wide range of flaws.

✔ Some people think that they're good intuitive decision-makers and others pride themselves on being analytical in their approach. They're both wrong: the reality is that people constantly flip between the two styles. (That ability enables you simultaneously to chew gum, read the paper, listen in to that loud mobile phone call and maintain a sense of how long until you get off the train.) The downside of this cognitive juggling ability is that people sometimes jump to wrong (in retrospect) conclusions and make lousy decisions, especially when under pressure.

✔ When people are evaluating a situation in order to make a decision, they're constantly juggling three sets of forces: what they *expect* to see, what they *want* to see and what they actually *do* see. This causes accidents and so you need to check your own thinking because you *will* make mistakes.

✔ Decision-making by committee is tricky at best, but one of the tasks of a crisis leader is to encourage a wide range of participants with varying perspectives to express their views, offer their interpretations and suggestions, and challenge the understanding and assumptions held by others, including more senior staff. At the end of the day the decision is likely to rest with one person, but getting a range of different eyes and minds on the problem, encouraging alternative viewpoints and promoting challenge is likely to lead to better decisions.

At the end of the day, whatever the considerations to bear in mind, you need to make tough decisions that affect your company's future. Here is some hard-won and valuable advice:

✔ **Be sure of your facts:** Be rigorous and sustained in your efforts to build a thorough picture of what, so what and what may (from the preceding section), and yet also . . .

✔ **Move quickly:** Doing nothing, and certainly saying nothing, is usually more damaging that doing something. When considering what to do, be guided by the principle . . .

- ✔ **Do the right thing:** Focus on your reputation, protect your brand and behave in a way that reassures suppliers and customers and limits the ability of critics to attack you (see the nearby sidebar 'Doing the right thing'), while remembering to . . .

- ✔ **Check, check, check:** You're going to make mistakes, misinterpret evidence, jump to the wrong conclusions, take your eye off the ball or miss the main event, and suffer a range of other shortcomings. No one likes to hear this, but it's true; however, self-awareness is the best defence against such errors – you have been warned!

Above all, always strive to make defensible decisions rather than defensive decisions:

- ✔ *Defensive* decisions are usually made by people who are covering their backs and acting in short-term, narrowly defined self-interest.

- ✔ *Defensible* decision-making isn't perfect decision-making (no such thing exists); instead it's about making the best possible decisions on the basis of the available evidence and good judgement and at the time that a decision needs to made.

Find decision tools for risk and crisis management document online at `http://epcollege.com/epc/knowledge-centre/document-hub/`.

Doing the right thing

A number of years ago, a high-street retailer was found to be selling products for children that were a fire hazard. This incident was due to a lapse in the supply chain and not a deliberate act to circumvent legal standards.

When the story broke, media interest was immediate and intense, but no senior member of staff was available to face the cameras. A middle manager stepped up to the line and made arrangements to give a hastily convened press conference. When considering how she'd handle this situation, the manager reflected on the core values of the company, which were those things that external people expected the company to adhere to. Protecting the financial bottom line, within this frame, was subordinate to protecting the brand. With this in mind, and acting beyond her formal authority but with a clear awareness of the strategic interests of the company, she expressed regret and empathy, was open with the facts as she understood them, promised compensation, initiated an immediate recall of stock and launched an inquiry.

This solution was expensive in cash but in fact bolstered the reputation of the business as a company to trust. Communicating well during a crisis is critical to surviving without a loss of reputation. In Chapters 18 and 19, we take a closer look at internal and external communications in a crisis by offering our top tips to getting it right.

Moving On: Recovering from a Crisis

Experience is simply the name we give our mistakes.

– Oscar Wilde

When the dust begins to settle, you can all too easily snatch defeat from the jaws of victory by prematurely deciding that a crisis is over. Listen to your customers, suppliers, staff and others with an interest in what you do, because they're better placed to tell you when you can shift back to business as usual. A company that unilaterally decides that a crisis is over and behaves accordingly is very likely to alienate those it depends on for its business.

Don't appear uninterested in those who've suffered or been disadvantaged at this time. Of course you need to return to normality, but remember to do so with care and sensitivity and think carefully about how your behaviour looks from a variety of perspectives.

A critical, but often overlooked, part of managing the recovery is to close the circle: that is, to identify and learn the lessons from the whole experience. Many organisations use the terms 'lessons identified' and 'lessons learned' interchangeably, but they're quite different things:

- ✔ The process of identifying lessons is one of finding them, recording them and sharing them.

- ✔ The process of learning lessons is the cultural business of effecting change on the basis of that hard-won experience.

Reflect on the experience and feed it back into your risk assessments (as we discuss in Chapter 5), crisis plan, training and exercising (see Chapter 11), and all the other elements that make up your crisis capability (check out the earlier section 'Developing a crisis management capability' for more on this aspect).

Crisis checklist: Things to be thinking about

When preparing for crises you need to:

- ✔ **Look for trouble; don't wait for it to find you.** Crisis managers and senior staff need to exist in a state of 'controlled paranoia'.

- ✔ **Create the conditions for members of your own organisation to raise problems.** When they do, you need to act on the warning, and incentivise others to do the same.

- ✔ **Be clear on what needs to be done, allocate roles and responsibilities accordingly and make people accountable for them.** With this system in place, train the people and then test the plan.

- ✔ **Stress-test your arrangements.** Gear your thinking and testing to what you may conceivably have to deal with instead of what you're confident you can deal with. If your thinking throws up inadequacies, deal with them.

We provide lots more on crisis readiness in the earlier section 'Preparing for Crises'.

If you think you may be facing a potential crisis:

✔ Remember that how things look can be as important as how things are. Although all the objective audience may suggest that things are under control, if media lines and public perception suggest otherwise, you have to engage with, and change, that subjective perception.

✔ Never be tempted to bury bad news. Unfortunately, bad news is generally pretty hardy and more than likely to emerge at some point. You need to deal with events and issues that can cause a crisis rapidly, directly, thoroughly and openly. Having identified a problem, this is by far and away the best route to maintain the confidence of others and to signal your intention to staff to tackle robustly malpractice, low standards or other negative behaviours. Behave as if everything that you say and do is made public.

When responding to a crisis, remember that:

✔ **Information is essential to crisis management.** Ill-informed crisis responses appear inadequate and may well look deliberately misleading in their intent, even when this isn't the case.

✔ **Co-ordinate the actions of all those involved and don't assume everything is working in concert.** Avoid falling into the 'left hand not knowing what the right hand is doing' trap. You need to stay on top of this aspect.

✔ **Communication is central to crisis management.** Many crises have been handled at the 'technical level' in a very adept fashion by organisations that then forgot to tell interested parties such as staff, customers

and suppliers what they've done about it. Get the facts, make sure as far as humanly possible that they're right and then get them out there. Bad news is far less damaging when you release it yourself, when you release it all and when you release it early.

✔ **If you make mistakes correct them as quickly as possible and don't hide the fact.** Behave defensibly, not defensively (see the earlier section 'Making decisions under pressure'). If the blame is yours, take it, don't try and shift it, and above all don't lie – lack of honesty is almost certain to come out in a crisis and make matters worse.

Check out the earlier section 'Responding to a Crisis' for more details.

When recovering from a crisis, remember to:

✔ **Identify the lessons.** Speak not only to your top team and your staff, but also to customers, suppliers, sub-contractors, partners and others with an interest in what you do in order to get a full and rounded picture of what happened, why, what you did well and what you did badly. Record the responses and circulate them widely within the company.

✔ **Learn the lessons.** In the aftermath of a crisis, considering lessons may feel like looking backwards, but embedding them makes your company stronger.

✔ **Maintain communications.** Keep listening to what a range of people with an interest in your business are saying, and keep talking to them, telling them what you're doing in their interests.

✔ **Invest in trust.** A crisis can cause a lapse in trust, and you have to work very hard to re-build that trust; it's an investment in time, effort and money that you have to make.

The 'Moving on: Recovering from a Crisis' section, earlier in this chapter, has more on crisis recovery.

Chapter 11

Validating Your Business Continuity Plan

▷ Introducing business continuity testing

▷ Planning your exercise

▷ Carrying out an exercise

▷ Making your business more resilient as a result

*V*alidation (introduced in Chapter 10) is the process of assuring your readiness for a disruptive event or crisis. In this chapter, we break this important task down a bit so you can be confident that the business continuity (BC) system you're putting in place will work effectively when it matters.

Although people often use the terms 'exercise' and 'test' to mean the same thing, here's how we use them in this chapter:

✔ An *exercise* can be many different things (as we explain later), but all of them have the objective of exploring how your BC arrangements will stand up to the pressure of real events. An exercise needs to be a learning event that tells you about areas of strength and weakness, so make sure you listen and act on what you discover.

✔ A *test* is a specific type of exercise that you either pass or fail, or are otherwise graded on. If you're serious about knowing if your BC arrangements are up to scratch then consider bringing in some outside help to conduct a test exercise.

Don't confuse *training* (learning about BC arrangements, roles, responsibilities and actions) with *exercising*. Realistically, exercises always enable people to learn more about BC and that's a good thing, but don't treat exercises as a substitute for training - you need to get yourself and your team up to speed before conducting an exercise, and most certainly before a test, otherwise you'll only really learn that you haven't done sufficient training!

Whether you call something a test or an exercise, however, the crucial thing is that afterwards you can answer the following key questions:

- ✔ What have you learnt?
- ✔ Where are the gaps?
- ✔ What can you do to become more resilient?

If you can, you have lift off to greater challenges in future exercises.

To help you achieve this aim, in this chapter we discuss what a business continuity exercise is and why you need one. We talk about planning and running such exercises and guide you towards learning the required lessons in order to achieve resilience in the face of future disruptive events and forces.

Accepting the Need to Validate Your Recovery Procedures

Here's a straightforward question: why carry out exercises or tests to validate your business's recovery procedures at all? Well, because preparation is everything. The reality is that disruption doesn't strike bearing invitations to down tools and join in if you have time. More likely it arrives with a smack and your feet need to hit the ground running.

Exercising your recovery procedures allows you to discover gaps and weaknesses in your knowledge, understanding and planning of what you need to do and have in place to survive a significant disruption to the normal running of your business.

Without a regular test of your firm's resilience to disruptive impacts, neither you nor your staff can have confidence that you are ready to tackle things if they go wrong, and your business depends on how you respond and what you can do. Without exercising and testing, your expectations for business maintenance/recovery remain unrealistic at best, and at worst may well scupper your enterprise altogether.

A tested BC strategy adds confidence to your competence.

Above all, through validation you enhance the performance of your most valuable asset – your staff – by demonstrating to them (and to you) that you have confidence in their ability to put things right. Give them the tools to do the job by expanding their expertise to keep your business, and their livelihoods, on track.

Don't underestimate the value of any testing outcome, particularly the lessons you learn that you can feed back into your safeguard procedures.

If you don't test your plans and strategies, you can't possibly know whether they work if the wheels come off your business. You put a lot of time and effort into your planning and so you need to know whether you've covered all eventualities – or as many as you can think of – and the only way to find out is to test your response capability.

Examining what an exercise is

Practice makes perfect, of course, but validating your ability to respond to the unexpected and to the unknown can only ever be preparation for the real thing. No exercise presents you with an opportunity to earn a ten out of ten performance. They aren't meant to do that, and if they did, you wouldn't learn anything you didn't already you know.

Don't allow the prospect of validation to panic you or your staff: you run an exercise to learn. Never use an exercise as a stick to scold staff when you identify the need for improvements or as opportunities for smart Alecs to shine.

Exercises are programmed events from which you and all your staff can learn and you can discover something about every business process that exists: no matter how often you exercise, you always discover something new.

The huge point is to build every valuable lesson you learn back into your BC planning. If something doesn't go well, make sure that it does next time. Nothing stands still, and given changing circumstances – however small – something will be different next time. Your plans, policies, procedures and protocols – whatever – need to continue to evolve to meet your needs.

To help you run testing exercises, you have to get the basics right to begin with. Most exercises use scenarios; in BC terms, that involves a made-up set of disrupting circumstances designed to make life difficult and see how well you cope in maintaining your business.

When is an exercise not an exercise? Well, suffice to say that a comfortable ride to self-assured already-knowns is no use to you or your staff.

Discovering the different exercise levels

Although quite a few exercise styles exist, in essence you have four levels depending on how far you want to go and how tough you want to make the process. The levels are progressive to ensure that you can walk before you try running. You can make each level more or less difficult, but the best exercise isn't necessarily the hardest one you can devise. Instead, prepare one that suits your needs and makes your business more resilient.

In this section, we take a look at the four levels.

Level 1: Walkthrough

A walkthrough of your BC plan involves key staff sitting down together and asking themselves whether, based on their joint knowledge of the business, the plan has all it needs. They talk through all the different parts of the plan but without any great examination of potential variations you may need in different circumstances. This stage is really just a short step beyond what you did when you developed the plan and signed it off (check out the chapters in Part II).

Requirements for this stage are:

✔ A quiet room

✔ A relaxed atmosphere

✔ Key staff

✔ The plan

✔ A note-taker

Level 2: Desktop scenario

In a desktop scenario, the same people as in Level 1 sit down again, but this time they work through the plan to see whether it withstands a deeper examination under a specific set of identified circumstances. This stage is a sort of case study of what you'd do in a particular situation. You need a story that evolves during the exercise, getting worse and placing more demands on your plans. For example: bad weather is forecast . . . the storm arrives . . . the river floods your buildings . . . the roof blows off and lands on your coupé!

Requirements for this stage are the same as for Level 1, plus:

✔ A sense of urgency

✔ More time

✔ A detailed analysis of the outcomes

Level 3: Time-pressured desktop scenario

At this stage, things can get a bit sticky and you progress to tackle a disruptive impact on your ability to run your business over a short period of time. This stage involves developing a scenario with timed *injects* (added difficulties introduced by the exercise organiser), each one designed to make the task more difficult. For example, the scenario may focus on a postcode power failure that affects the area surrounding your premises; the first inject is to announce that power in the area has failed and the effects may last two or more hours; the second is that you store your business records on your information technology (IT) system. As a scene setter, ask your team to decide what to do first.

Requirements for Level 3 are as for Levels 1 and 2, plus:

✔ A key planner needs to draw up a timed schedule of play with injects that key players introduce: someone who has that 'burst through the door' news that adds vigour and purpose.

✔ The exercise involves a close-down session that records decisions for next steps and identifies outcomes.

✔ A final de-brief session gauges reactions to the exercise and records feedback from all staff for lessons learnt.

Level 4: Active exercise in real time

This stage is what we can call the *live play*; it's where nails get bitten rather than nibbled. All players down tools and concentrate on a time-pressured scenario with injects, tackled in real time with normal running suspended. The aim is to test whether people can do what's expected of them and within a timescale; for example, a day. You may be able to recite the plan: 'I'd move the stock into room 2.' But this stage is where you find out that those new shipping crates don't fit through the door and you need all night to solve the problem.

Live play is complicated to organise and can sometimes be unpredictable, and so this stage isn't the one to do first, but you certainly learn from this stage! Also, live play exercises are costly, but looking into a part of your plan in this way often provides the jolt you need to make people realise that your business, and staff livelihoods, may well depend on the outcome of a real situation.

Get senior management buy-in and participation before you do anything! Then think and stop before you involve the kitchen sink. Be thorough, but don't overload the exercise with too many twists, turns and catastrophes. Have sufficient thought-provoking injects ready, more than you think you'll need, and judge which ones and how many you'll use as the test unravels. By the time you get to Level 4, you know instinctively what you need to have in place.

The resulting de-brief needs to lead to an exercise report. You'll have lessons to take on board and good practice to share.

Making the exercise more demanding

As your experience grows and you progress through the levels that we discuss in the preceding section, you need to focus on exercises that are significantly beyond what's merely uncomfortable or inconvenient. You can make exercises more demanding in several ways without actually going up to the next level:

✔ Making the scenario more detailed/complex.

✔ Having more than one thing go wrong at the same time.

✔ Interacting with third parties; for example, an energy or service provider, or a supplier to your business.

✔ Piggybacking another exercise; for example, following up one of your earlier exercises, engaging with a supplier who might be testing a delivery function, or liaising with a local authority who may responding to an emergency scenario.

✔ Lengthening the time the exercise runs.

✔ Asking independent assessors or trusted observers to scrutinise your responses.

Planning the Exercise and Its Objectives

Of course, your dedicated BC leader needs to be fully involved in planning your approach to validation, but which other staff take part depends on the size, complexity and structure of your organisation. In a company with a small workforce, the business owner probably wants a hands-on role.

Where several departments represent the organisation's daily business, the business leader may want to nominate an exercise planner.

This planner can be your BC leader or a senior manager with a thorough knowledge of the organisation, in particular of the critical activities, processes and products, the business's strategy and priorities, and the interdependencies of the management processes that support the product or service you provide. If your processes are very complex, someone with technical expertise may need to provide assistance. These people often know where to put the spanner in the works to get the best (worst!) effect.

An exercise gets an added punch when staff don't know what disruption they're going to have to deal with. So decide who does know the scenario in advance – keep the number very small in order to protect the integrity of the exercise – and who's in for a surprise. This approach limits those involved in the planning and that's for the best.

Make effective use of your preparation time to ensure that everyone uses the exercise time well. Ask yourself whether anything's missing from your exercise plan. If so, can you fit that missing aspect in? If you do, make sure that any additions/changes you make to the exercise don't skew the objectives you may already have set. Disturbing the balance of the exercise that you thought you had in place, by over-elaborating or with second thoughts, is all too easy. Keep the first few exercises simple. (Experience will test ambition.) As your experience grows you can become more ambitious about what you want to test.

Identifying exercise objectives

Identifying your objectives is in essence deciding what you're trying to achieve. Your overall aims needs to include:

- ✔ Making your organisation more resilient by validating your response capability.
- ✔ Identifying ways to improve your BC system and related arrangements.

A bit of a mouthful, but by identifying these relatively straightforward objectives you make clear that your exercises are about finding ways to improve business performance, and not about putting people on the spot or worrying them to death.

You need system-specific objectives too, as we describe in the following two sections.

Setting quality objectives

Choose four or so clear and achievable objectives. For example, the exercise needs to demonstrate that you can identify:

- ✔ The likely impacts from (a variety of) disruptive events.
- ✔ How you intend to restore your business activities.
- ✔ The value – to everyone – of your BC system.
- ✔ That you have key staff ready and available.

You also need to be able to mobilise the necessary technological skills to survive.

Setting measurable objectives

Focus on specific measureable targets for your exercise, based on your plan, on previous exercises or on emergencies. These aims may include being able to demonstrate:

- A timetable for recovery and to respond to business/customer needs.

- Your speed of access to current data; for example, you reported on the number of X available within three hours.

- That you can recover those activities identified as critical to business; for example, you were able to meet your recovery time objectives for all critical tasks (you need your up-to-date register of critical business activities – see Chapter 4).

- Which staff you expect to respond and know for sure they can; for example, staff members were available for all roles in the disaster recovery plan and attended the meeting point within one hour.

- You've addressed previous exercise shortcomings and learnt lessons.

If your organisation hasn't learnt lessons, something needs urgent attention – before you exercise again!

Assessing the cost

'How much is the whole process going to cost?' you may well ask, and the flippant answer is, 'Less than a badly handled disaster!' A more useful response is that the cost depends on what you need and what you want to spend. The main cost items for a desktop test are likely to be:

- Planning time.

- Staff time away from normal work.

- Perhaps room hire and catering – getting away from your normal location can be very helpful (as can tasty sandwiches!).

Running a live exercise costs significantly more (a lot more if you stop production).

Choosing a format

All businesses are restricted in what they can exercise to some extent, with possible costs, location, equipment and knowledge of players being a problem. Ask yourself how these or other factors may restrict what you want to do.

Do you need senior management agreement (extra buy-in) to accommodate these or any other issues? If that's likely, secure that support now (factor them in now). Don't compromise the exercise by silly, avoidable planning defects.

Identify a record-keeper at the outset who records actions, problems, questions and outcomes as the exercise scenario unfolds and logs them by speaker, time and subject. Make the record-keeper's role clear and ensure that this person doesn't contribute or take any direct part in exercise play and talks to no one during the course of play. The record-keeper reports directly to the exercise leader after the exercise – unless invited to present a brief review at the finale. The person can have prior notice of the event but shouldn't be privy to any details in advance.

Selecting who takes part on the day

Here's a rough idea of the people who need to take part in your exercise:

- ✔ Executive director
- ✔ BC leader
- ✔ Key staff including business process leaders
- ✔ Facilitators (if you're doing a live exercise)
- ✔ Experts (if you're relying on specific knowledge or expert advice; for example, on power, or tackling fire or water damage)
- ✔ A record keeper or note-taker

Telling your staff

Inform your staff that an exercise is going to take place and that they need to be up to date with the business's recovery procedures and the roles and responsibilities those procedures identify for them. You may need to provide a brief explanation about what the exercise is going to involve, but details depend on the type of exercise. You may want to say something like:

> *We will be running an exercise to see how we would cope in a disruption. This is to see whether the plans we have been developing will meet our needs. We will be testing the plans and not individuals. All staff should update themselves on the plan contents and the roles they will undertake. The exercise will take place at . . .*

By now, of course, all staff are clear about your recovery procedures and their roles and responsibilities – aren't they? Don't forget that you shouldn't give staff scenario detail in advance. You may want to spring an exercise upon them (if doing so is feasible and doesn't damage your business activity for the time involved). That's your call, of course.

Some people may find a surprise exercise very stressful or may mistake it for a real emergency, and so take care. A good compromise is to say that sometime next week an exercise is going to take place. From the start of the exercise and throughout all emails, phone calls and so on, begin with the word 'Exercise' along the lines we show in Figure 11-1.

Figure 11-1:
A test
exercise.

EXERCISE   EXERCISE   EXERCISE

Batch no. _____ of _____ has been found to be unsafe. Please stop using these items immediately and identify which of our products they contain.

Emphasise that a desired outcome of the exercise is to give you – and staff – the assurances you all need that appropriate measures are in place to maintain your business.

Developing an effective exercise scenario

Part of your exercising preparation is to create a scenario, which is a bit like writing your own nightmare – a story of bad things that get worse. To work, a scenario needs to present a realistic set of circumstances, which means something that may reasonably happen to your business (no alien storylines please!).

All the included technical material needs to be accurate. The last thing you want is for people to dismiss the scenario as impossible or for someone with greater knowledge, or who's simply better prepared, to tell you that you're wrong about a critical item.

This eventuality can happen; don't let it because it sinks the exercise before it starts. Worse, the credibility of the facilitator – which may be you – vanishes and staff can start to worry about issues such as leader competence (definitely *not* something to encourage).

So, to develop your exercise scenario:

- ✔ Identify source materials and check out what you don't know with experts.
- ✔ Make it plausible and relevant.

✔ Create an appropriate trigger mechanism.

✔ Be specific and include enough detail to make it realistic: for example, consider location and collateral damage, denial of access, threats, damage to reputation, utility, and information and communications technology failure, staff access and so on.

✔ Prepare more event possibilities and added difficulties than you think you need – you don't want to exhaust all your options before you've explored everything you need to.

✔ Consider how the story's going to work with the questions you plan to ask.

A good exercise scenario achieves the following:

✔ Contains content that's appropriate to the objectives you set.

✔ Offers a challenge and is solvable – even if the solution is imperfect, its resolution shouldn't be impossible.

✔ Challenges but doesn't overwhelm.

✔ Involves all key players.

✔ Works with your key players or their deputies who should fit easily into their roles.

✔ Doesn't require the emergency services to answer questions, unless they're taking part or you know what they'd say.

✔ Unfolds to timescale within the time available.

✔ Carries minimal risk of causing real disruption (unless you want it to).

✔ Creates lessons to learn.

We provide a sample exercise in the later section 'Considering an Exercise Scenario'.

Knowing What to Test

At the start of the chapter we described a test as a specific type of exercise that has a pass/fail or otherwise graded outcome. The key difference is that while an exercise can be exploratory, helping you to feel out how things might work in various scenarios, a test is something you undertake when you need to find out whether your arrangements can stand up to reality. In common with any exercise, a test needs clear objectives.

When you've sorted out and planned your objectives (as we describe in the earlier section 'Planning the Exercise and Its Objectives'), you're ready to ask: 'What do we want to test?' Well, this is where you can really get colleagues involved. You'll have your own ideas; they, we hope, have theirs. We can make sensible suggestions to start you off on the right road. But remember, you know your business, we don't.

Start with simple topics and leave the prospect of Armageddon to another day. That doesn't mean the key issues for business should be simple, of course; no point in that. In this section, we look at your planks of support: that is, your business processes that you can't allow to fail and the questions you're very likely to need to address if disruption occurs.

Testing people

You can test:

- Access to HR data.
- Staff awareness of their roles in a disruption.
- Your access to up-to-date staff job descriptions/objectives.
- What potential points of failure exist.
- How you would cope with the loss of staff expertise.
- Key contributions to your business from other organisations.

Your concerns may include:

- Effective co-operation and working across the organisation.
- Quick and effective access to all data.
- Accuracy of your staff skills audit.
- How you can cope with loss of key staff.
- What tasks you may 'stand down' and for how long can you afford to do so.
- Accountability and accurate recording of the business during disruption.
- Identifying good practice and learning lessons.

Testing places and services (the workplace)

You can test:

- Loss of critical features your workplace provides.
- Your ability to find the same requirements elsewhere and quickly.

✔ Whether you've identified, agreed and recorded all key requirements.

✔ Implications of having to relocate and the possible effects on staff.

Your concerns may include:

✔ Informing staff that your premises are inaccessible.

✔ Loss of equipment, records and access to their source.

✔ Lack of suitable alternative premises.

✔ Staff access to a new site.

Testing your ICT

You can test:

✔ Your ability to effect safe and swift shutdown of your systems without data loss.

✔ Your callout contract with your IT provider that covers breakdown, network problems and other failures.

✔ How you'd re-negotiate the service contract if it doesn't include provision for BC options.

✔ Security of your systems, PCs and laptops.

✔ Security of your stored data.

✔ Your cascade call procedure – particularly if land lines are down.

Your concerns may include:

✔ Whether you can deliver without IT.

✔ How you access your recovery plans.

✔ Your ability to identify critical business activities and which may be jeopardised.

✔ How you are going to access data.

✔ How you are going to record activity and ensure safe electronic recording for normal running.

Testing communications

You can test:

✔ Suppliers, customers and media contacts.

- Your capability to ensure single point of message 'control'.
- Communicating with staff on- and off-site.

Your concerns may include:

- Isolation from critical contacts.
- Maintaining control of internal and external messages.
- Quick and effective monitoring of activity.
- Safeguarding your reputation and protecting the brand.
- Ensuring careful announcement of a satisfactory return to normal running.

Testing finance

You can test:

- Your ability to pay bills and receive payments.
- Your reliance on IT.
- Your ability to maintain records and manage financial data.
- Availability of skills needed operate your finance systems.
- Other staff operating your systems if key people are away.
- Whether you can pay your staff if systems fail.

Your concerns may include:

- Complete collapse of your financial systems.
- Loss of financial records.
- Your ability to operate manual systems.
- Loss of staff expertise.
- Payments of staff and non-receipt of payments.

Running an Exercise

In this section, we take a brief look at some aspects of the exercise itself.

Deciding who organises and runs the exercise

If you're the manager, it's probably down to you to run the exercise. You can, of course, delegate to a senior manager or your BC manager, depending upon the size of your organisation. But whatever you do, don't stand 'cocooned' safely in a corner outside the exercise: get involved so staff see you're involved.

Whatever exercise role you play, make sure that you have a record-keeper or note-taker: someone outside the exercise who records/logs the really important points of progress, what goes well and not so well and all the learning points that players identify. An essential part of the note-taker's role is to assist you at the end of exercise 'wash up' (as we describe in the later section 'Identifying Lessons: Ending Up Stronger').

Watching for potential pitfalls

You can head off some of the potential pitfalls at the pass by preparing your exercise players. Tell them that:

✔ They aren't being invited to judge the scenario (this point is crucial).

✔ The exercise isn't designed to catch them out.

✔ They aren't to prejudge what the exercise involves.

✔ How they react to the given circumstances and maintain business is a key point.

✔ The exercise allows flexible redirection as progress demands.

Identifying Lessons: Ending Up Stronger

The process of exercising is complex and time-confusing, no doubt. When it's finished, you have permission to be exhausted! But you want to get the most of the process, and so in this section we invite you to take a good look again. You may find that you can introduce other aspects to the exercise to suit your own circumstances.

Just a word of caution: don't skip any of the steps we give you in the preceding sections of this chapter. All the steps are good practice.

Unfortunately, no shortcuts exist to getting this procedure right. If you think you find any, don't be tempted to take them. Stick to this path and go through each part of the process. Share with your key people and then broadcast your plans across your organisation. Remind your people – at all levels of the business – that they must take testing seriously.

Invite people to contribute to the process, because someone may have a good idea you want to investigate. Even if you find that it may not work, don't brush the suggestion aside: explain your reasoning and invite further contributions for consideration.

People are your most important asset.

Tackling the de-brief

Ideally, a de-brief takes place immediately following the exercise and before people leave the exercise location (known as a *hot de-brief*). All that means is that people tell you how the exercise was for them while their memories are fresh. Let them speak in turn and make sure that you get brief notes from everyone before they leave the exercise. You may want to invite them to list, say, three things that for them went well and three that didn't and get them to record lessons they learnt. You can share these items among players as the dust settles, before memories fade.

You need to follow up the hot de-brief with a measured cold de-brief from the desk. This de-brief allows players to write down more mature comments as they reflect on their actions, experience and interaction with other players. Tell staff they have, say, 48 hours to do this – and make sure that everyone responds.

Learning the lessons and sharing best practice

This stage is really important. What have you and your staff discovered about the way, and how well, your organisation responded to the disruptive event? These issues need your immediate attention. You need to tackle some quicker than others, but address them all promptly before necessity becomes the mother of invention. Have your record-keeper draw up an action checklist to share with staff, which you distribute to key people to complete. Give them deadlines for action and make sure that people meet them.

None of the above, of course, is any good to you unless you then update your procedures and plans to reflect the improvements you need to make. That may sound obvious, but you'd be surprised how easily you can forget that bit. Don't waste all the effort you've put in – you can't afford it!

The next step is to re-read thoroughly all your procedures, not just those you directly update through your action checklist. Also, have your key people do the same, because one head is never enough and interdependencies are bound to exist between your various procedural documents – a change or improvement in one has a knock-on effect elsewhere. At the very least, an inconsistency between documents can lead to delays, and at worst, to disaster. All the hymn sheets need to carry a joined-up message.

Updating plans

Updating your plan is essential: if following an exercise you've identified changes to make or new procedures to introduce, make doing so a priority task. You need to:

✔ Update your plan(s) and amend any written procedures or guidance.

✔ Update all interdependencies.

✔ Ensure that all key staff agree the amendments.

✔ Share each revision with all staff.

✔ Make sure that your master copies are made available to all.

Now, make sure that your next exercise embraces all the changes you've made. If the amendments are crucial to recovery, you may want to run a new quick test on how well the new requirements work.

Don't wait until things go wrong and you need to use your BC plan for the first time!

You may want to record amendments to your plan(s) as version changes and give the date that this happened. In this way, you provide currency to the plans people are holding or working to and have a helpful aid in retrospect if you're trying to recall progress and so on.

Ensuring good practice

This book is steeped in good practice and we hope that you find it full of sound advice and helpful hints that you can spark on. It's geared to sharing with you guidance and procedures that have a track record of proven accomplishment by many users; it doesn't lay claim to being of a 'formal standard' and doesn't need to. Good practice evolves from practical, commonsense applications, and what can be more helpful to a BC exercise scenario?

Ask yourself the following question: if one of your business processes boasts a smart piece of advice or demonstrates a more effective way of doing something – for example, an effective cascade call system or a sharing of expertise or a skill – can your other key business process staff adopt it?

Just imagine how much more a thorough review of your exercise results can add to that stock of proven and valuable experience. You're bound to uncover evidence of good practice – your good practice. From wherever or whoever within your company it comes, if the exercise helped you, don't hide it. Share it with everyone in the workforce. This opportunity is the point to hand out pats on the back and, more to the point, reinforce to staff the importance of having a strong BC system built on the things that you all do well – and on everything you've achieved together in your exercise.

After sharing, you may be surprised at the results for managing your current system and, what's more, creating a learning culture geared to maintaining your business in the face of real trouble. (We cover spreading the culture in Chapter 9.)

Using exercise forms

Creating some forms with details of some key points and desired outcomes, which you can share with your key players, is very useful.

The examples in Tables 11-1 and 11-2 provide a simple structure you can use in your first exercise to list key points and desired outcomes. Give these forms to test players to help create added focus and ease of reference. The listed items aren't exhaustive, but they cover some essentials; of course, you can identify and add other aspects that better suit your organisation. Just take the forms as examples to start you off.

Table 11-1   Suggested Form with Key Exercise Points

Key Points	Comments
Delivery of critical business activity	
Delivery via a business process subjected to disruption	
Joint working between business processes	
Access to current activity data	
Availability of key staff	
Meeting action deadlines	
Supplier and customer contact	

Table 11-2	Suggested Desired Outcomes Form
Desired Outcomes	*Comments*
Effective joint working	
Successful delivery of business	
Quick and effective access to data and contacts	
Full accountability and accurate recording	
Readiness for resumption of normal business running.	
Identification of good practice and lessons learnt	

Considering an Exercise Scenario

In this section, we provide an exercise called 'Autumn Grey'.

You get much more value if you customise this exercise to include the real circumstances of your business, local geography and actual risks.

Introductory comments

[Add your own facilitator's comments.]

Stage 1: 10 November

The I.C. Day clothing company is working hard in the run-up to the important Christmas period. Major roadworks are taking place in the areas of I.C. Day's Boghollow warehouses, causing minor delays. Staffing absences are 10 per cent higher than normal because an unusually severe flu is going round. Weather forecasters are predicting heavy rain and strong winds across the country in the next week.

Questions

1. **What are our main priorities at this time of year?**

2. **Can any of these issues be a cause for concern for our business continuity?**

3. **What can we do to reduce the likelihood and impact of possible disruptions in our department?**

Stage 2: 13 November

The predicted bad weather starts to arrive with a lot of surface water on roads and the wind is gusting to 100 kilometres per hour (60 miles per hour) in places. Storm damage to I.C. Day's main building means that offices/workshops on the north side are leaking and taking in water. They can't be used. Other parts of the region have suffered power outages (but not here). The main car park is under 15 centimetres (6 inches) of water and the roadworks have been affected, doubling the time deliveries and pick-ups are taking to access the warehouse and main site. The bad weather is forecast to continue for several days.

Questions

1. **How can we operate without the offices/workshops on the north side of main building? (Do these areas house any important or valuable items? What should we do about them?)**

2. **How are the disruptions going to affect staff members? (Does this affect them getting to and from work? Would they be asked to do different tasks or work to different priorities? How is this to be co-ordinated?)**

3. **What are the implications for delivering products and services? (Are any urgent functions going to be delayed and if so which ones? How will our customers view this disruption?)**

4. **What should we do to prepare for the days ahead?**

Stage 3: 15 November, 9 a.m.

The bad weather continues with less wind but more rain. River water is at high levels and the ground floor of building X has been flooded. (If all your buildings are on the crests of hills, replace this with water due to storm damage or (in winter) overnight burst pipes.) A local TV news item showed the flooded car park and a boarded-up window. Customers are phoning to ask when you're going to correct delayed deliveries. Priority/vulnerable customers and service users feel that I.C. Day hasn't been looking after them. Supplies from (place your key supplier here) have not arrived for three days. Power failures didn't materialise; telephone land lines are down, but are expected to be back by this evening. The local primary school has been forced to close. Staff have worked hard, putting in extra hours, but they're getting tired.

Questions

1. **What are our priorities for the next 24 hours? (What are the priorities for our department?)**

2. **Who are the key/priority customers and service users and how can we address their concerns?**

3. **How are we going to manage communications (with suppliers and customers/service users) and correct bad publicity?**

4. **How are we going to address the practical problems of flooding in building X and the loss of phones?**

Stage 4: 17 November

The bad weather has passed and the sky contains some blue. Flood water is receding but the damage it causes still remains. The repairs to the main building are underway and you're engaged in a clean-up operation. Staff have worked hard, putting in extra hours, but they're clearly tired and staff numbers are down. Calls from frustrated customers continue.

Questions

1. **What are our priorities for the next month? (What can we do to get back to normal business quickly?)**

2. **How damaging has this event been?**

3. **Have we learned anything that may strengthen our business?**

4. **Is it going to be a white Christmas and what happens if it is?**

Part IV
Examining Business Continuity in Specific Contexts

"I think Dick Foster should head up the business continuity plan. He's got the vision, the drive, and let's face it, that big white hat doesn't hurt either."

In this part . . .

*W*e take a practical look at specific areas relating to business continuity, including some issues that require expert help and how you can go about obtaining it. We provide direct recommendations for manufacturing businesses, retailers and professional services firms, and simplify the issue of insurance, showing how to make your insurance work for you.

Chapter 12

Calling in the Experts

*I*n business, countless pieces of the puzzle can go wrong – and at some point most parts are going to try to. In certain situations you may need expert help concerning a matter beyond your control or understanding; after all, you can't be an expert in everything.

As part of business continuity (BC), in this chapter we show you how to rec-ognise when you require expert help. You may be sitting there thinking that only a crisis would make you consider calling in a specialist, but the guid-ance, advice and approval that you get from professionals can be invaluable to your business at all stages. From advice on preventative measures before a crisis and counsel on actions to take during an incident, to guidance on salvation and recovery techniques afterwards, you're not admitting defeat by asking for help from someone who knows. Experts are there to help.

In certain situations, getting in the experts is mandatory, because of legisla-tion, design or service standards, or because you're contractually obliged to do so. We identify in this chapter where this is the case.

While reading this chapter, keep in mind the most significant parts of your business – the critical activities that keep your key products and services going from your Business Impact Analysis (BIA) in Chapter 4. These essential aspects may at times need expert help to protect them. Supporting essential, vulnerable or problem areas with expert help can only strengthen the resil-ience of your business.

Taking Preventative Actions with Expert Advice

Everyone knows that prevention is better than cure wherever possible, and you won't be surprised to find that this section forms the major part of this chapter. You can consult plenty of different experts to help you take preventative measures to protect your business. In this section, we describe situations that require you to get the experts in – perhaps to advise on things such as preventative measures that give protection to your critical activities. Some of the measures we describe are required legally, but even those that aren't are pretty much essential as part of business continuity.

In certain situations and at certain times you may have no choice but to call in the experts. These areas are the ones bound by legislation, regulations or legalese and of course you need to be aware of them in advance of any disruption. In this section, we examine the most common areas for small and medium-sized businesses: health and safety legislation, trading standards compliance and the specific issue of hazardous materials.

All these considerations perhaps sound a little daunting, and if you don't adhere to them, or you misunderstand them, they can prove very costly. You need to consider these issues, however, because they more than likely apply to your business no matter what size it is.

Fear not, though: expert help is available, and we aim to set you on the right track to finding it.

Health and safety legislation

All businesses that employ anyone must have in place employers' liability compulsory insurance, which protects you against any accidents that occur at work (turn to Chapter 16 for all about insurance). The Health and Safety Executive (HSE) enforces health and safety laws in the workplace (check out the HSE website at www.hse.gov.uk). Local authority inspectors check over businesses to make sure that they comply with appropriate laws. They have the right to enter your business premises unannounced to inspect health and safety in the workplace and with your work activities, and ensure that you're managing health and safety in accordance with the law.

You're required to take measures such as:

✔ Displaying the HSE standard health and safety law poster at work and/or issuing all members of staff with a HSE leaflet. The HSE produces these in a number of different formats so you can choose the one that best suits your business.

✔ Documenting and reporting any injuries at work. Don't worry, these aren't to be used against you; the results are required to improve advice and preventative measures for health and safety in the workplace, and help you to identify any patterns of incidents that occur. The minimum requirement is that you have first-aid equipment appropriate to the nature of your business and someone appointed to administer basic care.

If you're found to be in breach of the health and safety laws, you can incur a penalty depending on the severity of this breach. Local authority inspectors can take photographic evidence of, for example, faulty machinery or inadequate working conditions, and you may be prohibited from carrying out an activity until conditions are improved: in extreme cases you can even be fined. Ultimately, however, these inspections are there to provide advice and assistance with your health and safety management, and to protect you, your employees and your customers in the workplace.

All businesses with five or more employees require a health and safety policy statement, which assesses risks and ways that you can manage dangers effectively (www.hse.gov.uk offers advice in producing a policy for your company). Common risks are things such as slips, trips and falls. You can take simple action to stop these risks becoming real hazards: for example, painting the steps with a non-slip paint to help employees keep their grip after rain, and having a mop available to clean up spilt water to prevent the floor becoming slippery when wet, as well as signs warning of the danger. Keep your assessment of the risks updated and alter your policy if any changes warrant it. The HSE website guides you, but you have an obligation to provide the appropriate health and safety training and personal protective equipment (PPE) needed to use the machines and equipment in your building.

Don't get caught thinking that these obligations apply only to manufacturing plants; offices with computer equipment are also covered. You also need to contact your local fire brigade to find out what you must do to fulfil the current fire-safety regulations in your business; those conforming to the Fire Safety Order 2006. As an employer or owner of a building you're responsible for carrying out a risk assessment for fire on your premises.

If you employ five or more people, you also have to record and show evidence that you're reviewing this fire-risk assessment. You're also required to have a fire emergency plan that states exit points, meeting areas and evacuation procedures during the event of a fire. You're obliged to maintain fire precautions, such as extinguishers and fire blankets, and record the outcomes of any fire-related incidents that occur.

Every business, even those employing less than five people, needs to provide adequate fire-safety training for anyone who works in that building. Your staff need to be aware of:

- ✔ Exit routes from the building in the case of a fire, and how to keep these clear at all times. You need to refresh this awareness at certain intervals and make new staff aware of these points when they join your company. They also need to know where staff and customers should congregate in the event of a fire.

- ✔ Training to support your staff in their fire-safety duties. Ensure that you train and appoint a fire-safety manager, or at least someone who'd lead the group if an incident occurs and who's trained in health and safety.

- ✔ The different types of fire, and the appropriate fire extinguisher for each.

- ✔ How to raise the alarm if they discover a fire, and what to do if the fire alarm goes off.

Trading standards compliance

Local authorities provide trading standards services up and down the country. Part of this service involves inspection of local businesses to ensure that they're maintaining standards in the workplace, and that the quality of the products they're producing meets the latest regulations. These standards give customers assurance that a competent body is overseeing the goods they buy.

The regularity of inspection from trading standards depends upon the nature of your organisation and the key products and services that you provide. Organisations that produce or handle food are likely to be more regularly inspected than a bookshop, for example. Inspections check that you're meeting hygiene regulations, storing food at the appropriate temperature and clearly labelling food with best-before dates. If an inspection finds that your business is in breach of any of these, you can be subject to an informal or formal warning.

Hazardous substances

The Control of Major Accident Hazards (COMAH) regulations control and keep records of businesses and institutions that deal with hazardous substances. They set tiers indicating how much and of what substance a business can deal with. These regulations obligate businesses to put measures in place such as plans and procedures for when an incident involving hazardous substances occurs.

If you deal with any hazardous substances, you must declare this to The Competent Authority that co-ordinates and manages the COMAH regulations. The Competent Authority is formed by the HSE and three government bodies: the Environment Agency (in England and Wales), the Scottish Environment Protection Agency (Scotland) and the Northern Ireland Environment Agency (Northern Ireland). You can locate and contact your nearest HSE office and inspectors at www.hse.gov.uk/contact/maps.

Common dangerous substances that COMAH covers are:

✔ Arsenic pentoxide

✔ Chlorine

✔ Explosives

✔ Liquefied petroleum gas

As you may imagine, the more hazardous the substances that your business uses, the more is expected of you. The Competent Authority grades your business according to the level of danger that the use of hazardous substances poses to people and the environment around you. This grading ranges from lower-tier sites using little amounts or less-dangerous substances, to top-tier operators dealing with large volumes and the most dangerous chemicals. The category that your business is given determines the COMAH regulations to which you have to adhere. For example, a low-tier site is required to provide information on its use of hazardous substances to The Competent Authority and write an accident prevention policy. All graded businesses are expected to take necessary precautions to avoid an incident and limit any consequences to the surrounding inhabitants and environment.

Even if your business doesn't deal with hazardous substances, don't disregard the usefulness of COMAH from a BC viewpoint. Finding out whether any companies near to yours deal with hazardous substances is well worthwhile, because if your business is within the 'danger area' of a company that stores and/or uses hazardous substances, you need to be aware of the emergency planning procedures and BC plans. If the risk is high, your local authority will have given you some information already, but push to find out as much as possible.

In the same vein, if you identify a supplier that you rely on and is essential to delivering your key products and services, look into whether its site is affected by COMAH, directly or indirectly. After all, if the supplier is involved in a large-scale accident, the impact on your business can be just as severe as if it's your own site.

Reports of previous incidents are available from The Competent Authority, which can also provide assistance and guidance to anyone concerned about the use of hazardous substances. The Competent Authority publically reports on emergency plans and safety-management measures and ensures that businesses minimise risks and alleviate accidents with planning.

Taking Common-sense Measures

Adhering to legal requirements is, of course, a no-brainer, but knowing when to get preventative expert help can be more difficult when you're not compelled by law to do so. Experience, sometimes bitter, can play a part, but more often than not you need to make a judgement call.

Often, some of these decisions are just like those sensible precautions that you make in everyday life to keep you going and help you avoid grinding to a halt. For example, you wouldn't drive your own car long distances without first contacting a specialist company and getting breakdown cover, or have your car serviced by someone who isn't an expert in that area. Your BC is very much the same, and getting experts in helps to ensure that you don't find your business coming to a stop in rush hour.

We look at a few non-legally-required but certainly sensible areas in which to contact experts in the following sections.

Maintaining premises security

A burglary or break-in can be devastating to any business and, depending upon what's taken or damaged, can affect your ability to maintain business as usual. Don't fall into the trap, as many businesses do, of avoiding getting in expert security services or outside help because you think it's too expensive and unnecessary for the size of your business. When weighed up against the potential losses that you can suffer, you should at least consider the possibility; before a disruption is upon you and it's too late.

Professionals can put in place a number of measures, such as simple and effective deterrents to stop thieves getting into your business premises. Installing CCTV doesn't necessarily stop intruders but can discourage them by recording images and alerting security staff or police of the intrusion.

The level of security that you require depends on your vulnerabilities, and so look at the issue in conjunction with your BIA's critical activities and dependencies (which we discuss in Chapter 4). Think about the consequences of the worst happening and someone breaking into your business. Are your resources, data or equipment all contained in the same building? If so, what would happen to the output of your business if this building was raided?

Simple measures such as door code locks are a useful way of restricting access to your workplace, and changing or rotating these numbers in case someone else does find out the code is advisable. If the turnover of your staff is high or you have large numbers of people working for you, personal identity passes can also be useful. Restricting unauthorised access to your building is the best way to prevent unwanted visitors.

Ensuring that you protect your staff

You may want to consider tackling risks in the workplace for the health and wellbeing of your employees that go beyond your legal obligations. For example, if you have small numbers of staff working in your shop premises at any one time then you may want to get a professionally installed panic button that staff can press if an incident occurs, train staff in how to deal with potentially disturbing customers and ensure that they know what to do if faced with this situation. Not only can this make staff feel safer, but it also deters thefts, which can be devastating to your business.

Considering a business IT partner

Almost all businesses rely on some form of IT in their organisation and your company is unlikely to be different. You probably store plans, records and client contact details on your computers and so they're certainly worth protecting. But you don't want to look after only the physical machines. Although you may not be able to see the evidence of your IT security, as you can a physical padlock or CCTV camera on a fence, it's no less important. If your cyber security is compromised or manipulated, you may well feel the same impact as if someone pours a bucket of water over your laptop.

Dealing with the dangers of cyber space can be complicated; sometimes the threat of malicious software, viruses and firewalls is enough to make you feel like turning off the power socket and going back to pen and paper. But expert help is available.

Get Safe Online (www.getsafeonline.org) is an organisation that works with the government, businesses and law enforcement to provide free and independent advice for staying safe on the Internet. It offers useful and accessible guidance for individuals and small businesses and aims to show you how to stay safe with minimum effort and time. Get Safe Online recommends the minimum level of security and firewall specifications that you need for your business:

> *A software firewall is a bare minimum; however, if a business holds sensitive data a more robust hardware firewall will be necessary. Professional help will be required to configure this effectively.*

This statement leads to our next point. Get Safe Online suggests that small businesses link up with a business-class IT partner to save 'wasting time' on the technical side of things. A professional who understands business and technology can ensure the safety and wellbeing of your cyber and information strategy, and be invaluable in recovering your computer systems after a disruption (check out the later section 'Solving IT-related problems'). If nothing else, an IT partner gives you peace of mind and allows you to concentrate on other areas of your business.

Involving local authorities

Local authorities recognise that smaller organisations may be new to BC or not have the expertise or experience to know the most effective route to take. Under the Civil Contingencies Act, they're obliged to provide advice to businesses within their authority area on business continuity. Have a look at your local authority website for more information and specific advice for contingency planning specific to your area.

Contacting local talent

One of the most daunting things can be finding a tradesperson you can rely on and trust to handle matters crucial to the survival to your business. A lot of great people will go the extra mile in ensuring that you get what you need; seek them out *before* the time comes to make that important emergency call.

Maintain a list of reliable contacts that you can call upon to tackle any situation you and your staff find yourselves in.

Word of mouth and other recommendations are always a great start, but also consider the Trustmark service, which is an independent and government-supported service that enables you to search a database of trusted and reliable tradespeople in your local area. Start at www.trustmark.org.uk, an easy way of finding a trusted plumber, builder and so on nearby.

Hiring a business continuity consultant

Business continuity consultants are a useful resource to get you started in any particular part of BC, and to provide an extra pair of hands when you don't have sufficient staff and other resources to develop your BC plans alone. Usually, you hire such consultants on a contract basis for a set period; some are willing to be hired on a day-to-day basis. The length of time that you hire a consultant for depends on your business, and how confident you are in instilling your business continuity: but either way, getting an expert in is likely to get your plans moving more quickly. Just make sure that you retain ownership of the plans otherwise you'll find it difficult to generate enthusiasm amongst your staff and harder to promote the BC culture throughout your company.

BC consultants can be particularly helpful in:

- ✔ Carrying out the initial BIA
- ✔ Suggesting strategies
- ✔ Training
- ✔ Testing and exercising

Try to hire a consultant who has specific BC qualifications and a general management qualification too, because this indicates a full, more rounded understanding of business.

Beware of consultants who send an impressive partner along to the initial meetings and presentations and then less-qualified consultants to do the hard work. Make it a requirement that the consultant you interview is going to be the consultant provided.

Deciding 'Who You Gonna Call' After a Crisis

If, following an incident, you find that you can't perform a recovery yourself, you may need professional help to restore the important parts of your business.

Your first consideration when tackling an incident is safety, and nothing should compromise that.

If your workspace is damaged by a disaster, such as a fire or flood, don't allow anyone to enter until a structural engineer checks the building. In the event of a flood, don't attempt to turn the electricity on or off – call an electrician. In this sort of situation you'll be glad that you already established the contact details of a reputable local electrician to make life a whole lot easier (as we advise in the earlier section 'Contacting local talent').

Solving IT-related problems

One of the expert contact names that you need to maintain to help your business recover after a disruption is that of an IT specialist. If you have an IT partner, as we describe in the earlier section 'Considering a business IT partner', you're well set up to respond quickly to the problem. Flip to Chapter 17 for loads more useful tips on looking after your IT systems.

Repairing physical damage: Salvage and restoration

Even if the results of the disruption leave your workplace looking in a sorry state, all isn't necessarily lost. The first stage is to try to retrieve anything salvageable from the building in order to prevent further damage. If you suffer a flood, for example, perhaps the files on the top shelves are worth retrieving or the folders locked away in cabinets are still in fairly good condition.

As regards the building and equipment, countless stories exist of business owners and managers attempting to recover after a disruption but simply inflicting further damage by being too heavy-handed with damaged machinery. Always consider whether expert salvage help is the better solution in the long term. Unless you're some sort of hidden expert, or run a small business in restoration and salvation, this job can be a complicated and delicate task where good intentions can do more damage than good.

We list a few considerations in this section, but we can't overemphasise that safety remains your first consideration:

- ✔ If safe to do so, alleviate the lasting damaging to your building by removing standing water, ventilating with fans and disinfecting any areas previously covered by water. Ensure the security of the building by boarding up or replacing any windows or doors that have been damaged.

- ✔ If your carpets can be saved, get in a professional cleaner to dry them out and save them from going mouldy. Generally, carpets that have been underwater or soaked for more than two days are beyond repair, but trying to salvage any that have had less exposure is worthwhile.

✔ If water damages any vital papers or records, don't panic. Scientific techniques and procedures can now restore documents, though you'll undoubtedly need an expert to do it for you. Processes and drying techniques include:

- Cleaning

- Desiccant freeze-drying

- Mould remediation

- Stabilisation

If fire and/or smoke damages documents, salvation techniques are also available to help save them. This process involves careful cleaning to remove all particles of soot in order to prevent the spread of contamination. Think too about any areas of the building that may have been damaged by water used to extinguish the fire. These documents need careful handling by an expert in salvation of documents destroyed by water. A number of private document salvation companies offer specialist advice. The best way to find a reputable local company is through word of mouth; or contact your local authority, use the Trustmark website (www.trustmark.org.uk) or try a more general Internet search engine. As always, have a contact in place already, in case the worst happens.

Another advantage of getting independent specialists in is that they may be able to help you provide evidence to support your insurance claim. Discuss this subject when you first engage the firm.

Chapter 13

Viewing Business Continuity from a Manufacturing Perspective

---

*A*lthough the essential business continuity (BC) principles that we describe in Parts I, II and III of this book remain the same, certain sectors of business need to apply additional considerations when thinking about and implementing BC. We aim this chapter at manufacturers, and particularly provide practical and useful information for smaller firms.

Like all businesses, your BC needs to ensure the continued delivery of your key products and services by identifying your critical activities and then focusing on keeping them going, or getting them back up and running within your set time periods. If you haven't already carried out a Business Impact Analysis, turn to Chapter 4 and identify these key items and critical activities through one now.

In this chapter we look at the areas relevant to you as a manufacturer, which most likely revolve around your production line, and offer some thoughts on practical ways to ensure that you can keep going if disruptions occur. We also examine the BC strategies and considerations within manufacturing and highlight some of the difficulties, in the process illustrating why BC isn't only relevant and achievable, but also essential for manufacturing businesses.

Focusing on Manufacturing and BC

For your manufacturing business, BC is about ensuring that products continue to reach customers regardless of any problems you experience along the production line. Your mantra needs to be: 'Even if I have a problem, my customers don't.'

Your *inputs* are the raw materials or parts that you turn into your *outputs* (the goods or finished products you supply to others). BC is simply about continuing to deliver the outputs no matter what spanner (metaphorical or literal) gets thrown into the works.

Therefore, understanding your supply chain is imperative, because as a manufacturer you're likely to have upstream and downstream worries as part of being a supplier and a customer. (For more about identifying vulnerabilities in your supply chain and positively influencing it, flip to Chapter 6.)

The basic principles of manufacturing involve converting inputs into outputs within a certain timeframe. Usually, some form of labour, tools or equipment is involved along the way to making this happen. To clarify a couple of things:

- ✔ **Components** are your inputs – the materials, ingredients or chemicals that you modify in your business processes.

- ✔ **Products** are the outputs of your business – the goods or produce that you sell to others to make money.

The components have to be available when you need them to ensure the continuity of the production process. Therefore, you need to co-ordinate your processes to ensure that you deliver your products on time and to the agreed standard.

For example, take the process of baking a cake (and we'll tackle the onerous task of eating it). The ingredients are the components and the finished, delicious Victoria Sponge is the product. As part of the cooking process you check the cake halfway through to make sure that it's rising well and have a look towards the end to see whether it needs a bit longer in the oven.

Breaking this process down a bit more, consider one component in your cake: milk. Many stages go into modifying milk into its final form ready for consumption. This production involves a number of different processes, not necessarily all done by the same business but all under time pressures to co-ordinate with another:

1. **The farmer milks the cows.**

2. **The milk is chilled and transported for processing.**

3. **The milk factory checks the milk for quality control.**

4. **The milk is treated.**

5. **The milk is packaged.**

6. **The milk is transported to retail outlets.**

7. **Shops sell the milk.**

All these stages in the manufacturing process give rise to the final output: the bottle or carton of milk for sale. Many things can impact on these various stages and interrupt the process. In this case, an additional specific and fairly restricted shelf-life issue applies because milk is no good after a few weeks. If you fail to get the milk to the retailers, the consumers can't buy it and, ultimately, the result is a glut of inputs but no outputs.

The manufacturing process is part of a cycle in which a delay can, and normally does, have a knock-on effect further down the line. To minimise the likelihood of this happening, you require a carefully considered production plan to help ensure that you deliver products on time. Your products and the delivery of them to the final customer are normally key to hitting your sales forecast or plan.

Your business's products may well in turn be essential components for someone else's business. As a manufacturer you know that successful delivery (or otherwise) is often a lot to do with timing; a seemingly insignificant problem early on in the process can cause significant problems later along the line.

Understanding What's Important to Your Manufacturing Business

In order to run your manufacturing production line, you need to avoid disruptions in three areas: staff, materials and machinery. We describe these main contributors to your manufacturing process in this section and what you can do to keep it going from beginning to end – leading you from components to products.

Thinking about staff issues

Your staff members are integral to keeping your production line running. They can be the key to surviving a disruption but also the cause of disruptions. Here we look at some of the things to consider with your manufacturing staff.

Whether they're directly employed or part of an agency, ensuring that your staff members have the proper training is essential. Mistakes when operating machinery that occur through lack of training can result in disruptions and even a complete standstill while you put things right. Investing the time and money in proper training is well worthwhile, because these mistakes are likely to cost you far more in downtime and repairs.

Also train your staff in the areas of health and safety. Obviously, you want to do so anyway as a responsible employer, but note that you have legal obligations in this regard as well. (For more information about your legal health and safety requirements, take a look at Chapter 12.) In addition, the loss of a key member of staff through injury can mean that you're unable to fulfil orders. In this same vein, ensure that all staff members have the correct personal protective equipment (or PPE as it's known). This provision helps to avoid unnecessary injuries that can have a significant impact on your business.

Think about what you'd do if a key member of staff were off from work at a busy time. Be careful that you don't create single points of failure with your staff by asking yourself whether any of the following situations apply to your business:

- ✔ Is one member of staff solely responsible for a particular part of machinery?
- ✔ Does just one person have access to certain items?
- ✔ Does only one person has the necessary experience to oversee operations?

If you answer yes to any of these questions, consider cross-training to ensure that you can cover all functions forming part of your critical activities in the event of the loss of a vital employee.

You may wonder about the cost of cross-training while the 'sun is out', but believe us, when clouds gather, it begins to rain and you lose the only production operative who can mix a vital solution, you'll be thankful that you put measures in place when the pressure was off.

Another consideration is what happens if you lose a number of staff simultaneously. This situation can be a challenge for your business, even if all your staff members can cover each other's roles. In this case, you need to consider options such as pulling in agency workers and temporary staff. Doing so is much easier and quicker if you've identified a suitable agency (or two) that can fulfil your needs in advance and already made some initial contact with them to gauge what support you can obtain.

Don't neglect the training of the new staff. Prepare a training package in advance that enables you to get temporary staff up and running as soon as possible and also helps in avoiding any mistakes or injuries, especially in the stressful environment of a disruption.

If you have recently retired staff members who can still operate your machines and would be valuable when you're short-staffed, stay in touch with them informally or through a retainer. Keep them trained and up to date with company developments so that they can slip more or less seamlessly into temporary roles or back into their previous jobs to help out. Make sure that you keep this list of suitable staff current and ask them to keep you informed of their arrangements around childcare or how quickly they're able to get into the office at short notice. This precaution can bring a high reward for a low cost, especially when the pressure is on.

In manufacturing you need your staff to maintain control of what's going on and recognise the early warning signs of any problems. Therefore, put a structure in place, with supervisors overseeing the overall process and making sure that quality standards don't drop. Consider who has the skills to replace your supervisors if they're unable to perform their duties and create a continuity plan to keep operations running smoothly.

Bearing in mind materials

Resources are important to any business but manufacturers especially rely on them. In this section, we describe some precautions to consider making.

The important aspect is working out exactly how much material you need. As we talk about in Chapter 7, carrying contingency stock means that even if a supplier does let you down, you still have a sufficient supply of inputs to maintain the production line and produce the outputs necessary to keep your customers happy.

The availability of suitable raw materials can certainly jeopardise the manufacturing process. The raw materials that you choose are likely to be suitable because:

- ✔ They meet a precise specification.
- ✔ They meet a certain quality level.
- ✔ They're readily available.
- ✔ You can purchase them at an acceptable price.

A problem with any of or all the above requirements may mean that the raw material input isn't available and that you suffer a subsequent interruption to the production process. In this situation, dual sourcing can help you out.

As we describe in Chapter 7, maintaining multiple sources of key raw materials means that you can source materials from one or more alternative sites in the event of your primary one letting you down. This precaution minimises the risk and impact to your manufacturing process as a result of a failure within the supply of a raw material. You don't want to have to suffer for someone else's mistake or misfortune.

Weighing up just-in-time manufacturing

Some organisations work on a *just-in-time* model for manufacturing and delivering goods, which involves ordering in just enough input or raw materials to cover what you need. This approach can save you using up money and valuable space at your premises because you have no wastage of materials and no need for mass amounts of storage space. But just-in-time is only just-in-time when it works, and if your supplier fails to deliver to you in time, you have no contingency stock to fall back on. A failure of this type can result in staff being unable to commence work and, ultimately, in missed deliveries and failed orders.

Consider what you'd do when faced with a telephone call to say that your goods are going to be delayed (apart from feeling suddenly queasy!).

We aren't suggesting that you necessarily avoid just-in-time manufacturing altogether: it can be valuable to avoid tying up money in warehouses full of stock. But do be mindful that if the approach was to go wrong, it would go very wrong! Have a backup strategy such as a mutual arrangement with a local, like-minded business where you agree to help each other out if a delivery fails.

Dual and multiple sourcing is about knowing your business and industry, and then using this knowledge to forecast your likely sales and ensure that you have sufficient resources to cope with this demand. Turn to Chapter 7 for what forecasting involves and how this helps you predict your monthly sales and stock requirements.

As a supplier, you may have to meet contractual commitments and service level agreements. Keep these obligations firmly in your mind, and if potential penalties – reputational or otherwise – apply, decide on what action you need to take if you can't produce the required output.

One such strategy that may combat this is obtaining a similar product to the planned one and delivering that to the customer as an alternative. In this way you may be able to maintain the sales relationship with a customer that obliges you to offer an alternative source of input.

The best time to start searching for potential alternative suppliers for your key components is now, while things are calm and you have the time to look around for the best option.

Don't limit your search to the UK, but consider diverse alternatives; the disruption that causes you problems is less likely to affect businesses outside your locality, at least not at the same time.

Think about the area in which you store your components and goods. Naturally, you need them to be near to your machinery and plant, but at the same time consider alternative locations. Even locations on the same site may be less prone to, say, flooding, decontamination and fire.

Upon receiving goods, always carry out a full quality inspection. If you don't, you risk coming to use your components only to discover that they're sub-standard and you've lost time in which you could be sourcing replacements or alternatives. This advice is also important for any solution that you receive from tankers: make sure to analyse it before allowing it to be poured into your vat, contaminating your existing stock and rendering it unusable.

If you use a supplier that's essential to your business and can't find an alternative, work with the firm and encourage it to put its own BC in place or strengthen any existing arrangements. This may seem like quite a time investment, but the supplier is crucial to your business and its failure is ultimately going to be your failure.

Some of the resources that are essential to your business are often less obvious than tangible components. One example is the electricity that powers your plant, the loss of which would result in operations grinding to a halt. In this case have a backup generator available to keep going, or at the very least know where you can hire one in the event of a power shortage.

Protecting against machinery problems

You need to have your factory, equipment or tools available and fully functioning in order to carry out the manufacturing process. As a result, maintaining and checking that certain pieces of equipment – such as presses, electrical machinery, robots, IT and business vehicles – are safe to use is essential. These are the types of equipment that you really have to keep on top of, whereas others just require sensible maintenance.

You need to spend enough to keep you safe and within legal standards, but you may not want to go much further than that. If you're sweating your assets with punishing 24/7 schedules, however, and the loss of a machine is costly for every minute it's off-line, you may want to pay rather more attention to preventative maintenance.

If the emphasis of your BC is on continuity of product supply, recovery of facilities may be less important in the short term if you can transfer manufacturing, or parts of it, to an external subcontractor or competitor. This option may be necessary to keep your customer happy, even if you're temporarily handing some work to a competing business – and it's clearly preferable than to risk losing the customer permanently by letting them down.

Some level of preventative maintenance is a must for all manufacturing businesses. Preventative maintenance works on the same principle as having your car serviced, except that the machines producing your key products and services are likely to be a lot more costly. Create a preventative maintenance schedule to ensure that you don't forget it or push it back until the devastating moment when something snaps (that is, too late).

Ideally, you want to select the best time for your business to carry out maintenance, instead of being forced by a snapped widget to strip the entire line down and lose several hours at a crucial time.

If when carrying out maintenance you find that parts are wearing thin, in most cases replacing them when you have the opportunity is worthwhile rather than having to do so when time is tight. Consider what components and spares to carry as well, because even a short trip to the local wholesalers can be costly in lost output if a vital component breaks. Base your considerations on which items are likely to snap or wear out most frequently and which items have a long lead time when you order them. This decision is down to your experience and judgement. You don't want to hold ten diamond cutters at a £1,000 each, but you may want to have one in the store if they have a two- to three-week lead time.

Reciprocal agreements or mutual help schemes with other local businesses can be hugely beneficial when you or they get in trouble. Just make sure that you have a written agreement and mutual understanding of what both businesses expect from the arrangement. No point finding out during a crisis that the people you thought would provide you with a solution have just taken on a new contract and no longer have the capacity to help you out. You need to carry out a regular review process to ensure that such agreements remain valid and realistic, especially if they aren't based on legal agreements.

Generally, manufacturing organisations are good at responding to problems and do so every day, and so the response strategies of your BC can reflect and build on these existing abilities instead of creating structures that are alien to normal business practice. Try to identify those staff members within your business who usually come up with innovative solutions and 'workarounds', because if they're absent during a disruption, you may be struggling. Consider adopting a mentoring system where the more experienced employees, such as vital engineers, pass on knowledge and ways of working to others.

The best way to maintain continuity in manufacturing is always to keep your own equipment and machinery going (maintenance and well-trained competent staff are key to this aim) and to ensure that staff treat equipment with respect and are careful. Achieving this ideal situation at all times, however, isn't always going to be possible, no matter what you do. Therefore, you need to have to hand a number of other options for alternative machinery. Here are a few possibilities to consider:

- ✔ Know what your manufacturing priorities are so you can swiftly re-prioritise them to ensure that you use facilities for your most important products.

- ✔ The easiest solution is to buy duplicate machines that you can use when your main machine breaks down, but to be honest for most firms this is going to be unjustifiably expensive.

- ✔ If you replace or are intending to replace your machines, keep your older ones in working order and available to call upon if needed.

- ✔ Identify options for hiring machinery and equipment. Although possibly impractical for larger machines, do explore while the pressure is off and you have the time.

- ✔ If none of the above options are feasible, consider subcontracting work to a competitor.

The harsh reality is that customers have little or no interest in understanding problems that manufacturers face, just as you probably react to any issues that your suppliers have; all you care about is that they're late. Customers need their products, and if they can't have them from one source, they're going to find another (the sensible ones already have options lined up as part of their BC!).

Chapter 14

Developing a Retail Business Continuity Programme

*B*usiness continuity (BC) is all about maintaining business as usual and encouraging the resilience of your organisation; or as Chapter 4 discusses in BC terms, ensuring that you can deliver your key products and services if disruption hits. Therefore, BC is perfectly suited to the needs of the retailer.

In this chapter, we look at BC from the retailing perspective, providing practical and useful advice for small firms in particular. We describe the specific vulnerabilities, critical activities and aspects that need protecting, and examine how BC is essential for supporting and managing them effectively.

As a retailer, these priorities are likely to concern protecting your trading outlet, securing your stock against theft and ensuring that you have sufficient stock to meet demand. Essentially, BC makes sure that you can always meet the requirements of your customers and protect yourself against loss of profit caused by external risks and threats.

Considering the BC Specifics for a Retail Business

Retailers come in various shapes and sizes but they all have one thing in common: they sell or supply products or commodities. For this to happen, they need the products (stock) to sell and somewhere to sell them from.

Managing the right amount of stock can be more difficult than it sounds. You need to balance the need of maintaining enough to meet the demands of your customers, without wasting any perishables or out-of-date products, against how much room you have in your warehouse. Your *critical activities* – the absolute essential processes of your business – inevitably revolve around the supply of products or goods to customers.

In addition, the *outlet* – which can be a shop premises or other means of selling your products – is the basis that drives your entire business. You need to ensure that customers, staff and suppliers can always gain access to your outlet, and that you have an alternative location to trade from if your property is damaged or destroyed.

Deciding What's Important to Your Retail Business

The first thing you need to do when building your BC system is to consider exactly what your retail business needs. As we discuss in this section, BC for the retailer concerns the supply of goods to your customers and inevitably centres on stock, outlet and theft – you don't want to waste scarce time and resources on protecting anything that isn't essential.

You identify your own business's precise key products and services, and the critical activities that underpin them, through a Business Impact Analysis (BIA). We talk about this process in Chapter 4, and it's the first step to take in building the foundations of your BC system. After you've identified where the vulnerabilities of your business lie, you can think about how best to support them.

Riot!

The inner-city disturbances of summer 2011 are an example of how an unexpected incident can have widespread and devastating impacts on retailers. Over several days, shops in areas of London and cities across England were looted, raided and vandalised to varying extents. Whole streets were damaged and lines of shops were left in bad repair. Many had to close for several days, losing immediate business, but things were worst for the retailers who had stock and premises destroyed and those that were unable to return to business.

The British Retail Consortium (BRC) Retail Crime Survey 2011 estimates that the riots affected more than 20,000 staff in retail businesses, and that the average cost per incident was £8,157.

During this time, retailers had to put resilience plans into action (if they had some) or struggle to cope with not only the riots as they happened but also recovering in the aftermath and returning to business as usual. Shops with alternative premises, extra stock contingencies and secure crime prevention measures no doubt found that continuing business as usual and maintaining the running of their organisations was much easier. The consequences for those that hadn't taken these precautions were severe.

Despite being a nightmare scenario for retailers, think about what you'd do when faced with the summer 2011 riots (see the nearby sidebar 'Riot!'). Identifying where your business's weaknesses are, supporting vulnerabilities and having BC plans ready to come into play are all part of making your retail business more resilient and better able to cope with such incidents.

Securing your supply of stock

Your customers are the source of your profit, and so a significant part of your BC planning is ensuring that you always have the means to supply and satisfy them so they don't have to shop elsewhere because you've run out of stock. If customers travel to your shop only to find that you've sold out of what they're looking for, you may well lose their business to a rival company. Whether you sell individual units to customers or crates of products at a time, you need to ensure that you have the contingency plans in place to meet the demand.

Estimating stock levels can be tricky, especially when you're dealing with perishable goods or products that are likely to remain popular in the market for a short amount of time only:

- ✔ Ordering too much of a product can lead to wasted goods and wasted money.

- ✔ Ordering too little can result in the loss of customers when they're forced to take their custom elsewhere.

Getting used to estimating sales figures accurately and using past trends to guide how you order and carry contingency stock are helpful for every retailer.

Such forecasting doesn't have to involve anything too complicated and you certainly don't have to be a mathematical genius to work it out. We describe the general process and figures you need in Chapter 7, but in its most basic form, forecasting simply involves looking at different factors, such as current and past sales and things that are likely to have an impact on sales numbers (not forgetting to take into account any promotions or voucher schemes that you've been running). We discuss a few particulars of forecasting for retailers in the rest of this section.

Compare the average unit sales in months at a time to iron out any disruptions to profits caused by short-term issues such as roadworks or employee sickness. But remember to take note of any significant or anomalous events that may cause monthly figures to deviate from the norm for that time of year. If February 2011 was plagued by unusually heavy snow, for example, this may have impacted the whole month's profits: but that doesn't necessarily mean you should expect sales to be quite so bad this February.

Looking for clues to retail fluctuations

Market trends and national advertising campaigns can have a huge impact on the fluctuating successes and dips of your retailing business. For example, the National Health Service five-a-day fruit and vegetable campaign is undoubtedly a great endorsement and most likely a boost for grocers, and yet may well affect sweet shops and fast-food outlets quite differently. But for how long? Keeping an eye out for various market movements and trends can help you pre-empt retail fluctuations so that you can adjust your marketing strategies or vary your stock accordingly.

Forecasting is only an estimate comprising last year's figures, but it does help you to average out how much stock per week you're likely to need and predict the peaks and troughs that are natural to the retailer. You can also learn from these patterns: did you at times under- or overestimate the amount of stock you needed, and if so why didn't your actual sales meet your estimations?

After you estimate your forecasting, you can decide how many *weeks' cover* (extra stock) you think you need to carry. For example, if you have a number of suppliers who work locally and you know that you'd be able to get products from alternative business if your primary supplier lets you down, you may not need to carry more than one week's extra stock in case of your main supplier suffering an incident and taking weeks to recover. Therefore, you simply use your estimate of the stock that you need for the next month and divide it by four.

The amount of contingency stock that you decide to carry also depends on how much space you have to store it. If you sell non-perishable goods and have a spare warehouse to fill, you can look to carry enough stock to see you comfortably through a snowy winter (although, of course, you do need to factor in the cash you're tying up). If you're limited on space, however, and you sell, say, fresh food that won't last longer than a few weeks, you can't carry more than a week's worth of cover.

As with all aspects of BC, discover what's best for your firm and adapt your strategies accordingly. We've no right or wrong answers here, just a means of planning what works best for you.

Protecting your retail outlet

As a retailer, you have to consider what would happen if you could no longer operate from your present premises. Do you have another location to sell from or would you have to close business until your original premises are fit for use again? Access to your outlet, for staff and the public, is essential to running your business, and so ask yourself: if only one small road leads to your shop, what would you do if it were blocked by snow or two weeks of major roadworks?

Investigate the possibility of trading from an alternative location, or having some staff work from home. For example, employees can do tasks such as ordering stock, speaking to customers and arranging deliveries from home. If a shop is an essential part of your business and your usual premises become unfit for use, however, having a similar alternative is a must.

Consider the things that you can put in place now to source this alternative premises. What equipment, communications lines and information technology (IT) would you need to keep trading?

Alan Sugar began his successful trading career by selling from the back of a van. If you don't have any other place to operate from, this option may be a suitable alternative for your business. Or, in this day and age, use technology, and look into whether selling the same volume of goods over the Internet may be a viable backup for your business. You want to explore the option now while you have time on your side, instead of finding yourself setting up a website during a disruption while simultaneously trying to deliver your products and keep your customers satisfied.

When investigating alternative premises, think about whether you have somewhere you can store your stock if your warehouse floods. Consider the practicalities: would your suppliers be able to deliver to a different location at short notice, and would they be confronted by access restrictions if, for example, they were unable to drive their delivery vehicles down a small country road? In addition to considering the risk of hazards and disasters to your premises, the security of your outlet is something to assess regularly. Eliminating as far as possible the chance of a break-in is a big part of BC planning and a consideration you need to keep updated (flip to the later section 'Tackling theft and damage' for details). You also need to factor in the maintenance of clear fire escapes into your risk assessments and BC plans.

You have a level of responsibility to customers while they're in your shop and so don't forget to ensure that your premises are a safe and comfortable environment for them. Not only are you legally obliged to uphold a safe environment for your customers and staff, but you also want to protect yourself from the legal implications if a customer slips and is injured in your shop. Check out Chapter 12 for more on your legal responsibilities in this area.

When thinking about the health and safety of your premises and the associated risks, don't neglect to take the simple measures and assessments that you make around your home and in everyday life. For example, does the smoke detector have batteries in, does your burglar alarm work and are your windows secure? Do you have a spare set of keys for the back door and are fire exits clear?

Make sure that all your contacts and paperwork are up to date too. If the worst happens, such administrative information can be critical to your business continuing to operate. You need access to insurance details, customer information, tax returns and other essential paperwork. When is a good time to review all your documentation and insurance policies? Now! Lack of backed-up or up-to-date documentation was a particular problem for retailers making claims following the aftermath of the summer 2011 riots that began in London (check out the earlier sidebar 'Riot!'). Make sure that you aren't caught out and discover too late that you weren't protected as well as you hoped.

Tackling theft and damage

The goods and products that you sell are the basis of your business. They're the focus around which you base your organisation, the things that you advertise and the market that attracts customers to your outlet. Therefore you need to do everything you can to protect your stock against theft and damage. Customer theft can have a particularly devastating impact on small businesses, and investing in secure crime-prevention measures can avoid a burglary or break-in that can see the loss of your most important assets. (For the associated but slightly different problem of employee theft, read the later section 'Combating staff who steal'.)

As a retailer, you're particularly vulnerable to theft, and so it's a good place to start your BC considerations. Crime-prevention measures are especially important to the retailer; losing even small amounts of stock at a time can cost the small business dearly. Interestingly, although the BRC Retail Crime Survey 2011 shows that fewer incidents of crime were reported in that year, 2011 did see an increase in organised and higher-scale crime – which is where the impact to the retailer is more financially devastating.

Of course, the level of crime prevention that you need depends on the type of products that you sell. For example, if you run a furniture shop, customer theft is perhaps less of an issue than if you sell jewellery, because legging it with a sideboard under each arm is pretty tricky.

Protection such as CCTV is a huge deterrent to a criminal, and having cameras carefully placed can help catch someone if you do become an unlucky victim.

Seek advice from your local Neighbourhood Policing Teams and build good relations with the police. They can advise you of local crime trends and provide crime-prevention advice that you can adapt to the specifics of your business. These authorities exist to provide a service and make your local area a safer place to live and work, and so take advantage of any information they have on offer. Check out the useful website `www.met.police.uk/crimeprevention/business.htm`.

Look into whether you have a local crime prevention officer (CPO); this is a bit of a postcode lottery but many local authorities do offer this service. A CPO can help you conduct a security risk assessment, which involves having a walk around your premises and identifying any threats to your business property. You can also examine your community risk register, which contains advice and information for small businesses. The local authority can advise you on your BC plans in a way that's specific to the risks and hazards of your local area. Research the type of retail crime that's common in your area and to which your type of business may be at risk.

Report all instances of burglaries or thefts to your local police. Providing information about any victims, damages and the value and nature of the losses helps the local authorities to build up an accurate idea of the crime risks in your area. This information in turn informs businesses of any crime patterns or trends; for example, indicating the methods of entry that thieves use or the type of shops they target.

Don't believe that stock is the only thing of value for a thief. Consider where you store all your valuable information too. If everything is at your shop premises, without a backup, how are you going to recover your important data if thieves break in? Do you have any systems in place to ensure that your information is available when you need it? Simple measures such as having hard copies or photocopies of contracts stored safely at an alternative location can save you vital time and labour if you lose the originals.

A good approach to security is to consider how your premises appear to thieves. Play Columbo (raincoat optional) and try to view your property and arrangements from a criminal's point of view:

✔ Think about whether your premises look like a secure unit or as if it's 'inviting' in unwanted visitors:

- A large amount of clear window space, so that staff can see out and customers see in, puts people off attempting to break in because they feel like people can easily see them or interrupt.

- Too much advertising on the windows limits exposure from the inside and means that certain areas of the premises are concealed from the outside view.

- Lights on in your shop at night suggests to criminals that they've nowhere to hide inside.

✔ Reduce the amount of cash that you have in your till and don't 'advertise' it. Having a till full of notes coming into view every time you make a transaction is advertising money to potential thieves. Make sure that you visit your bank frequently but irregularly. If you can, try to go to the bank to cash earnings at different times of the day in case potential thieves take an interest in you; not carrying the money in the same bag each time is sensible and use an inconspicuous one.

✔ Consider the location of your shop: if you're situated along a main road with other outlets around and people walking past both day and night, perhaps you're less likely to have your front window smashed and someone breaking in at night. However, with lots of customers coming in and out all day, you may be vulnerable to low-level, opportunistic theft. On the other hand, a quiet local shop may not be a target for thieves during the day, but they may try their luck to see whether you've left cash in the till overnight.

Crime prevention isn't only about keeping your stock and premises secure; you also need to ensure that your staff members feel safe and comfortable in their workplace. This security encourages greater productivity and allows employees to go about their work unhindered by worry for their safety.

Combating staff who steal

Theft by members of staff is something that no manager ever wants to have to deal with. For a healthy working relationship between you and your staff, you need to be able to trust each other. Unfortunately, dishonest people exist and you may find yourself in a situation where you have to install an added level of security if you suspect your business is in jeopardy.

CCTV is useful for recording customers and visitors in and around your premises, and it also allows you to keep an eye on staff if you need to. Positioning a camera facing the till, for example, covers both angles in a way that doesn't automatically accuse staff or make them believe that you see them as untrustworthy. (Guidelines exist to protect customers' chip and pin details, and so you need to think carefully about how you position the till camera.)

Having a signing-in system that requires staff to record when they enter and leave the building means that you can log the presence of your employees. If an instance of theft occurs, knowing who was where makes it easier to get to the bottom of the problem. Again, this doesn't have to be an accusatory method and in fact it's just as useful for roll-call reasons in the event of a fire or evacuation (something we discuss in Chapter 3).

As with much of BC, prevention is better than cure and identifying weaknesses in order to correct them means that you're less likely to find yourself in a situation where vulnerabilities end up snapping under pressure.

Chapter 15

Using Business Continuity with Professional Services Firms

In This Chapter

▶ Assessing professional firms and BC

▶ Focusing on essential aspects of professional firms

*W*e design this chapter for small, professional service firms. All the general business continuity (BC) information and advice that we give throughout this book is applicable to these companies too, but here we concentrate on focusing BC to suit the specific characteristics of these businesses.

Instead of dealing with a tangible product and maintaining a series of processes or business functions – for example, as with manufacturing or retailing – professional firms are more likely to offer a service or skill. This difference doesn't mean that BC is redundant to such firms, however. On the contrary, as a professional firm you rely heavily on your reputation for delivering these services, and so being able to continue the critical activities that underpin them during a crisis is essential.

As we describe in this chapter, the main concerns for the professional firm are effective, reliable communication, availability of key staff and premises, the backing-up of vital documents and contracts, and maintaining a consistent service even through a disruption. Protecting client confidentiality and making sure that you meet the standards and obligations expected of you are of the utmost importance, and all part of maintaining a reputation that draws new clients in rather than warning them away.

Examining Professional Firms and BC

Professional firms face the same problems as any organisation as regards potential interruptions in providing services. Some events are common and happen as part of everyday business, and some are more unusual and difficult to prepare for.

The principles of a professional firm are based around providing advice, consultation and expertise to clients and customers. This service can be in a number of sectors, including:

- ✔ Accounting
- ✔ Advertising
- ✔ Engineering
- ✔ Financial services
- ✔ Legal
- ✔ Media
- ✔ Medical
- ✔ Public relations

Firms often give advice on a one-to-one basis and clients expect an expert and professional opinion based on the experience and education of the consultant.

In this section, we take a look at some general areas in which BC can prove invaluable to professional service businesses.

Accepting that BC is essential for the professional firm

Just like any other business, starting your BC journey involves looking at the key products and services that you carry out in your business.

When you identify where the vulnerabilities and any single points of failure lie (through a Business Impact Analysis, as we discuss in Chapter 4), you're better able to see how BC can protect what really requires protection (your critical activities) and so ensure that your key services can continue functioning in the event of a disruption. You can begin to see how these vital processes can go wrong, what the impact would be if they did and how you can go about preventing this from happening.

A key overall area for professional businesses is communication. In past times, communicating with a client involved sending a letter and waiting patiently for a reply. The letter at either end of the correspondence could get lost in the post, dropped on the way to work or eaten by the same dog that ate your child's homework as it came through the letter box: and eventually the letter would be sent again. With the abundance of technology and communication services today, however, if you don't acknowledge an email within minutes, or swiftly return a missed call, clients want to know why.

Most likely you correspond with clients via text messages or personal mobile phones, and little excuse is available for not being contactable 24/7. In addition, online filing of accounts and responses to requests and invitations mean that the timescales for doing business and dealing with clients are tighter than ever before. Although this technology makes business quicker and communication more efficient, it also means that the required recovery time following a disruption is greatly reduced.

Therefore, you need to be able to communicate quickly and securely with your clients and be available when they need you. Being without email contact for even one day can leave you out of the loop with a client's situation, lose you a potential customer or annoy another business that's trying to get hold of you for some advice.

Focus your BC on strengthening your IT system and decide on an alternative means of communication in case your primary one isn't available. Even if you communicate primarily over email, back up clients' contact details so you can give them a call, or offer to go over to their office and speak to them personally if they'd rather not discuss issues over the telephone. BC is essential in the information technology (IT) arena, as we describe later in the 'Backing up data' section.

In addition, your relationship with clients is likely to be fairly sensitive to them, their business or both. As a result, you need to file information securely and make sure that no unauthorised members of staff or intruders can gain access to confidential records or details. For how BC assists in this aspect, check out the later section 'Fulfilling your obligations'.

BC can encourage the resilience of your professional business so that if you're faced with a disruption, you're able to cope and maintain business as usual far more efficiently. You can meet obligations, fulfil agreements and remain within the contract that you agree as part of maintaining a professional and consistent service. In turn you uphold the reputation that's so important to the professional firm (for more, see 'Protecting your reputation', later in this chapter).

Understanding how BC can help your company's flexibility

The nature of your service, whether you're a doctor, accountant or engineer, means that clients probably come to you because something is going wrong or they need some sort of help. After all, when everything is going well and under control, people don't need to pay for your advice. Faced with plunging profits or confused accounts, however, they're going to phone you for professional help.

Therefore, business from individual clients is likely to fluctuate according to their situations. If they're experiencing a crisis or coming up to a big event, you may find yourself seeing a client three times a week, but after the situation stabilises you may not hear from them for a month. You need to be flexible in your approach, and have the capacity to take on the extra demand when it presents itself.

According to your sector, seasonality may also affect the business. Accountants are busiest just before the financial year-end and advertisers have a surge in demand before Christmas. You need to find a balance between providing a highly individual and specific service, and being adaptable and able to take on new work or increased demands at particular times. This flexibility is largely dependent on your workforce and the experience and expertise of your staff.

BC can help your firm ensure this valuable flexibility by assessing your workforce, making sure that you always have the appropriate staff available to carry out the essential services and knowing where you can source extra help if the pressure really starts to pile up (see the later section 'Considering staffing issues').

Discovering What's Important to Your Professional Services Business

In its most basic terms, your professional service firm requires a professional or consultant, a client, a means of external communication between the two, a contract or agreement and a place to meet. Of course, you also rely on the support of your team, the use of an IT system and a method for storing and retrieving contact details and original documentation. These key areas are what you need to protect through your BC.

More specifically, the fundamentals of your professional firm are based on providing a consistent and high level of guidance and building a strong working relationship between your staff and clients. The latter rely on you for professional guidance in the running of their business or an aspect of their personal life. Perhaps their own BC plan requires them to talk through, say, their accounts with a professional in order to better understand what they're spending and where and how much money they can afford to put into contingency stock.

Providing this type of service to your customers relates to the reputation that forms around your business and determines the relationships that you have with your clients. The service extends beyond the time you spend with your clients in the office to maintaining client confidentiality and being available for clients to contact you when they need to.

We focus in this section on some specific aspects of concern to the professional service firm and show you how BC can help.

Considering staffing issues

Employees are vital to a professional firm. Their advice and guidance is the service you're providing and it's unique to each client. Although employees may follow a general business strategy or formalised advice system, such guidance is ultimately dependent on the client's individual situation.

The nature of the professional firm means that staff and clients work closely with each other, and so you often try to match partnerships suitably when clients first approach your business. As a result, complications can arise when employees are unwell or on holiday. The loss of a key member through unplanned leave or long-term illness can have a huge effect on a small professional firm. When staff members leave unexpectedly and establish their own company or go to work for a competitor, you can face some sudden client retention challenges.

As part of your BC programme you need to consider whether clients are happy to deal with someone else in the firm and whether another member of staff is available with the expertise to deal with specifics of the client's organisation or query.

 Contractual agreements can even require that clients work with a specific member of staff and they may object to compromising on a one-off consultation with someone else, even if that person has similar experience and is from the same team.

To deal with such staff issues, consider temporarily contracting in someone of similar experience and expertise, or asking another professional for guidance on how to advise your client. Perhaps get in touch with a past employee or colleague who's had experience in this area. Being on good terms with others in your line of expertise can be mutually beneficial in sharing contacts and experience.

Endeavour to retain 'ownership' of the relationship with the client, and don't simply hand over a customer to a rival firm because a member of your staff is on leave.

Your BC plans need to include how you manage changes in staffing and ensure that you always maintain a professional and efficient client service. Think about the experience of your team and how you're equipped to deal with different clients and situations. Try not to have all the most experienced members of staff on a fortnight's holiday at the same time. If regular clients have a crisis and need expert advice during this period, they may not be satisfied with a temporary worker who's helping out in your firm.

Backing up data

As with most businesses, IT is likely to form a key component of your firm. Whether you use it every day to update your company website and communicate with clients, or just now and again to update client records and check your accounts, continuing business as usual when your IT fails is going to be difficult. Make sure that you have a backup system for the contact details of your clients and know how you can get through to them if you're unable to access email.

Your portfolio of information on clients – including contact details, certain personal details and perhaps information about their business or occupation – contains valuable material. Even if clients have since left you or seem to have been a one-off consultation, keep a record of your correspondence because it may prove useful if they return later for advice. An accountant, for example, may have a record of the progress and developments of a client's accounts, and previous advice given along with any difficulties faced.

This information is confidential and sensitive and been entrusted to you, and it may not be easy to retrieve if lost. For example, a client with an ongoing mortgage application may store the original deeds in a legal firm to complete the transaction. Not only is the relationship between you and your client dependent on the safe-keeping of this information, but so is the status of your client's mortgage.

You're responsible for keeping this type of documentation safe and secure. Storing, say, contracts safely is a way of making sure that the payment of your fees remains according to the agreed arrangement. This type of original documentation is hugely important. Keep copies of originals and records of customer liaisons somewhere safe so that if a fire in the office destroys the cabinets filled with previous meeting actions, and reviews of the progress of a long-term customer, you have backups to refer to.

Even simple measures such as photocopying contracts and storing them at an alternative location is better than nothing, and provides some evidence of a formal agreement if you're unfortunate enough to lose everything else.

Looking after your premises

The office or workspace is the hub of your professional firm – the engine that drives the services delivered to your clients. You file documents, base technology and keep resources at your premises. Here clients may arrange to meet you and potential customers discuss whether you're suitable for providing the service they want. The space itself provides a visual representation of your business and what you do, often giving an invaluable first impression to visitors.

Your BC needs to include plans for how you continue time-critical activities without losing clients if you're unable to access your workspace for whatever reason. You may need to arrange an alternative location to meet clients and/or a means of accessing details and information on your clients from outside the usual office.

Consider options such as additional virtual hubs through remote working, which enable the operations of the firm to continue as much as possible during the disruption. You can then work from alternative sites and access your IT system from outside the now inaccessible office.

Protecting your reputation

Ensuring client satisfaction is important for building a positive reputation in your local area and business sector. Where competition is fierce, clients are most likely to go with professional firms recommended by friends or businesses that are well known for being reputable and reliable. Your reputation is built on a combination of factors such as word of mouth, positive media and press releases, sponsorship from other companies and positive statements from your bank.

In today's litigious world, the buck stops with you. Suffering an interruption is devastating enough for your business, but the effect that it can then have on your reputation is something from which you may never recover. A good reputation takes a long time and hard work to build, but a single off-day or mismanaged case can destroy it. You're seen as the fulcrum and focus of the business, and in the event of the business failing to meet its clients' demands, you're the one who's tarnished and identified with that failure.

This all sounds rather daunting, but fortunately having a firm BC plan in place helps to protect your reputation, by maintaining the continuity of your organisation and preparing it for any disruption.

Look at the practices of other small firms in your sector and learn from their success (and failure) stories. The understanding that you have of your staff, profession and business undoubtedly puts you in a position of power over your competitors. Understanding competitive rates for the local area, the job market and what the clients who come to you really need from your service means that you can appeal to the right people. Talk confidently to potential customers by addressing the right market for your capabilities.

Seek out the knowledge of experts and local authorities as well as other professional firms. You enrich your understanding of where your professional firm fits into the local business market, and form an effective and appropriate BC plan by comparing your programme to ones devised by similar businesses. Starting off with realistic goals and actions allows you to build and expand your BC programme progressively without becoming disheartened or uninterested. You then see immediate results and benefits, which helps to embed the culture firmly among your staff and within the organisation.

Maintaining your fees

The survival of your business relies upon the income it receives. When the business stops delivering services due to a disruption and has increased expenditure, it can suffer a decline in fee earning and collecting capability.

For some small businesses income is fairly steady and doesn't vary particularly from month to month. For professional firms such as legal advisors, however, fees depend upon client numbers and the nature of the services that clients require. As a professional firm you strive to make sure that your fee income meets or exceeds your outgoings, which makes fees a key element to include in your BC plan.

The best way to protect your fees income is to maintain the services that are chargeable to clients. Clients pay for the service provided, and an indication that the quality, content and speed of the work has suffered may compromise the scale of the fees. Afterwards, restoring confidence in your firm is hard and so a downwards spiral can begin. Maintaining the quality of service your firm provides is the best measure to ensure continued deliverance of your fees.

Fulfilling your obligations

When you set up and run a professional firm you take on a number of obligations, including commitments to your profession, clients and staff. Your firm is likely to be governed by a professional body, which has expected standards that you're obliged to meet and hopefully exceed. The ability to maintain your business to these professional standards is paramount in meeting quality requirements.

Your clients entrust you to deliver and provide a service, and you have an obligation to meet their demands and deliver what they require and expect. As a key aspect of your business, you want to make sure that clients are kept happy. Having a BC system in place provides clients with a sense of security and illustrates that you've thought about, prepared and tested a continuity system and are strengthening the resilience of your business. For instance, the potentially sensitive business or personal matters that you may be dealing with require your BC plan to ensure that client confidentiality is secure. Assess how you record and store your client's details and make sure that they're protected from theft or hacking.

You also hold a level of responsibility to your staff: you offer them a contract of employment and they expect to build a career and income upon what you provide for them. Maintain the integrity of this expectation and endeavour to provide them with continuous and rewarding work. In return they work consistently for you and provide the framework from which your business is built.

Chapter 16

Making Insurance Work

In This Chapter

▷ Examining insurance required by law

▷ Getting the insurance you need to have for your business

▷ Deciding on the right level of cover

▷ Enjoying an easy insurance experience

*I*nsurance is a critical part of your business continuity (BC) system. Although you don't always see the obvious, real-life, tangible benefit of insurance until you have to claim, it plays a major part in protecting the future of your business and preserving the assets and jobs of your staff. Insurance provides financial protection, helping to reduce a business-threatening incident down to an inconvenience.

The insurance world can sometimes seem filled with terms, conditions, jargon and obscure acronyms, but it doesn't have to be that complicated. As we describe in this chapter, insurance is about knowing the following:

✔ **What you're legally required to have:** Making sure that you abide with the law.

✔ **What you really need to have:** Taking out the essential cover for your type of business.

✔ **What you may want to consider having:** Deciding on any appropriate extras.

When selecting insurance, you want to get the balance right between the amount you want to spend and the level of cover that you think you need.

To help you obtain suitable cover, avoid any pitfalls and save you valuable time, we provide some key insurance tips and information. This chapter guides you towards getting the most from your insurance and finding the best cover for your small business.

Meeting Your Legal Responsibilities

Insurance and BC need to go together hand in hand, complementing each other's strengths and weaknesses. The main aims of your BC plan are to protect vulnerabilities, do what it can to stop something going wrong and encourage your business to cope with emerging threats. Insurance exists to cover you when the unavoidable does happen and you need reimbursement following an incident.

Try to find a balance between what you can protect with BC and/or what insurance needs to cover.

In this section, we take you on a quick trip around the insurance that the law requires you to take out as an employer and business owner/manager.

Covering staff risks: Employers' liability insurance

Having employer's liability insurance is a legal requirement and protects you as an employer against the costs and compensation if an employee has an accident at work or is injured as a result of working for you. The law requires you to have this insurance, with a minimum limit of £5,000,000.

You have to arrange cover for all staff including those on temporary contracts, volunteers or any previous employees that you bring back to help out during busy periods.

Having regular engineering inspections

You're required by law to have regular inspections carried out if you have items such as forklift trucks, pressure plants (such as boilers) and ventilation systems. The insurer doesn't necessarily have to carry out these inspections; it can provide an independent 'competent person' who can advise on the legal requirements and provide the inspection service.

These persons can also inspect non-statutory items and provide management systems to issue reports and monitor areas of breaches. In addition, engineering insurers can provide optional insurance cover for loss or damage to equipment, including breakdowns and resultant loss of profit.

Covering your firm's motor vehicles

If you use a vehicle for delivery or transportation in your business, you're legally required under the Road Traffic Act to make sure that your vehicles are insured while in use on a public road.

The Continuous Insurance Enforcement 2011 Regulations means that even if the vehicle is laid up off the road, the owner still needs to insure it or obtain a Statutory Off Road Notification (SORN; form V890) from the Driver and Vehicle Licensing Agency (DVLA; see www.dft.gov.uk/dvla/forms).

Although you need to have only the minimum Road Traffic Act cover to protect against the cost of damaging or injuring a third party, you can extend cover to 'third party, fire and theft' or 'comprehensive' (to cover accidental damage costs to your own vehicle).

Ensuring You Have the Insurance You Need

According to the nature of your business, different levels of cover or types of insurance are applicable to you. We recommend that you speak to an expert in the form of an insurance broker or intermediary, to see whether policies are suitable for the needs of your business. The Association of British Insurers (ABI) produces a booklet with insurance advice for businesses, which you can find at www.abi.org.uk/information/business.

Although the insurance products we describe in this section aren't compulsory, you really do need to consider taking them out to protect your profits and keep your business safe.

Covering against other business risks

Many of the risks facing your business don't legally require insurance but are still very important to insure against.

Small and medium-sized companies commonly find that insurance 'package policies' are available to their sector, which bundle in many of the basic covers they need into one simple policy. However, because every business is different, take advice from your insurance broker or intermediary to see whether such a policy is suitable and sufficient for your needs. We list some of the key cover available in this section.

Property insurance

Property insurance is probably the most important insurance that you don't legally have to have, but really should have. Property insurance protects you against fire, storms, flood, theft, riot, vandalism, lightning and even the occasional earthquake, which are the most common incidents that give rise to claims by businesses.

You can get additional add-ons with property insurance to offer terrorism cover, which is worthwhile for businesses situated in major cities. Other possibilities include protection for glass, goods in transit, machinery, stock and frozen food. Depending on the nature of your business these can be important aspects of your key products and services that you need to protect (see Chapter 4 for identifying critical activities).

You can also cover the costs of alternative accommodation, in the event that your original business premises become uninhabitable. Your insurance broker can advise you in relation to insurance requirements for leased premises.

Public liability insurance

Public liability insurance needs to be high up in your insurance priorities. It covers your business against compensation claims made by the public in case of any damage, injury or even death caused by your negligence. For example, imagine a customer walks into your shop and slips on a wet floor in a room with dim lighting and no warning signs that the floor has just been mopped. If the customer's legal representative proves that the business had a duty of care to the customer, failed in that duty and the customer suffered a loss as a result of that breach then the business is negligent (not the customer).

Business interruption insurance

Business interruption insurance is often linked to your property insurance and you should consider it an important part of your BC arrangements. It offers financial support for the periods when your business may have a reduced turnover following a claim or loss that damages your property or prevents access to it, such as a fire.

You can extend business interruption insurance to cover the financial impact on your business following a claim for an insured loss at the premises of your customers or suppliers.

Don't underestimate your business interruption indemnity period. The British Insurance Brokers' Association recommends minimum cover of no less than two years.

Environmental liability

New European laws introduced in recent years covering pollution mean that even if a business isn't negligent in causing pollution it can still be liable in law to pay for the loss. Therefore any business that deals with products that can potentially cause pollution should have environmental liability insurance.

Professional indemnity insurance

Professional indemnity insurance provides financial protection following negligent advice or poor architectural design given to third parties. For some professionals, such as architects, surveyors, lawyers, insurance brokers, financial advisers and accountants, the professions regulators usually require minimum levels of professional indemnity insurance.

Many professional indemnity claims involve complex legal disputes and can be extremely costly. Cover includes compensation payable and legal costs, up to a specified policy limit.

Product liability insurance

This cover is a non-compulsory but recommended policy for manufacturers or suppliers of goods that carry the risk that a defect in their product may cause injury to someone or damage that person's property.

This insurance is for companies that deal with products such as electrical goods that can catch fire or items that turn out to be faulty after being sold.

Product recall

This insurance provides financial compensation for the withdrawal costs of recalling a faulty product. It's particularly important for manufacturers and firms that may not realise a product is defective until after they've sent it out.

Legal expenses insurance

Increasingly used and very popular with small businesses, this insurance covers the cost of pursuing or defending a legal action that wasn't insured by a more specific liability policy. This cover often provides a useful legal helpline, which can be beneficial in situations such as employee disputes.

Protecting your employees

Depending on the size of your business and how many people you employ, you may want to consider various policies that protect your workforce. Not only does such insurance cover the needs of your staff and protect you if any legal issues arise, but also it can be an attractive incentive in encouraging people to apply to work for your company.

Personal accident and sickness insurance

You can arrange cover as an employee benefit or as financial protection to the company to meet the costs of employing replacement staff during illness or adapting premises for an employee disability. Benefits can be a fixed sum or multiple of salary, payable for a specific period following an accident. Cover can be payable on death, or permanent or temporary disability.

Private medical insurance

This insurance isn't only a welcome benefit for staff, but also important to the business. It assists with the welfare of employees and can minimise their time off work by paying for private medical treatment quickly while they're under your employment.

Travel insurance

If your employees travel overseas on behalf of the company, you may want to consider a travel insurance policy. Most policies cover the key areas of medical expenses and repatriation, cancellation and curtailment, baggage, money and personal liability to anyone who suffers a loss due to your actions (for example, the motorcyclist who crashes his bike because you stepped off the path without looking).

Employees should always take a summary of the policy with them when they travel, along with the details of the 24-hour emergency line in case they do find themselves in trouble.

Limiting your financial exposure

You can arrange policies to help protect your company's financial risk.

Trade credit insurance

If your customers are unable to pay you or fulfil their end of your agreement, this cover protects your financial loss due to the bad debt and can even include a debt-collecting service.

This insurance is particularly important if you rely on only a small number of customers and one of them letting you down would significantly impact on your profits and ability to buy in more stock.

Fidelity guarantee

This protects your business against an employee stealing stock or money from you. When you have a particularly high turnover of staff or take on a lot of temporary employees at short notice, this cover may be worth having.

Money insurance

You're likely to have to carry or transport money in some form, whether cash or cheque. Money insurance covers you if someone steals money, cheques or similar from you while on your premises, in transit with an authorised employee or stored externally. It doesn't cover cash being sent by post or courier, but can cover staff for personal incident; for example, an employee injured during a theft.

Arranging the Appropriate Cover for Your Business

No doubt you want to know how to locate and purchase the insurance cover that's appropriate for your business; at least we hope so, because that's what we discuss in this section. As part of your BC programme, look into identifying the insurable risks to which your business is exposed. You're then able to discuss your requirements for a suitable policy with your insurance broker or insurer. Of course, the business that you're in dictates what other cover may be necessary. For example, manufacturers need product liability and professional advisers need professional indemnity (the earlier section 'Covering against business risks' has more on these covers).

Deciding on the right level of cover

Make sure that you arrange the legal and contractual 'needs to have', along with property and public liability as your minimum cover.

You need to get the balance right, and so make sure that you don't carry an excess that you can't afford. An *excess* (sometimes called a deductible) is the first portion of a loss or claim that the policyholder agrees to pay on that claim. It can be voluntary (to obtain premium benefit) or compulsory (imposed for underwriting reasons).

Add the voluntary and compulsory excesses together to come to the total you must contribute to each claim, to make sure that you can afford the sum.

Insurance works on an *indemnity basis*, meaning that you're put back into the same position you were in before the claim occurred (and not a better position). You may be able to arrange for *replacement as new* on property insurance, but it's more expensive.

Wondering why a claim may be rejected

Insurance policies are contracts of 'utmost good faith'. The insurer relies on you as the customer to disclose all 'material' facts that may influence its decisions. Therefore, you must be open and honest and never conceal any information that may be deemed relevant by the underwriter. In particular:

✔ **Don't underinsure:** If you don't arrange sufficient limits on your property insurance, the *average* clause may apply. In real terms, this clause means that if your £200,000 property is underinsured by 50 per cent, your final claim sum is reduced by 50 per cent. So if you suffer a loss of £80,000, the maximum that your insurer pays is £40,000.

If you're in any doubt about the correct sum insured, speak to your insurance broker, bearing in mind that you're insuring for the rebuild costs and not the market value of the property. Your insurance broker can advise on the correct definition of *value* in this case; for example, including debris removal costs, professional fees and value-added tax (VAT).

✔ **Don't forget to update your details:** If you don't advise changes to your circumstances, such as a new vehicle, premises or activity, you run the risk of invalidating your policy and the provider reducing or rejecting any claim.

✔ **Don't fail to report historical claims:** Commercial premiums take into consideration the previous claims data, which you must disclose.

✔ **Do keep to warranties or conditions on the policy:** For example, if you don't activate your burglar alarm one night and doing so is a condition of the policy, you aren't covered if you suffer from a break-in.

Above all make sure that you have a written agreement. Often insurance providers (whether brokers, insurers or banks) have a Service Level Agreement with you, making clear at the outset who's responsible for what, the full contractual obligations, who deals with mid-term charges and important factors such as who's responsible for updating the Motor Insurance Database (a central database of every motor insurance record in the UK). Make sure that you agree to the content and are familiar with it.

Accessing the right insurance for you

You can buy insurance from your bank or direct from the insurer, although they most likely have only their own products and are usually unable to give independent advice. For this reason, the main route for commercial insurance is through an insurance broker. The difference between an insurance broker and an insurer or bank is that brokers are in law the *agent of the client*. This means that they owe a duty of care to their customer and give independent advice on a suitable policy for you to protect your business and to fit your budget. Also, they can offer choice by searching the available products on the market.

After identifying the risks you're exposed to, work with your insurance provider to give all the information it needs such as proposal forms, employee data and vehicle data. Take plenty of time to prepare your application.

Online comparison websites focus mainly on personal insurance and if you use one check the suitability of the product with the seller; they often offer low-premium policies because the cover is minimal.

Ask to see any proposal that a broker puts in on your behalf to the insurance company or underwriter to check that your BC arrangements are mentioned. You can always try a different broker for an alternative quotation because that broker may deal with different markets. Also, always read the policy and surrounding documentation before committing; get a copy from the insurance company or your broker. You need to know the extent of your cover. Don't skimp on cover, because your business may well need it.

Saving money

The insurance industry uses a system of *risk-based pricing*, which means that the lower the risk is to them, the lower the premium is to you. Prices are dependent upon the level of risk exposure to the insurer as well as your track record – that is, your previous loss frequency and severity.

Your insurance provider looks to identify the risks to your business. Depending on the size of your firm, this risk identification can be through inspection, surveys, checklists, documentation, auditing or just a standard proposal (application) form.

If you can demonstrate that you're a well-run business with a good claims record and all your risk assessment is up to date (for example, control of substances hazardous to health (COSHH), fire-risk assessment, reporting of injuries, diseases and dangerous occurrences regulations (RIDDOR)), you're going to have a smoother insurance experience and find that more doors are open to you.

Record keeping

Record keeping is of vital importance in proving claims experience and when filling in an application. Evidence of robust BC is attractive to your business interruption insurer (flip to the earlier section 'Covering against business risks' for more on this insurance).

Security

Some insurers give discounts if you fit approved security devices or systems to your vehicles or property. Consult with your insurance broker to see which systems are approved and whether an official expert needs to install them.

Instalments

Paying by instalments can spread the cost and help with cash flow, but beware the APR interest. Your insurer or a specialist premium finance company may provide premium payment facilities. Finance companies can look at incorporating several policies with different insurers, so you can easily identify and manage each through your bank records.

Renewal

Reflect on your insurance programme at renewal. Things change over the year – turnover, staff, assets and so on – and you need to tell your insurance broker about all these changes. The changes may mean that a different insurer is now more suitable for you, and so ensure a market review with your broker occurs every year in the months leading up to the renewal. If you insure direct with an insurer or a bank, make sure that you get a second opinion because they only deal with their own product.

Getting the best out of a claim

Here we provide some suggestions to help any claim that you need to make go as smoothly as possible:

- ✔ Always notify your claim quickly and provide as much information as possible.

    Your policy contains time limits within which you must report a claim.

- ✔ Take photos to record evidence of damage or breaking and entering, and record as many details as you can.

- ✔ Make sure that you go through the official channels (your insurance broker or insurer's claim line) and work constructively with the loss adjustor. *Loss adjustors* are independent claims specialists who investigate, negotiate and agree the conclusion of insurance and any other claims on behalf of insurers and policy holders. The insurer usually pays for loss adjustors.

✔ Check with your insurer before you appoint someone and make any repairs yourself, to avoid arguments later, and try to mitigate any costs wherever possible. A loss adjustor can help you put together a costing of your overall claim, but first check what your broker can offer in this area.

✔ Keep hold of damaged items until the insurer confirms the amounts payable and gives you permission to dispose of them. You may also consider appointing a loss assessor who can act on your behalf in negotiating your claim, although you can't always recover that fee and you may have to absorb the cost.

✔ Ensure that you comply with any specific policy conditions relating to claims reporting: for example, you must report travel baggage claims to the police or airline to make them valid and you may need report claims under RIDDOR (1995) to your insurer.

✔ Remember that you must report any liability claim received from third parties or solicitors representing employees to your insurer immediately, to ensure that it can comply with timescales laid down in law, so reducing the cost of the overall claim.

Knowing what not to do

When looking for an insurance policy or provider don't try to keep secrets. Don't be fooled into thinking that by withholding information from your insurance providers you may get a cheap deal: they're likely to find out eventually. Make sure that you disclose previous claims, convictions, correct valuations and details of all stock, even if that does mean paying a higher premium. Likewise, if something does go wrong in your business, be truthful; don't inflate claims in the event of a loss to try to get a larger amount.

Strike a balance with your insurance: remember that the cheapest may not be the best, but also that you need to be realistic about what you can afford. Do make sure, however, that you buy insurance from an appropriate and legitimate source. Don't cut corners.

When buying your insurance policy ask whether your insurer is regulated by the Financial Services Authority (FSA) or 'passported' from outside of the UK.

If the insurer isn't FSA regulated, check where it's situated and whether the policy is written under English law or not. Make sure that you clarify details about the position if you have cause to complain, what compensation system the insurer offers if it fails and the legal jurisdiction that applies (a UK court or one in the insurer's own country).

Don't be afraid to ask your insurer questions: it's there to provide assistance as well as financial security.

Following Quick Tips for Easy Insurance

Here are some tips to help make your insurance experience as hassle-free as possible:

- ✔ If you want to use an insurance broker, choose a suitable one and agree terms.

- ✔ You can access a broker through the British Insurance Brokers' Association; find a broker service at www.biba.org.uk or call 0870 950 1790.

- ✔ Identify the risks and exposures to your organisation.

- ✔ Put a risk-management and BC plan in place to ensure that your risk is as attractive as possible to an insurer; test the plan and keep it up to date.

- ✔ Identify the insurance products that you absolutely need to have, including legal and contractual requirements. Make sure that you identify your most valuable and important property so that they can be protected, and be sure to discuss the appropriate business interruption period with your insurance broker or insurance company (this is the period you require financial support while your business is unable to trade or suffers a reduced turnover due to an insured incident).

- ✔ Complete the proposal forms with as much relevant information as you have, including correct sums.

- ✔ Obtain quotes and a suitable policy with a manageable excess and ensure that you can easily comply with the policy conditions. Check out the earlier section 'Arranging the Appropriate Cover for Your Business' for more on excesses.

- ✔ Ensure that you advise your broker/insurer promptly of mid-term changes.

- ✔ Respond to claim queries quickly, thus maintaining close relationships with your insurance providers.

- ✔ Always ask questions if you don't understand something you're being told about your policy or something included in your documentation.

- ✔ Don't assume that the cheapest policy is the best.

- ✔ In the event of a disruption, never admit liability to a third party without approval from your insurer.

Reaping the benefits of always being prepared

Tagish, a software company based in Alnwick, Northumberland, had a fire at its head office in February 2006. The blaze started on a Saturday morning, apparently caused by an electrical fault. Within hours of the fire starting, all the staff were in the crowd of several hundred people watching the fire burn. The office, including Tagish's facility for hosting many websites for customers, was completely destroyed. Nothing was retrievable from the building.

Staff members overcame the initial shock and immediately invoked the pre-prepared disaster recovery plans, which were good as a basis for moving forward with staff knowing who to contact, what to do and being able to establish teams to focus on the key elements of service recovery and restoration of service relatively quickly. The important lessons learnt were in

✔ Knowing what's in the office – Tagish now regularly films the contents of the office.

✔ Considering a loss assessor to assist with the insurance claim.

✔ Purchasing adequate insurance coverage, including business interruption cover.

✔ Backing up all data, including that on local PCs, safely on computer servers away from the premises.

✔ Copying key paper-based information and storing it off-site.

Despite the disaster having a massive impact on the business in terms of the loss of information and the time taken to fully restore services and normal business operations, Tagish retained 98 per cent of its customers during this time. The key to this success was thorough preparation, with a pre-disaster recovery plan, a suitable insurance policy, the hard work of the staff and excellent communication throughout the crisis.

Part V
The Part of Tens

The 5th Wave   By Rich Tennant

"Remember when Bruce wanted to practise the evacuation procedure we all just got a memo in e-mail?"

In this part . . .

*W*e provide a collection of reminders, hints, observations and warnings about what to do – and not to do – as you travel along the business continuity path, including protecting your IT assets. We also describe the vital tasks of maintaining internal communication with employees and external communication with, for example, the media and stakeholders.

Chapter 17

Ten Top Tips for Keeping Your IT in Great Shape

*I*n some form or another, information technology (IT) is a key component of most businesses, something you don't realise how much you rely on until it's gone. Luckily, you can reduce the stress and damage that any disruption on your IT causes if the worst happens. As with everything, having a plan gives you somewhere to turn to when things go wrong, and such a plan can make the difference between suffering a mild disruption and, ultimately, the loss of your business.

In this chapter, we present our top tips for keeping your IT system healthy and making sure that you're protected as effectively as possible.

Back Up Your Data

The single most important measure you can take to improve your IT continuity is to back up your data.

The process doesn't have to be complicated: simply copying documents to a USB device, photocopying a contract or even just emailing a document to yourself to pick up on a different computer. The key thing is to have more than one copy.

Keep backup copies at a different location so that they aren't destroyed in the same flood or whatever ruins the originals. Many suppliers offer a remote backup service at low cost, and utilities and service providers also provide automated backup services.

Create a system for backing up to remind you to do so regularly. For example, email important documents to your personal email address every other Monday morning so that if your system crashes you don't lose too much essential data.

Send Data Securely

If you have to send confidential or sensitive data electronically, make sure that you do so securely. *Encrypting* is a much more secure way of sending data than a standard email and involves converting information using a code that only authorised systems can read. Encrypt sensitive and confidential information to ensure that only you and the intended recipients can access it.

A range of products allows you to encrypt emails sent from your IT network, laptop and mobile devices such as smart phones. These ensure that even if an intruder breaks into or manipulates your system, he or she can't decipher your information; and these products cater for anyone from the individual to the large business.

Minimise Human Error

No matter how much you train your staff, the possibility of human error remains. Sending an email to the wrong person, for example, can be not only embarrassing but also a detrimental mistake. Take precautions, such as:

- ✔ Having shared contacts groups for employees to reduce the possibility of staff entering the wrong email address into the 'To' section.

- ✔ Having a staff email list containing all employees in a group that only members have access to. Staff can send emails or event invitations to the whole team without accidentally including a client or stakeholder who's next to an employee alphabetically, or who has the same surname.

- ✔ Restricting access and editing ability to files to ensure that staff can't accidentally or absentmindedly amend an important document.

- ✔ Limiting access to Windows files for certain users, and locking Excel documents with passwords to stop others from viewing the information. This is particularly important if you have documents on a shared system that the entire office can access.

Having locks or editing restrictions as a default denies access to the majority of your staff. You can always remove the restrictions if a particular team is working late or requests to see the information: the restrictions just mean that you have some control over who can see what.

Protect Passwords

Despite warnings to the contrary, many people still set their password as their favourite pet, date of birth or the place where they were born. A few simple precautions can make the process of guessing a password – and in turn gaining unauthorised access to your business's IT systems – more difficult:

- ✔ **Set a password specification:** Specify that the password has to be a mixture of letters and numbers, or capitals and lowercase letters, which makes guessing it much harder.

- ✔ **Arrange expiry dates for passwords:** Staff then have to change their passwords or access codes regularly, which reduces the time that someone has to guess a password.

  Don't require the change to be too often, however, so that staff members have to write down multiple passwords, which compromises security.

- ✔ **Substitute numbers for letters:** For example, if you make the password 'sandwich', modify it by substituting the '@' symbol for 'a' and the number '1' for 'i'. Add some numbers at the beginning or end of the word to make it around ten characters long. Using this method your password becomes '8s@ndw1ch8', which is as easy to remember as a word but far harder to guess.

Restrict Staff IT Access

Restricting staff from accessing systems or documents allows you to keep information confidential and secure. Prohibit staff from viewing or changing certain information by placing a restriction on their accessible rights.

Delete employees' accounts as soon as they leave the business to prevent them from being able to log on to your system.

If you have staff working away from the office environment, you may need an Internet system that people can access using home broadband or mobile devices.

If you don't secure your connection with a password, unauthorised people within the wireless signal range can use your Internet service.

Protect Your IT System

Computers and the Internet bring significant benefits to everyday lives and businesses, but they do come with hidden dangers, most commonly viruses that attack computer systems from the outside. They're often hiding in email attachments, Internet downloads or external drives and USB sticks inserted into your computer, and for this reason they're known as *Trojan* viruses. Opening or downloading a virus can slow down the performance of your computer, track your online activity or even copy your sensitive information.

Protecting your computer is essential, but not as hard as it may seem. Here are four simple methods:

✔ Install a firewall onto your computer, which acts as a barrier and monitors any information going in or out of your Internet connection that may be harmful; most computers come with a firewall already installed but search around if you want some added protection.

✔ Use anti-virus software, which prevents, detects and removes *malware*, or malicious software, along with regularly updating your computer to keep on top of new threats. You can accidentally download viruses to your computer via a USB device or disk. Malware cause harm to your computer and can disrupt and destroy systems and copy information.

✔ Keep an eye out for and download software updates or *patches* that are designed to repair flaws or points of entry that emerged with the previous version.

✔ Don't open or download anything of which you're unsure.

Nothing makes your computer untouchable, but by taking these four simple precautions you're less likely to fall victim to viruses.

Seek Expert Help

If you find the whole IT business a bit too complicated and you don't have an in-house expert, get yourself an IT business partner (which we discuss more in Chapter 12). Finding someone who's experienced in business and IT alleviates the stress of maintaining a complicated system and allows you to concentrate on running your business, which can be difficult enough at the best of times.

Talk through with your partner exactly what you need and the level of confidential data that you deal with in your business. The expert can advise you and keep software updated, which is something that can easily slip your mind when you're busy with other priorities.

Form a Business Continuity Plan for Your IT System

If you rely heavily on IT in your everyday business, perhaps it deserves a Business Continuity Plan of its own. Take a Business Impact Analysis (BIA) of your IT systems (we describe the general process in Chapter 4) to indicate where your priorities and vulnerabilities lie. For example, ask what you rely on the most and how you'd cope without, say, email for the day. Think about how you'd activate and implement the plan, who'd be in the team and who'd take control of the situation.

In some circumstances, full IT recovery may not be an option. In this case you need to understand where systems rely upon each other and make as much as you can safe. Decide your required level of data backup and keep this updated so you can pick up and start again from there if necessary.

Having a clear plan and recovery strategy reduces possible ambiguities, provides everyone with a clear direction and commitment, and establishes roles and responsibilities. Be clear about what information staff can access and what personal access they have to business-owned equipment or infrastructure. Think about what areas of your system store sensitive or confidential data and which people you want to have access to that information. Consider any external data storage devices you have and who in your business is able to use them.

In addition, consider how your IT relates to other areas of your business; more than you think at first glance may rely on IT in one way or another. Bear in mind these other business processes that may be affected, and put measures in place to work around them if possible.

Whatever happens, protect the confidentiality of your staff, customers and suppliers even when everything else in the office is in chaos.

Practise Restoring Your Systems

As with any BC plan, practise restoring your IT recovery plans. Imagine how devastated you'd feel if, having backed up all your data from the start and created an IT continuity plan, your business suffered from a serious incident and you found that your backup files were corrupt. You need to be able to reload applications and get systems back up and running, all within the timescales you previously identified.

Practice provides valuable insight into the potential problem areas of a restore plan and increases recovery awareness among your staff. Without regular testing you can't understand realistic timeframes or become familiar with the recovery processes that can make such a difference to the extent to which you're able to salvage your system. We discuss testing and carrying out exercises in Chapter 11.

Educate Your Staff in IT

You're wasting effort in maintaining the security of your IT system if your staff don't know how to use it safely and keep it secure. Make sure that all employees who use the system understand the dangers of opening spam emails and the like, and of downloading applications that they don't recognise.

Nominate the most IT-friendly of your staff to give a lunchtime workshop to others who aren't so knowledgeable, and encourage all employees to take some element of responsibility for the safety of their computers and the system. For example, ensure that staff delete all data on previous clients properly. Remind people that moving documents from the desktop to the recycle bin doesn't permanently delete information, and that a computer thief can still access such files.

Chapter 18

Ten Tips for Communicating Internally During a Disruption

Your staff members are the most valuable, but sometimes the most underestimated, resource in a crisis. Communicating effectively with them during a disruption makes all the difference to the recovery of your organisation. You need people to work longer and harder than normal under pressured conditions, and yet still maintain positive, helpful relationships with each other and your customers.

This chapter takes you through our top ten tips for maintaining good communication with, and strong management of, your staff. Check out Chapter 9 for more on working with staff and building an effective team.

Keep Your Staff Fully Informed

Your first priority must always be the safety of your people. Health and safety legislation still applies, even during an emergency.

Effective internal communication with staff is always important, even more so during a disruption; people want to know about the disaster, how it affects them and what they can do to help. They know that something is wrong, and if you don't tell people what's happening, you allow a space for the rumour mill to invent something that may be distracting and even harmful.

Instead, you need to lead, support and encourage your staff in a professional and calm way, even when the situation is unclear. You may have many demands on your own time, and in such situations mistaking a brief pep talk or group email for effective conversation can be all too easy.

Communicating is a two-way process and failure to communicate effectively creates more work in the long run.

Think Carefully about What You Say

Before you can communicate the facts, you need to know the facts. Make sure that you collect all relevant information and look at it critically before you make any statement. In a crisis everybody is anxious and looking to you for reassurance. You can formulate a plan for the key messages that you want to deliver in a crisis, but in reality, finding a way to deliver them isn't quite so simple.

While remaining calm and compassionate, try to break down what people need to do into manageable tasks, using simple language that avoids jargon and management phrases. Make yourself available for questions, and remember that effective communication depends as much on non-verbal factors, such as tone of voice and body language, as on the delivered facts.

Be Honest about Difficulties

Resolving to tell the truth in stressful times is more easily said than done. But whatever is happening in your organisation, honest and open communication is the foundation of an effective social group. Bad news doesn't get any better by ignoring it, and people genuinely respect and appreciate honesty, even when they don't like the message. Asking others for help may well yield useful advice.

Take Care of Hurt or Seriously Affected Staff

Personal safety should be paramount throughout your entire business continuity planning, but in the event of a crisis the disruption can still pose serious harm and distress to staff. We aren't for a moment suggesting that you try to do the work of the emergency services or put yourself at risk, but make sure your staff know you're prioritising their safety before anything else. Don't allow them to enter a damaged building without the go-ahead from a professional that the premises are safe, and always emphasise that people are more important than equipment.

During an incident communicate fully with your staff and be able to account for where staff are and identify anyone who's missing. Reassure your staff that you're doing everything you can to help those who are affected or hurt, pass details on to the emergency services if necessary and record information for any casualties in order to inform relatives.

After an incident staff may suffer fatigue or shock, so allow people to take some time off if they need so they can recover properly. Arrange meetings with people particularly affected, and make sure team leaders are providing adequate support and advice. Rushing employees back to work isn't beneficial in the long run and doesn't help your recovery phase if your team are unable to perform well.

Encourage Staff to Be Flexible in Their Roles and Responsibilities

You may have particular people in mind for handling certain tasks in an emergency, but things may not go quite to plan in reality. Encourage your staff to multi-skill in their everyday roles so that they adapt more easily during a crisis. Incentivise taking on different positions by offering extra pay or emphasising the experience that this adds to employees' CVs. Communicate the benefits of multi-tasking and taking on new responsibilities, and offer temporary promotions to take over from absent staff.

Encourage staff to work in different teams and put new combinations of staff together to facilitate wider communication throughout the workforce. Don't create single points of failure by having only one person trained to understand a certain system. Also, remember that people act differently under stress, and just because someone performs well in an exercise doesn't mean that the person won't need help on the day.

Plan in advance and communicate that plan clearly: prepare a shift pattern or think of a way of incentivising overtime, such as with added pay or responsibilities. Test the practicalities of working from a different location and explain clearly to staff how to organise the set-up and machinery of your organisation at an alternative premises. Chapter 11 contains loads more useful information on testing and exercising.

Provide Clear Guidance to Staff Working in Different Roles

Employees normally know what's expected of them, understand where they can go for help and appreciate where their role fits into the bigger picture of the company. During a serious disruption, however, all these guides can go missing. The workforce's priorities are likely to change and people may be working with others they don't know as well. Working in a different position can cause uncertainty and confusion, and if you aren't firm, clear and realistic about what you're asking of people, they waste time as they try to decipher their roles.

During a disruption communicate firmly who's in charge and where people should turn for help or advice. This is particularly important where roles and responsibilities have changed, and if staff aren't entirely sure who answers to whom. Ask staff to keep you updated so you know they're on track, and remind teams where equipment and documents are kept in case staff are working outside of their usual areas.

Listen to Staff Concerns and Suggestions

After a disturbance, people may want to talk about what happened to express how they feel, voice concerns, ask questions and offer solutions. Each of these is a reason to make and take the time to listen and hear concerns, both personal and work-related.

Unresolved worries and uncertainties draw energy from your workforce and generate ill-feeling, which customers and clients can pick up on. Conversely, listening to and dealing with problems creates a positive cycle that strengthens team-working at a difficult time.

Use People's Skills and Abilities

The pressures of a difficult situation can cause you to forget the individual strengths and skill sets of your staff. People can be a great source of innovative solutions to difficulties, and those with experience or specialist knowledge may have ideas to offer that you can build into the larger business continuity response. As part of effective communication, solicit views from a broad range of staff during planning to produce a variety of options; individuals may well have valuable skills or ideas that come to light only during an unusual disruption.

Don't forget to look after yourself – you can be expected to do only so much. Consider your individual strengths and weaknesses and don't be afraid to delegate responsibility.

Look After Your Senior Staff

Like everyone else, senior employees react differently in abnormal situations. Even people who are outstanding under the pressures of their normal position can have difficulties responding in a disruption. If senior staff members are unable to fulfil their roles effectively in a crisis, for whatever reason, communication is central to ensuring that they can maintain their credibility with other staff both during the disruption and when the incident is over.

Make clear to senior staff what you expect of them throughout a crisis, and where their responsibilities lie: friction can result if you're unclear about who's in charge. Take steps to assert this so that everyone in the team is sure which person they should be responding to and that you've placed people in the most appropriate role for their experience. Support senior staff by keeping them updated on the situation so they're able to lead and direct their teams accordingly.

Hold a De-brief

A *de-brief* is a meeting where the people involved in an incident get together to review and discuss what happened. The meeting allows you and your workforce to mark the end of a period of disruption and look forward to a return to normality. It also provides an opportunity to voice any issues that arose and give and receive feedback. During a de-brief, you can identify lessons that may make a reoccurrence of the situation less likely or the response better if something similar happens again.

Most of all, a de-brief is an opportunity to recognise that you've all made it through a difficult patch and have done so together. Say thank you to the people involved and acknowledge their personal sacrifices.

Chapter 19

Ten Tips for Effective External Communication in a Crisis

In This Chapter

▷ Deciding on an external communication strategy

▷ Keeping information relevant

▷ Knowing what to say and how to say it

*O*ne of the key considerations to manage when dealing with a disruption is your external communications. How you present information to the public, press and stakeholders can make the difference between recovering with your reputation intact and struggling through an incident only to find that you've lost previous loyalties.

Deciding what, how and when to provide information during an incident deserves some serious thought, and so in this chapter we give you ten invaluable tips to help you get the right messages across.

Have a Communication Strategy

Before you even get close to a crisis point, you need to have already thought out an external communication strategy: this forms part of your crisis response, which we talk about more widely in Chapter 10. The strategy doesn't have to be complicated, but it needs to fit in with your business continuity plans and therefore be tested and exercised as part of them. Plan in advance details you want to tell the public during a disruption, such as whether your business is currently able to take on new orders and whether you're offering any sort of compensation or discount as a result of the disruption.

If you have communications- or media-trained staff in your firm, use them; even if they don't speak in front of the public, they can advise senior staff how to respond to questions and what they do and don't need to say. The details of your communication strategy depend on the specific nature and severity of the incident, but think about how you're going to get the message out and whether you have any contacts within the local media who you can call upon to help out.

Inform the Key Players

Part of your external communications strategy involves thinking about a list of people you need to inform in the event of a disruption. Depending on your business, these may range from stakeholders and suppliers to customers and partners. They've all invested in your organisation and want to know if you're in trouble, particularly if it has a knock-on effect for their business.

Don't keep key players in the dark because they won't thank you for it afterwards.

Create a list of important contacts and prioritise those who need informing first. If the dark day arrives you can check through this list and give people the information quickly before the disruption causes too much damage at their end.

Get Your Side of the Story Out First

If you aren't quick with your decisions, and don't act fast, the disruption can come to control you, not the other way round. On the other hand, a professionally and calmly managed crisis can work well in your favour.

Releasing information yourself is preferable to being pushed into disclosing details from the pressurising media. Being upfront, admitting difficulties and getting your message out early, consistently and repeatedly shows that you've nothing to hide – in fact, people may well soon lose interest.

Stories heard via the rumour mill, however, can be fabricated, and you become bombarded by calls from worried parties and annoyed investors.

Get the media on side by contacting them with a story instead of letting them come to you. Otherwise they inevitably will, and typically, when everything is at its most chaotic.

Think About the Channels of Information

You need to communicate across the same media that are covering and carrying information about the incident. Local television, radio and newspapers are obvious, but social media have also become increasingly prolific in communicating news. They're probably the quickest way of getting information out to a wide audience, and mean that you can provide updates as you want without relying on someone else to publish the information. Social media also allow you to decide the content, whereas you're in the hands of the journalist with traditional forms.

Provide information and a helpline on your business's website and have an appointed member of staff to take calls from any concerned members of the public or suppliers.

Keep Information Updated

Make sure that you regularly update public information. In a crisis, situations change very quickly and the information that you put on your website yesterday morning may contain a completely different picture to how your business looks a day later. In addition, seeing a regular update progress convinces the public that you're working hard to put the situation right and doing your best to get back to business as usual.

Judge Your Timing

A fine balance exists between issuing facts as they're received and taking the time to check and verify them. Silence is filled quickly with speculation, and so keep people in touch, but make sure that, as far as is possible, the information is correct. Better to wait an extra hour until things become a bit clearer than have to recall a previously released email or change your statement to the press. We talk more about the importance of getting accurate information out quickly in Chapter 10.

If you're dealing with uncertain facts, make this clear to avoid people flagging the information as incorrect later. Avoid precision and promises and acknowledge the uncertainty, providing reassurance that you're taking all steps to provide solid information and firm guidance.

Focus on Simple Messages

You don't want your statement to become the victim of rumour in which the information is distorted and exaggerated. Providing long reports and complicated updates increases the possibility of people mis-communicating and exaggerating information.

Keep messages simple, and state the facts along with the actions you're taking to rectify the situation. If possible try to give realistic timescales for recovery, or when you'll be able to resume deliveries. Overestimating the length of this time is better than having to keep pushing back deadlines, which annoys and worries people who depend on your organisation.

Display Sensitivity

Any disruption is bad for your company, but it can affect other people as well. Be sensitive to people's misfortunes when circulating information about the incident – the fire may have lost you a warehouse of stock and yet completely burnt down the factory next door, injuring several employees. Releasing statements complaining about how much the incident inconveniences you when people have been seriously injured next door is insensitive to say the least.

Acknowledge the effects on the local community, and remember that people are more important than premises and goods. Accept responsibility if appropriate and offer condolences rather than lament over the impact on your own business.

Put Out a Consistent Message

When breaking the news of a disruption, some phone calls are inevitably harder than others. You may be straight on the phone to your insurance company or loss adjustors, but you may not be quite so keen to break the news to the businesses to which you're due to deliver later that day.

But with external communications everyone must be on the same page. Suppliers, stakeholders and other local businesses will lose faith in you if you give out mixed messages or alert some suppliers to the disruption without telling others – especially if they're likely to discuss the situation among themselves.

In order to get a consistent message out there, make sure you brief your staff and define what they should (and shouldn't) say outside of the workplace. Bring some discipline to the operation by going through responses to predictable questions, and ask staff to refer difficult queries to you so you can control what is and isn't said. And make sure you remind off-duty employees to think before talking to their friends in the pub or on the bus home.

Record What You Said

A lot can happen in a short time during a disruption and after a few days you may have difficulty recalling your own name let alone everything that you did in response – and, more importantly, what you did or didn't say.

Your external communication strategy can lay out the information about your business that you want to circulate after an incident. Your response should therefore follow this communication strategy, but try to keep a record of what you publicly said because in the heat of the moment you can struggle to remember the exact details that you promised. Make sure you record whether another update was scheduled, and any specific questions that you said you would confirm in advance of this.

Recording information that you released minimises the likelihood of miscommunication. You don't want to be offering customers 10 per cent off if they place an order in the next week after your colleague advises people that you can't deal with orders for the next fortnight.

Consistent information is essential for retaining the reputation of your business, which the crisis itself may already have put in jeopardy.

Index

• F •

• G •

• H •

• S •

About the Authors

Stuart Sterling is one of the Assistant Directors within the Civil Contingencies Secretariat in the UK Cabinet Office, which provides central support to the British Prime Minister; Deputy Prime Minister; Cabinet Ministers; and coordination of the Government's response to emergencies. Stuart heads up the Infrastructure and Corporate Resilience area within the department and is author of the National Risk Register's guidance to businesses and business continuity guidance that accompanies the Civil Contingencies Act. Along with being chair of the government estate business continuity forum, Stuart oversaw a group set up to provide support to businesses in preparing for the Olympics. Stuart has spent most of his career in public sector law enforcement and is a law student with a short but successful period within the business environment in the day-to-day running of a business and steering it through the exit process.

Brian Duddridge is the Business Continuity Manager for Welsh Government and is based in Cardiff. He is responsible for corporate business continuity, having introduced a business continuity management system from scratch; the system has since successfully aligned to BS25999. Brian advises a team of six business continuity co-ordinators who are responsible for business continuity arrangements for their respective directorate's business, across the Welsh Government estate of some 65 buildings. He has prepared a set of strategy working documents including a corporate business continuity plan and a directorate plan template for generic application. Brian is responsible for whole organisation exercising and has written and delivered exercises annually since 2007. Brian is a member of the government estate business continuity forum, of the BSI BCM/1 working group and an organising committee member of the south west BCI Forum. He is currently engaged on facilitating business continuity tests across the Welsh Government estate and is exploring support for a business continuity working group for Local Resilience Forums across Wales.

Andrew Elliott is a Policy Adviser and External Business Continuity Lead in the Resilience Division of the Scottish Government.

After graduating in economics at Cambridge University, Andrew moved into healthcare and worked as a registered general nurse, before taking up posts in diabetes research and public health. He worked in emergency planning at NHS Lothian then as their Business Continuity Lead, where he was involved in training and exercising with the emergency services in Scotland's capital, including preparation for several major international events. He has practical experience of responding to emergencies – both regional, health incidents, and as part of SGoRR, the Scottish Government's emergency response centre, which supports Ministers and emergency responders at a national level. He has been involved in responding to incidents as varied as extreme weather, fuel strikes, transport disruptions, disease outbreaks, the recovery of military casualties and contaminated fatalities. Andrew has extensive experience of policy development, and is currently revising the Scottish Government's external business continuity policy. As part of the Community Resilience Unit, which promotes personal and community resilience, he also has responsibility for developing policy on recovery following emergencies, care for people and managing mass fatalities.

Michael Conway is a founding director of Renaissance Contingency Services. The company was established in 1988 and is the leading independent provider of Business Continuity consultancy in Ireland. Michael has been involved in the preparation and review of Continuity and Crisis Management Plans for many of the leading organisations in Ireland, the UK and Mainland Europe. He has a commerce degree from University College Dublin and has lectured extensively on the preparation of Continuity and Crisis Management Plans, developing Continuity and Crisis Strategies and Testing of Continuity and Crisis Plans.

A Fellow of the Emergency Planning Society of Great Britain, Michael was also a founding member of the Emergency Planning Society in the Republic of Ireland and has served as Secretary and Chair of the Branch along with being a long standing committee member. Michael is a member of the Business Continuity Institute, the international Professional Body for Business Continuity Practitioners and the Irish Computer Society. He has lectured extensively on Business Continuity, Influenza Pandemic, and Emergency Management and has contributed on this subject to TV, the print media and various radio shows, including appearances on Irish National TV News, Current Affairs and Irish National Radio news programmes.

Anna Payne has worked in Policy Development in the Infrastructure and Corporate Resilience Team within the Civil Contingencies Secretariat in the UK Cabinet Office. After graduating with a BA and MA from the University of York and undertaking doctorate study in 17th-century history at the University of Bristol, she has dedicated her time to business continuity and strengthening the resilience of SMEs. Anna currently works in Ministerial Private Office.

Authors' Acknowledgments

This book was born out of the Government's Strategic Defence and Security Review commitment to improve the business continuity of Small and Medium Sized Enterprises (SMEs). SMEs can suffer disproportionately from civil emergencies but have a potentially significant contribution to make to the resilience of communities and essential services.

The project was a joint effort between a number of parties, representing the full spectrum of business and business continuity views. It was sponsored by the Cabinet Office, Business Continuity Institute and the Emergency Planning Society.

The authors and Wiley would like to thank all of those involved and in particular the following people and organisations.

Sponsors

John Tesh and Christina Scott, Civil Contingencies Secretariat (Cabinet Office); Lyndon Bird and Lee Glendon, Business Continuity Institute; Marc Beveridge and Thomas Croall, Emergency Planning Society.

Simon Whitbourn, Cabinet Office Legal, for his invaluable guidance on the legal aspects of the project.

As members of the authoring group

David Adamson, British Standards Institution; Jim Barrow; Nestor Alfonzo Santamaria, City of London Corporation; Mark Henry Beale, Metropolitan Police Service; Maureen Bradley; Colin Ive, Codrim; Hugh Leighton, Aon Global Risk Consulting; Robert MacFarlane, Cabinet Office Civil Contingencies Secretariat; Ron Miller, SunGard Availability Services; Norman Powell, Cheshire Local Authorities; Helen Peck, Cranfield University; Russell Price, Continuity Forum; Graeme Trudgill, British Insurance Brokers' Association; Piper-Anna Shields, SunGard Availability Services; Ian Speirs, Harrogate Borough Council; Sue Stallard, T-Systems Limited; Andy Tomkinson, Adtapt.

As members of the reviewing panel

Mike Adcock, Department of Communities and Local Government; Catherine Bowen, British Retail Consortium; Kevin Brear, University of Portsmouth Business School; Richard Bridgford, Santander; Dominic Cockram, Steelhenge; David Cairncross, Confederation of British Industry; Amy Carson, Association of British Insurers; Steve Daniels, Detica; Tom Endean, British Franchise Association; Hilary Estall, Perpetual Solutions; Martin Fenlon, Emergency Planning College; Andrew Fisk, Tagish; Andy Harrison, Department for Business, Innovation and Skills; Ceri Harrison, Cabinet Office Legal; Anne Hayes, British Standards Institution; Jim Haywood, Business in the Community; Gary Hibberd, Irwin Mitchell LLP; Alexander Jackman, Forum of Private Business; Clive Lewis, Institute of Chartered Accountants for England and Wales; Tim Liggins, Partners in Enterprise; Therese Loveday, Office of Cyber Security and Information Assurance (Cabinet Office); Richard Maddison, Financial Services Authority; Tim Marjason, Metropolitan Police Service; Kathy McCarthy, Bank of England; Steve Mellish, Sainsbury's; Alex Mitchell, Institute of Directors; Craden Moulds, Metropolitan Police Service; Phil Orford, Forum of Private Business; Michael Paisley, Santander; Samantha Ramen, Association of British Insurers; Deborah Ritchie, CIR Magazine; Andrew Rogan, British Bankers Association; Linda Stephens, Department for Business, Innovation and Skills; Matt Stockdale; Phil Storr, Department of Health; Carolyn Williams, Institute of Risk Management; Ian Weatherhead, London Chamber of Commerce and Industry; Sajid Younis, Department for Communities and Local Government; the members of the Securities Industry Business Continuity Group (SIBCMG).

Publisher's Acknowledgments

We're proud of this book; please send us your comments at http://dummies.custhelp.com. For other comments, please contact our Customer Care Department within the U.S. at 877-762-2974, outside the U.S. at (001) 317-572-3993, or fax 317-572-4002.

Some of the people who helped bring this book to market include the following:

Acquisitions, Editorial, and Vertical Websites

Project Editor: Rachael Chilvers

Commissioning Editor: Claire Ruston

Development Editor: Andy Finch

Assistant Editor: Ben Kemble

Proofreader: Charlie Wilson

Production Manager: Daniel Mersey

Publisher: David Palmer

Cover Photos: ©iStock / TommL

Cartoons: Rich Tennant, www.the5thwave.com

Composition Services

Project Coordinator: Kristie Rees

Layout and Graphics: Joyce Haughey, Erin Zeltner

Indexer: Dakota Indexing

FOR DUMMIES

Making Everything Easier!™

UK editions

BUSINESS

978-0-470-97626-5

978-0-470-74737-7

978-1-119-97527-4

REFERENCE

978-0-470-68637-9

978-0-470-97450-6

978-1-119-97660-8

HOBBIES

978-0-470-69960-7

978-1-119-99417-6

978-1-119-97250-1

Asperger's Syndrome For Dummies
978-0-470-66087-4

Basic Maths For Dummies
978-1-119-97452-9

Body Language For Dummies,
2nd Edition
978-1-119-95351-7

Boosting Self-Esteem For Dummies
978-0-470-74193-1

British Sign Language For Dummies
978-0-470-69477-0

Cricket For Dummies
978-0-470-03454-5

Diabetes For Dummies, 3rd Edition
978-0-470-97711-8

Electronics For Dummies
978-0-470-68178-7

English Grammar For Dummies
978-0-470-05752-0

Flirting For Dummies
978-0-470-74259-4

IBS For Dummies
978-0-470-51737-6

Improving Your Relationship
For Dummies
978-0-470-68472-6

ITIL For Dummies
978-1-119-95013-4

Management For Dummies,
2nd Edition
978-0-470-97769-9

Neuro-linguistic Programming
For Dummies, 2nd Edition
978-0-470-66543-5

Nutrition For Dummies, 2nd Edition
978-0-470-97276-2

Organic Gardening For Dummies
978-1-119-97706-3

FOR DUMMIES®

Making Everything Easier! ™

UK editions

SELF-HELP

978-0-470-66541-1

978-1-119-99264-6

978-0-470-66086-7

STUDENTS

978-0-470-68820-5

978-0-470-974711-7

978-1-119-99134-2

HISTORY

978-0-470-68792-5

978-0-470-74783-4

978-0-470-97819-1

Origami Kit For Dummies
978-0-470-75857-1

Overcoming Depression For Dummies
978-0-470-69430-5

Positive Psychology For Dummies
978-0-470-72136-0

PRINCE2 For Dummies, 2009 Edition
978-0-470-71025-8

Project Management For Dummies
978-0-470-71119-4

Psychometric Tests For Dummies
978-0-470-75366-8

Renting Out Your Property For Dummies, 3rd Edition
978-1-119-97640-0

Rugby Union For Dummies, 3rd Edition
978-1-119-99092-5

Sage One For Dummies
978-1-119-95236-7

Self-Hypnosis For Dummies
978-0-470-66073-7

Storing and Preserving Garden Produce For Dummies
978-1-119-95156-8

Study Skills For Dummies
978-0-470-74047-7

Teaching English as a Foreign Language For Dummies
978-0-470-74576-2

Time Management For Dummies
978-0-470-77765-7

Training Your Brain For Dummies
978-0-470-97449-0

Work-Life Balance For Dummies
978-0-470-71380-8

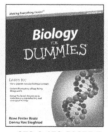

FOR DUMMIES

Making Everything Easier! ™

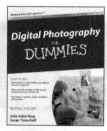